# Organism-Oriented Ontology

# Organism-Oriented Ontology

Audronė Žukauskaitė

EDINBURGH
University Press

Edinburgh University Press is one of the leading university presses in the UK. We publish academic books and journals in our selected subject areas across the humanities and social sciences, combining cutting-edge scholarship with high editorial and production values to produce academic works of lasting importance. For more information visit our website: edinburghuniversitypress.com

© Audronė Žukauskaitė, 2023, 2025

Edinburgh University Press Ltd
13 Infirmary Street
Edinburgh EH1 1LT

First published in hardback by Edinburgh University Press 2023

Typeset in 10/12pt Goudy Old Style
by Cheshire Typesetting Ltd, Cuddington, Cheshire

A CIP record for this book is available from the British Library

ISBN 978 1 3995 1054 7 (hardback)
ISBN 978 1 3995 1055 4 (paperback)
ISBN 978 1 3995 1056 1 (webready PDF)
ISBN 978 1 3995 1057 8 (epub)

The right of Audronė Žukauskaitė to be identified as the author of this work has been asserted in accordance with the Copyright, Designs and Patents Act 1988, and the Copyright and Related Rights Regulations 2003 (SI No. 2498).

# Contents

*Acknowledgements* vii

Introduction: Towards an Organism-Oriented Ontology 1
    The Thinking of the Organic 2
    Autopoietic Systems 6
    Organism-Oriented Ontology 11
    Outline of Chapters 14

1 Gilbert Simondon: From Ontology to Ontogenesis 19
    Physical Individuation: Transduction 20
    Biological Individuation: The Membrane 26
    Psychical Individuation: The Transindividual 31
    Conclusion 37

2 Raymond Ruyer: Organic Consciousness 38
    Morphogenesis: Between Preformationism and Finalism 39
    Equipotentiality 44
    Types of Forms, Types of Consciousnesses 47
    Self-Survey without a Self 50
    Conclusion 55

3 Gilles Deleuze and Félix Guattari's Philosophy of Life 57
    Individuation as Differentiation 58
    The Deconstruction of an Organism 64
    The Brain: Between the Mental and the Cerebral 71
    Conclusion 75

4 Catherine Malabou: Plasticity of Reason 77
    Plasticity and Potentiality 77
    Damasio: From the Neuronal to the Mental 82
    Malabou: Between the Neuronal and the Mental 85
    Epigenesis and Reason 90
    Conclusion 95

| | |
|---|---:|
| 5 General Organology: Between Organism and Machine | 96 |
|    Simondon on Technical Objects | 97 |
|    Stiegler's General Organology | 102 |
|    Hui's Cosmotechnics | 108 |
|    Conclusion | 113 |
| 6 Planetary Organism | 115 |
|    The Gaia Hypothesis | 116 |
|    Gaia and the Theory of Autopoiesis | 119 |
|    Gaia and Actor-Network Theory | 123 |
|    Gaia and the Theory of Sympoiesis | 128 |
|    Conclusion | 132 |
| 7 Hybrid Organism | 134 |
|    Sympoiesis as 'Making-With' | 134 |
|    Immunity and Contagion | 139 |
|    Hybrids and Chimeras | 145 |
|    Conclusion | 151 |
| Conclusion: Organism-Oriented Ontology | 152 |
| *Bibliography* | 158 |
| *Index* | 169 |

# Acknowledgements

The title 'Organism-Oriented Ontology' was first presented in my talk on the Anthropocene that I presented at the conference in the Lithuanian Culture Research Institute, and it felt as though it opened some important perspectives into contemporary philosophy. I presumed that the notion of organism connects the most interesting theoretical works, such as newly translated and reinterpreted philosophies of Gilbert Simondon and Raymond Ruyer, together with the most intriguing aspects of Gilles Deleuze and Félix Guattari, and also relates to the contemporary philosophy of Catherine Malabou, Bernard Stiegler, Bruno Latour and Donna J. Haraway.

This book is the result of a research project 'Posthumanist Theory: Objects, Problems, and Methodologies', which took place from 2017–20. The project received funding from the Research Council of Lithuania (agreement no. S–MIP–17–32). The book also includes modified excerpts from previously published articles, which have been significantly rewritten. Some aspects of Simondonian philosophy were discussed in 'G. Simondon's Theory of Ontogenesis: Between Organism and Technical Object', published in Lithuanian in *Problemos*, 94, 2018, pp. 22–34; Simondon's and Ruyer's influence on Deleuze was elaborated in 'Multiplicity as a Life: Deleuze, Simondon, Ruyer', in *Deleuze, Guattari and the Art of Multiplicities*, ed. Radek Przedpełski and S. E. Wilmer, Edinburgh University Press, 2020, pp. 35–49; the connection between Ruyer and Deleuze was elaborated in 'Interspecies Sonification: Deleuze, Ruyer, and Bioart', in *Aberrant Nuptials: Deleuze and Artistic Research 2*, ed. Paulo de Assis and Paolo Giudici, Leuven University Press, 2019, pp. 421–8; and the connection between Ruyer and Malabou was discussed in 'Other Minds: Ruyer, Damasio, and Malabou', in *Shared Habitats: A Cultural Inquiry into Living Spaces and Their Inhabitants*, ed. Ursula Damm and Mindaugas Gapševičius, Transcript, 2021, pp. 271–92. The notion of organology was examined in 'General Organology: Between Organism and Machine', published in Lithuanian in *Athena: Philosophical Studies*, 16, 2021, pp. 52–68, and in 'Planetary Assemblages: From Organic to Inorganic and Beyond', in *Machinic Assemblages of Desire: Deleuze and Artistic Research 3*, ed. Paulo de Assis and Paolo Giudici, Leuven University Press,

2021, pp. 297–308. The notion of Gaia was introduced in 'Gaia Theory: Between Autopoiesis and Sympoiesis', in *Problemos*, 98, 2020, pp. 141–53. Different aspects of immunity were discussed in 'The Notion of Immunity in the Philosophies of Jacques Derrida and Roberto Esposito', published in Lithuanian in *Athena: Philosophical Studies*, 13, 2018, pp. 81–95, and some aspects of hybridisation in 'Hybrids, Chimeras, Aberrant Nuptials: New Modes of Cohabitation in Bioart', in *Nordic Theatre Studies*, 31.1, 2019, pp. 22–37. The notion of immunity was also examined in 'Sympoiesis, Autopoiesis, and Immunity: How to Coexist with Nonhuman Others?', in *Text Matters*, 12, 2022, pp. 380–96. Different ideas in this book were presented at many conferences in Lithuania and abroad. I want to thank the first readers of the manuscript, Naglis Kardelis, Kristupas Sabolius and S. E. Wilmer, and also the anonymous reviewers.

# Introduction: Towards an Organism-Oriented Ontology

My previous research on biopolitics posed for me an unresolvable theoretical question: does biopolitical power ever reach its end and is it at all possible to resist biopolitical power? Is biopolitics such an assemblage of micropowers that it incorporates every attempt to resist it? Michel Foucault and Gilles Deleuze provide an answer that doesn't seem very elucidating or obvious: it is life itself that can resist biopower. As Deleuze points out, quoting Foucault, 'when power in this way takes life as its aim or object, then resistance to power already puts itself on the side of life, and turns life against power: "life as a political object was in a sense taken at face value and turned back against the system that was bent on controlling it"' (Deleuze 2006a: 76). When power starts to interfere with different domains of life, not only manipulating the human species but also re-engineering all other species and environments, it is the potentiality of life that allows one to resist it.

> When power becomes bio-power, resistance becomes the power of life, a vital power that cannot be confined within species, environment or the paths of a particular diagram. Is not the force that comes from outside a certain idea of Life, a certain vitalism, in which Foucault's thought culminates? Is not life this capacity to resist force? (Deleuze 2006a: 77)

More recently, Catherine Malabou makes similar claims by pointing out that 'a resistance to what is known today as biopower – the control, regulation, exploitation, and instrumentalization of the living being – might emerge from possibilities written into the structure of the living being itself' (Malabou 2016b: 429). She suggests that there might be biological resistance to the biopolitical which is revealed in new developments in biology and medicine such as epigenetics, cloning or regeneration. All these developments propose new transformations, such as reprogramming, replicating or regenerating the body through a combination of external factors and its own genetic material. These transformations imply that a body is transposable, changing and full of potentialities, hence it might evade the grasp of power. As Malabou observes,

The articulation of political discourse on bodies is always partial, for it cannot absorb everything that the structure of the living being is able to burst open by showing the possibilities of a reversal in the order of generations, a complexification in the notion of heritage, a calling into question of filiation... (Malabou 2016b: 438)

It is the capacity of living beings to self-organise, self-generate and change that might help them to evade the control of biopower. This makes me ponder whether the biopolitical paradigm can be opposed by the organic, and whether one could conceptualise the plastic and transformative properties of living beings as enabling them to evade biopolitical power.

## The Thinking of the Organic

This thinking about the living being is not something absolutely new in the history of philosophy. As Yuk Hui points out, since Immanuel Kant's *Critique of the Power of Judgement* (1790), the concept of the organic has been a new condition for philosophising (Hui 2019: 2). Thinking about the organic arose as a reaction to the mechanism of that time, and developed in different directions, such as vitalism, organicism, systems theory, cybernetics, the theory of autopoiesis, organology and the Gaia hypothesis. What connects all these theories into one current of thought is the idea that the organic being is not reducible to a mechanical model of linear causality. Instead, it follows its immanent causality, which is not linear but recursive. This means that the organic being constantly refers to itself and evaluates itself in order to maintain and prolong its being. Thus, the organic being expresses a special kind of organisation, which is determined by its immanent causality, and functions by not simply referring to itself but by constantly changing and integrating contingency into its functioning.

In *Critique of the Power of Judgement*, Kant discusses teleological judgements and, in this context, defines organisms as 'natural purposes' or 'natural ends'. In §§64–5 of the 'Analytic of Teleological Judgement' Kant argues that an organism is a natural purpose because it is 'cause and effect of itself' (Kant 2000: 243, 5:371). Kant gives the example of a tree, which can be considered as a natural purpose in three respects. First, the tree generates another tree according to a natural law, but the tree it produces is of the same species. Thus, it 'generates itself as far as the *species* is concerned', so it continually preserves itself as a species. Second, the tree also generates itself as an *individual* by taking matter from the outside and converting it into a substance of which it is made. This is nothing other than generation (Kant 2000: 243, 5:371). Third, one part of the tree generates itself in such a way that the preservation of one part is reciprocally dependent on the preservation of another part: one part helps to preserve another part and the whole (Kant 2000: 244, 5:372). In §65 Kant specifies the condition for something to be a natural purpose. 'Now for a thing as a natural end it is requisite, *first*, that its parts [. . .] are possible only through their relation to the whole' (Kant 2000: 244–5, 5:373) – this condition is valid not only for organisms but also for artefacts, such as a watch, in which each part serves the whole. 'Then, it is required, *second*, that its parts be combined into a whole by being reciprocally the cause and effect of their form' (Kant 2000: 245, 5:373). This condition is met only by living beings but not by artefacts, because a watch cannot replace its parts or repair itself on its own. By contrast, 'An organized being is thus not a mere machine, for that has only a *motive* power, while the organized being possesses in itself a *formative* power' (Kant 2000: 246, 5:374). This formative power propagates itself in matter and organises itself. Thus, organisms are both organised and self-organising.

What is important to point out here is that Kant's understanding of organisms as self-organising beings is based on an analogy with reason's own existence as both the cause and effect of itself. As Jennifer Mensch argues, 'ascribing purposiveness to an organism was something that was done in the service of reason's own investigations and that purposiveness was ultimately an idea generated by reason for the sake of itself' (Mensch 2013: 143–4). Kant regards natural organic processes as analogous to reason's intentional purposeful activity. Is this interest in the organic just a digression, or is it a turn towards thinking about the organic? Mensch argues that 'Kant found epigenesis to be attractive for thinking about reason because it opened up possibilities for thinking about reason as an organic system, as something that was self-developing and operating according to an organic logic' (Mensch 2013: 144). Kant's interest in the theory of epigenesis is also at the centre of Catherine Malabou's work, where she discusses Kant's attempt to reconcile the biological and the transcendental. As Malabou points out, 'The meaning of the epigenesis of and in critical philosophy derives from the long rational maturation of the relation between the transcendental and that which appears to do without it, to resist it: the living organism, which self-forms and has no need for categories' (Malabou 2016a: 161). Thus, the self-organising power of living beings is revealed here as capable of resisting biopower.

Kant's fascination with living organisms encourages thinking about the organic, which is later adopted by different philosophers and biologists. As Hui points out, 'Kant's *Critique of Judgement* sets up [. . .] the organic condition of philosophizing. This means that philosophy, insofar as it wants to exist at all, has to become organic' (Hui 2021: 51). This new condition of philosophising can be traced back to the debates between mechanism and vitalism: mechanism explains living beings according to the laws of physics and chemistry, whereas vitalists argue that to understand living beings we have to presume the existence of some non-physical, vital force, such as Henri Bergson's *élan vital* or Hans Driesch's *entelechy*. In *The Science and Philosophy of the Organism* (1908), Driesch distinguishes between aggregates and organisms: aggregates appear as the result of external forces, whereas organisms are driven by *entelechy*, meaning that they have their end or goal in themselves, and express an unexpected capacity to rearrange themselves at certain moments in life. Although the idea of *entelechy* was often explained as a causal factor that enables the process of biological organisation without being part of this organisation, that is, as being transcendent to the living being, in fact Driesch asserts the autonomy of life in the sense that life has the faculty of giving laws to itself. Driesch discovered that organisms have the faculty for the rearrangement of their material, and, in this sense, his notion of (neo)vitalism can be seen as a precursor to organicism and systems theory.

Organicism, which appears as a special trend in the philosophy of biology in the twentieth century, is associated with authors such as Ludwig von Bertalanffy, Joseph Needham, Joseph Woodger and Conrad Waddington. Organicism can be seen as an attempt to solve a contradiction between mechanism and vitalism: organicists argued that biological entities can be explained in terms of organisation, which has a hierarchical order and which can be seen as being autonomous. 'Von Bertalanffy [. . .] saw organicism within biology as having three major components: an appreciation of wholeness through regulation, the notion that each whole was a dynamic, changing, assemblage of interacting parts, and the idea that there were laws appropriate for each level of organization (from atoms to ecosystems)' (Gilbert and Sarkar 2000: 3). Organicists thought that the dispute between mechanism and vitalism could be resolved by acknowledging that every level of organisation has appropriate laws that cannot be reduced to the organisation of lower or higher levels.

Organicism is closely related to systems theory, where a system is understood as an advanced form of organisation. As Hui points out,

> Organicism is fundamental to thinking of an open system, which is different from a closed system for the reason that the former exchanges information with its environment, which defers its destruction according to the second law of thermodynamics. Systems theory investigates a form of organization of which organicism is an advanced form. If classical physics produces a theory of unorganized complexity, systems theory concerns 'organized complexity' . . . (Hui 2019: 74)

In *General Systems Theory* (1968), von Bertalanffy suggested that an organism is an open system because it needs a continual flux of matter and energy from the environment, which keeps it in a steady state. Thus, an organism is a system that is far from equilibrium. Therefore, it cannot be described by classical thermodynamics, which deals with closed systems at or near equilibrium. Bertalanffy also suggested another property of an open system – that of self-regulation. This idea was supported by Ilya Prigogine thirty years later when he formulated the thermodynamics of open systems in terms of 'dissipative structures' (Capra 1997: 49). The basic characteristics of systems – openness and self-regulation – led to the idea that these general principles might be applied to systems of a different nature (organisms and their parts, social systems and ecosystems).

At the same time, when Bertalanffy was trying to define general systems, Norbert Wiener was creating a theory of self-regulating machines, for which he invented the term 'cybernetics'. In his *Cybernetics: or Control and Communication in the Animal and the Machine* (1948), Wiener was also trying to overcome the opposition between mechanism and vitalism. He argued that 'The living organism is above all a heat engine, burning glucose or glycogen or starch, fats, and proteins into carbon dioxide, water, urea. It is the metabolic balance which is the centre of attention' (Wiener 1985: 41). In this respect, there is no clear division between a living organism and a machine:

> and hence there is no reason in Bergson's considerations why the essential mode of functioning of the living organism should not be the same as that of the automaton of this type [. . .] In fact, the whole mechanist–vitalist controversy has been relegated to the limbo of badly posed questions. (Wiener 1985: 44)

There is no difference between an organism and a machine because machines are able to simulate the functioning of organisms. However, cybernetic machines are very different from machines described by Descartes. The necessary element of cybernetic machines is feedback – a circular arrangement of causally connected elements so that each element has an effect on the next until the last 'feeds back' (Capra 1997: 56). Wiener acknowledged that feedback is an important concept to define not only cybernetic machines but also living organisms, which use feedback loops to maintain their homeostasis and balance. In this respect, the notion of feedback leads to another idea – that of self-organisation.

However, even if the phenomenon of self-organisation emerged in cybernetics, it was smoothly extended to living systems. In the 1970s and 1980s the phenomenon of self-organisation was elaborated by very different thinkers and researchers: Ilya Prigogine in Belgium, James Lovelock in Britain, Lynn Margulis in the United States, Humberto Maturana and Francisco Varela in Chile (Capra 1997: 85). Systems theory presented a more elaborated model of self-organisation which can be compared with that emerging from cybernetics in three respects. First, in contrast to self-organisation in cybernetics, a more elaborated model includes the creation of new structures and new modes of behaviour in the self-organising process. Second, self-organising models are open systems operating far from equilibrium, exposed to the flux of matter and energy. Third, in self-organising systems the components are interconnected in non-linear ways (Capra 1997: 85). What is important here is that self-organising systems have the capacity to create new structures and new modes of behaviour and integrate them into their internal order.

## Autopoietic Systems

The notion of self-organisation is creatively elaborated in Humberto Maturana and Francisco Varela's theory of autopoiesis, which can be taken as a starting point to discuss different theories of biological organisation. The theory of autopoiesis examines living systems both as organisationally closed and structurally open at the same time. Maturana and Varela proposed the term 'autopoiesis' in the 1970s. *Auto* means 'self' and refers to the self-organisation of living systems, and *poiesis* means 'making' (and comes from the same root as the word 'poetry'). Thus, autopoiesis means 'self-making', or the self-organising capacity of a living being. A simple example of an autopoietic system is a unicellular organism which is capable of maintaining and recreating its organisation despite multiple chemical reactions taking place in it. Thus, the main characteristic of an autopoietic system is its self-organisation, self-maintenance, and its constant self-reproduction within a boundary. Not every self-organising structure is autopoietic; only those organisations that are self-making, i.e. autopoietic, are considered to be alive. The idea of self-making and self-organising implies that a living system is *organisationally closed*, that its order is imposed not by external forces but by the system itself. However, a living being cannot survive without energy and nutrients and for this reason it is connected to the environment. The environment triggers an autopoietic system and engenders some changes within its structure. Therefore, it is said that every living system interacts with the environment through 'structural coupling'. However, even after undergoing some structural changes, the model of organisation of the system does not change. This is why autopoietic entities are said to be *closed* on the level of organisation but *open* at the level of structure.

Thus, Maturana and Varela define autopoietic systems as organisationally closed and structurally open at the same time. Such a definition might sound like a contradiction because closure and openness towards the environment move in different directions. However, what is important to understand here is that a living system needs the environment so as to obtain energy and nutrients to maintain itself and to keep its identity. As Evan Thompson points out,

> The self-transcending movement of life is none other than metabolism, and metabolism is none other than the biochemical instantiation of the autopoietic organization. That organization must remain invariant – otherwise the organism dies – but the only way autopoiesis can stay in place is through the incessant material flux of metabolism. In other words, the operational *closure* of autopoiesis demands that the organism be an *open system*. (Thompson 2009: 85)

In other words, to stay alive a system has to communicate with the environment and change, because a total closure would mean death. In this context it is important to understand the difference between 'organisation' and 'structure': 'organisation' means the relations between the components of a system that allow it to be a member of a specific class (e.g. a bacterium, an animal or a human brain). All living beings of the same class have a similar organisation. The term 'structure' means the actual relationships between physical components: a given organisation can be embodied in different physical structures (Maturana and Varela 1998: 47). In other words, living beings differ from each other in their structure, but members of the same class are alike in their organisation.

It is important to note that even if an autopoietic system is triggered by the environment, its organisation remains constant. In this sense, an autopoietic system differs from an allopoietic system, or a machine, which is dependent on external inputs and outputs. An autopoietic system 'makes' itself, and the changes within this system appear as emerging properties, in other words, properties that are not present in the parts but emerge from the interaction of these parts. Thus, in contrast to a mechanism, which defines a living being as the sum of its parts, and vitalism, which presumes that a living being is guided by some transcendent principle, the autopoietic entity is guided by its immanent cause. By referring to themselves and constantly restructuring themselves, living beings are driven by recurrent causality, or recursivity, which incorporates contingency into its functioning. In this sense, a living being does not have a final cause or teleology because it is open to change and contingency. In *Autopoiesis and Cognition* (1980), Maturana and Varela argue that teleology does not belong to autopoietic organisation: 'Living systems, as physical autopoietic machines, are purposeless systems' (Maturana and Varela 1980: 86). In later years, Varela explained that organisms do not require a transcendental cause in the Kantian sense and that organisms have their intrinsic teleology (Thompson 2009: 93, n. 52). His later revision of this theory was that organisms do not have a teleology but a sense-making, which emerges from an organism's coupling to an environment. In this regard we can argue that a living being is driven not by external causes (inputs and outputs as in the case of allopoietic systems), or by a transcendent cause (a teleology of universal reason), but by its immanent causality.

In this respect, a living system may be differentiated from a non-living system. If a non-living system, such as a cloud or a rock, is affected from the outside, it will react according to a linear model of cause and effect, whereas if a living system is affected from the outside it will react (or respond) through recurrent interaction within the system. The idea that a living being responds to the environment and can even affect it in a certain way led to the conclusion that a living being is interrelated to its environment through a 'structural coupling'. This insight challenges Darwin's idea of adaptation because the organism is not simply adapting to the environment but is also actively manipulating it. The idea that living beings can manipulate and change their environment allows Maturana and Varela to argue that self-organising activity, expressed at different levels of life, is a mental activity. '*Living systems are cognitive systems, and living as a process is a process of cognition.* This statement is valid for all organisms, with and without a nervous system' (Maturana and Varela 1980: 13, emphasis in original). Living systems are cognitive systems in the sense that they change their environment. For example, photosynthetic organisms create an oxygen-rich environment. Likewise, spiders and beavers, not to mention humans, create their own environments. All living beings interact with their environment in a cognitive way and create preferable conditions for their own being. This statement is valid for organisms at different levels of complexity: for example, a cell interacts with its environment by incorporating substances and making some internal changes; a nervous system interacts with its environment through perception, and every sensory perception initiates internal changes within it. Thus, an autopoietic system relates with the environment structurally; in other words, it relates through recurrent interactions that cause changes within the system (Capra and Luisi 2014: 135). This explains the difference between living and non-living systems: a non-living system will react to an external disturbance according to a linear logic of cause and effect, whereas a living system will respond according to recurrent causality which will engender changes within the system. Every change within the system influences the system's future behaviour. Therefore, Maturana and Varela assert that the interaction between a living system and the environment is structurally determined.

However, this does not imply that a living system is determined from the outside; rather, it is determined by its internal changes. The environment triggers some changes within the autopoietic system, but the system itself introduces changes into the environment. Thus, the living system and the environment are co-evolving and co-emerging. 'The emphasis and overall concern here is not to define cognition in terms of an input from the external world acting on the perceiver, but rather to explain cognition and perception in terms of the internal structure of the organism' (Capra and Luisi 2014: 141). According to Maturana and Varela, all interactions between the living being and the environment can be described as mental activity: 'The interactions of a living organism – plant, animal, or human – with its environment are cognitive interactions. Thus life and cognition are inseparably connected. Mind – or, more accurately, mental activity – is immanent in matter at all levels of life' (Capra and Luisi 2014: 254; Capra 1997: 168). The statement that living systems are cognitive systems radically changes our understanding of cognition and consciousness. Hence, the notion of cognition is applied not only to humans and animals with nervous systems and brains, but is expanded to all living beings. According to this theory,

> the brain is not necessary for mind to exist. A bacterium, or a plant, has no brain but has a mind. The simplest organisms are capable of perception and thus of cognition. They do not see, but they nevertheless

perceive changes in their environment – differences between light and shadow, hot and cold, higher and lower concentrations of some chemicals, etc. (Capra 1997: 170)

Thus, cognition involves not only thinking, but also perception, emotion, self-awareness and 'feeling of what happens'. Cognition and mental activity are associated not only with self-reflecting subjectivity but with diverse processes of life taking place in living beings.

The idea that living systems are cognitive systems not only extends the notion of cognition to all processes of life but also changes our understanding of what human cognition is. If cognition is embodied in all processes of life, this implies that the brain is not the only organ through which cognition is expressed.

The entire dissipative structure of the organism participates in the process of cognition, whether or not the organism has a brain and a higher nervous system. Moreover, recent research indicates strongly that in the human organism the nervous system, the immune system, and the endocrine system, which traditionally have been viewed as three separate systems, in fact form a single cognitive network. (Capra 1997: 171)

This insight allows one to conclude that human cognition and knowledge are rooted in biological existence, and that there is a certain continuity between different levels of cognitive systems, or different forms of 'self'. For example, Varela distinguishes between biological self, bodily self and cognitive self.[1] Varela's ideas are supported by Antonio Damasio's theory of consciousness, which relates conscious activity to continually changing neural mapping. These non-conscious nervous impulses form the 'proto-self', which is later encapsulated into the conscious experience of 'core self'; the 'core self', in its turn, is encapsulated into the 'autobiographical self' that is the equivalent of reflective consciousness. In other words, both Varela's and Damasio's theories reveal the continuity and discontinuity between different levels of biological, neurological and reflective self. However, the idea that cognition is rooted in living processes and that it can evade brain control – and simultaneously the grip of biopolitical manipulation – might be thought of as a potential site for resistance.

Maturana and Varela's notion of autopoiesis is a good theoretical model to start thinking about living beings and also to define their interactions with non-living beings, such as machines or the atmosphere. Maturana and Varela often describe living beings as 'autopoietic machines', thus pointing

---

[1] In 'Organism: A Meshwork of Selfless Selves' (1991), Varela distinguished between five levels: 1) cellular identity (biological self); 2) immunological identity (bodily self); 3) behavioural identity (cognitive self); 4) personal identity (sociolinguistic self); and 5) social identity (collective self).

out that living beings and cybernetic machines share the characteristics of self-organisation and recursivity. However, autopoietic machines literally produce 'themselves'. They are the product of their transformations, whereas allopoietic machines produce something different from themselves. Still, autopoietic systems and allopoietic systems are connected in 'structural couplings' and produce organism–machine hybrids. The notion of autopoietic system is also useful in trying to explain the interactions between living and non-living systems. For example, Gaia theory is based on the idea that plants and other organisms produce the atmospheric gases to make the Earth suitable for living. James Lovelock and Lynn Margulis recognised that planet Earth as a whole is a living-like, self-organising system. It was Varela who convinced Lovelock and Margulis that Gaia theory could be reframed from its initial cybernetic model into an autopoietic system. As Margulis and Sagan point out, 'There is little doubt that the planetary patina – including ourselves – is autopoietic' (Margulis and Sagan 1986: 66).

Thus, the notion of autopoiesis is a very useful theoretical model to explain the internal organisation of an organism, to define the interactions between organisms of different complexity, to demonstrate the interconnection between the human body and mind, or to discuss the interactions between living and non-living systems. However, the notion of autopoiesis might have its limitations, especially when trying to explain the production of change. As Mark B. N. Hansen points out, 'autopoietic closure remains insufficiently dynamic to grapple with the basic operation of change that is everywhere at work in the world' (Hansen 2009: 116). If autopoietic systems constantly reproduce themselves, how can something new emerge or happen? And in what way can one autopoietic system interact with another autopoietic system? Donna J. Haraway (2016) proposed a productive notion of sympoiesis, which accounts for the interaction between living beings of different species. Félix Guattari (1993) argued that autopoiesis can be rethought as machinic heterogenesis, which could break operational closure by coupling autopoietic systems with allopoietic machines. The tension between operational closure in autopoietic systems and the need to go beyond this closure to incorporate heterogeneous collective systems will be discussed later in this book. At this point we can agree with Hansen's idea that the notion of closure, or boundary, might depend on the scale being explored (Hansen 2009: 117). In other words, the closure and openness of autopoietic systems should be differentiated at different scales: 'whereas autonomy of the living requires organizational closure, autonomy of psychic and collective beings requires openness to alterity' (Hansen 2009: 126). A human being is composed of different levels of autopoietic systems: according to Varela (1991), it is made of a cellular autopoietic system, an immunological autopoietic system, a cognitive autopoietic system, and at the same time it belongs to social assemblages. Thus, even if the notion of autopoiesis works perfectly well in examining cellular identity, at different scales, such as that of immunological or social identity, the notion of operational closure might be insufficient and require the invention of the idea of operational openness.

## Organism-Oriented Ontology

At this point I would like to ask if the biological mode of existence can be defined in ontological terms? Is an organism just a domain of life, or is it an ontological mode of existence? Here I would like to propose a new concept of an organism-oriented ontology, which encompasses different threads coming from systems theory, the notion of autopoiesis, and the philosophy of biology, and relates them to actual and 'vital' ideas circulating in contemporary philosophy. An organism-oriented ontology pursues the Kantian idea that some characteristics defining living beings – organisms – might be helpful to reconceptualise ontology. In this respect, the notion of an organism-oriented ontology engages with the controversies concerning whether the living system is closed or open, whether it follows a certain teleology and purpose, or, on the contrary, is absolutely contingent and unpredictable. An organism-oriented ontology examines the relationships of continuity and discontinuity between different levels of a living system, and also between organisms of different complexity. It problematises the relationship between organisms and technological objects and extensions, asking to what extent these technological extensions can be seen as part of the organism. Paraphrasing Cary Wolfe's essay title 'What "The Animal" Can Teach "The Anthropocene"' (2020), I would like to ask what the organism can teach contemporary philosophy, and consequently, how the notion of the organic could help to resist recent challenges, such as climate change and the Anthropocene. On the other hand, I would like to ask whether some models of self-organisation and self-determination, specific to organisms, could be useful in resisting biopolitical power.

The notion of an organism-oriented ontology prioritises three main ideas: processuality, multiplicity and potentiality (the potential for qualitative change). In contrast to ontologies based on the priority of identity and substance, organism-oriented ontology examines organisms as developing, changing and evolving. This orientation towards processes follows Alfred North Whitehead's process philosophy, the notion of morphogenesis coming from Raymond Ruyer's philosophy of biology, and also from the notion of ontogenesis formulated by Gilbert Simondon. This means that instead of being instructed by some pre-existing form (as in the case of preformationism), or by a transcendent idea (as in the case of vitalism), the living being itself is inventing its immanent principles of self-organisation, self-generation and self-maintenance. For example, Simondon questions the idea of the bounded and pre-formed individual and proposes the theory of individuation, which examines both living and non-living beings from the perspective of permanent development. Similarly, Ruyer rejects the notion of preformationism and invents a new notion – that of a living form – which follows its own principles of generation and development. Simondon's and Ruyer's insights are incorporated into Gilles Deleuze and Félix Guattari's ontology of becoming.

The ontology of becoming, focusing on processuality, differences and changes, marks a radical shift in contemporary philosophy. Many philosophers, after Deleuze and Guattari, take processuality as the necessary condition of thinking. For example, processuality as the potential for change appears in Catherine Malabou's notion of plasticity, and also in her concept of epigenesis, which explains how organisms of different complexity are shaped by the environment. Processuality is also at the centre of Bernard Stiegler's examination of technological objects which allow us to memorise our past and to anticipate our future. Processuality is also central for Bruno Latour's thinking of the Earth, and generally, of nature, which should be reconsidered not as a universe but as a process.

The notion of processuality leads to the second principle, that of multiplicity. The notion of multiplicity can be seen as opposing that of identity and totality. Driesch described the organism as an extensive manifoldness, which develops from simple to more complicated forms, and also as an intensive manifoldness, which involves the differentiation and epigenesis of these forms. Here we can take into account the fact that organisms are composed of heterogeneous parts that are being constantly restructured; moreover, organisms are constantly coupled with the environment and compose with them certain kinds of assemblages. This image of an organism as a manifoldness can be discovered in the Deleuzian notion of multiplicity.[2] Metaphysical philosophy used to conceive things as being unified, timeless and eternal, whereas the Deleuzian concept of multiplicity allows us to examine them as being differentiated, unfinished and continuous, as if they were developing organisms. Deleuze extends the notion of multiplicity to different fields: multiplicities correspond not only to organisms but also to mathematical relations and realities, psychic structures, languages and societies.

Some biological theories, such as developmental systems theory or the theory of symbiosis, support the thesis that organisms are multiplicities that develop according to their interaction with environments and other

---

[2] Deleuze takes inspiration not only from biology, but also from the differential geometry of Friedrich Gauss and Bernhard Riemann. Riemann suggested a new approach to space by examining n-dimensional surfaces or spaces, which were defined through their intrinsic features and without embedding them into the global extrinsic higher-dimensional (N+1) space. Deleuze takes these main features of the manifold and extends them into a universal theory of multiplicity. As DeLanda points out, 'A Deleuzian multiplicity takes as its first defining feature these two traits of a manifold: its variable number of dimensions and, more importantly, the absence of a supplementary (higher) dimension imposing an extrinsic coordinatization, and hence, *an extrinsically defined unity*' (DeLanda 2002: 12, emphasis in original).

organisms. This thesis allows a major reconceptualisation of the notion of an organism: instead of thinking about organisms as Kantian wholes, we can interpret them as multiplicities, or assemblages, which can be examined not only vertically, according to their heredity, but also horizontally, according to their interaction with their environment (Bennett and Posteraro 2019: 12). This reconceptualisation of the notion of the organism contests the notion of biological individuality and anticipates the concept of the holobiont – the host organism plus its symbionts. Scott F. Gilbert argues that the notion of the holobiont is not limited to non-human organisms; it also radically changes our understanding of what it means to be a person (Gilbert et al. 2012; Gilbert 2017). Thus, a human organism can be seen as a multiplicity that includes other organic and inorganic components, such as micro-organisms or technological extensions. In this respect, the concept of multiplicity helps us to rethink the interaction between organisms of different species and the interaction between organic and inorganic components.

The ideas of processuality and multiplicity lead us to the question of potentiality. If the development of an organism is not defined by some prior form (preformationism), or by some transcendent principle (vitalism), how can we explain its development? How can something proceed, develop and change and still remain part of the same body, species or multiplicity? How do multiplicities emerge and coexist together? This can be explained by referring to the notion of potential, or potentiality, which explains how something new might emerge and thus change the existing structure or system. Simondon expresses this idea through a distinction between the preindividual phase and the process of individuation. Ruyer makes a similar distinction between equipotentiality, which is the reservoir of living forms, and the process of morphogenesis, which is an actual development. Deleuze encompasses both physical and biological notions of potentiality into his concept of the virtual and opposes it to the intensive and the actual. The Deleuzian ontology of becoming explains reality as the interplay between the virtual (the potential) and an actual becoming which accounts for the genesis of individuals and the process of ontogenesis.

The tension between potentiality and actuality also guides Malabou's work, where it appears as a struggle between plasticity and determination, epigenetics and genetic code, creativity and calculus. Malabou is looking for the potential for transformation and change not in the 'transcendental' realm but in the biological reality of an organism. Similarly, the notion of potentiality guides Simondon's and Stiegler's research into technical objects and technologies: it is pre-individual potentiality which explains both the development of technical objects and the evolution of technologies. The same question reappears in recent discussions about Gaia theory: is life on this planet something that can be measured and geo-engineered, as is implied in the Anthropocene theory, or is it an emergent property, an 'intrusive Gaia', which is potentially unpredictable and capable of eliminating humans from the surface of the Earth?

Thus, it is not difficult to discern that processuality, multiplicity and potentiality characterise any living being, or organism, if by organism we mean not a bounded and finite individual but something that is constantly developing, multiple and capable of change. In contemporary philosophy, the notion of the organism is often misinterpreted as a locus of identity and wholeness, and therefore it sometimes has negative connotations. For example, Deleuze and Guattari are hostile to the notion of the organism, which they understand as a principle of organisation and articulation, and to which they oppose their notion of the body without organs (Deleuze and Guattari 2004: 176–7). Thus, as Bennett and Posteraro point out, Deleuze and Guattari managed to reconceptualise the notion of the organism in such a way that it might be understood as an assemblage (Bennett and Posteraro 2019: 12). Such an understanding of the organism is consistent with recent developments in biology, such as the theory of autopoiesis, the notions of symbiosis and symbiogenesis, and the concept of the holobiont. Interpreted in this way, the notion of an organism can be significantly extended and used to account for the interactions between the different levels of the living system (internal organism), for the interaction between different species (a hybrid organism) and the interface between organic and inorganic, or technological, entities (an exo-organism). It also helps us to rethink the interactions between living and non-living systems on a planetary scale and to compare the quantitative approach to the Earth (the Anthropocene) and the qualitative theory of Gaia (interpreted as a quasi-organism).

## Outline of Chapters

This book, establishing the notion of an organism-oriented ontology, will try to bring forth an organic condition of philosophising as the necessary condition for contemporary philosophy. Chapter 1, 'Gilbert Simondon: From Ontology to Ontogenesis', introduces Simondon's theory of individuation. Simondon argues that philosophy should analyse not complete and self-identical individuals, but the processes of individuation. Individuation is understood as a shift from the pre-individual state to the continuous process of individuation, and the individual is seen only as a result, emanating from this process. In this respect, the theory of individuation tackles both the metaphysics of substance and traditional hylomorphism, and places processes at the centre of ontology. The process of individuation is seen as the potentiality for transformation, or change, when a metastable system is undergoing a phase shift under certain conditions. Simondon's theory is a good starting point for this book because it compares physical, biological, psychical and technical individuation. In contrast to physical individuation, which is completed when certain conditions are exhausted, biological and psychical individuation is in continuous transformation through the interaction both with the pre-individual and its milieu. Simondon's theory not only defines the unique trajectory of biological individuation but also reveals that psychical and social individuation, as well as technological individuation, are deeply rooted in the biological. The comparison between different kinds of individuation helps Simondon to develop a universal method of analogical paradigmatism. This method allows him to create a theory of ontogenesis which can explain both continuity and discontinuity between living and non-living, organic and inorganic systems.

Chapter 2, 'Raymond Ruyer: Organic Consciousness', discusses Ruyer's philosophy of biology. Like Simondon, Ruyer is interested not in bounded individuals, but in processes and becomings. In contrast to the theory of preformationism, which presumes that an organism is formed in advance and later changes only in quantity, Ruyer argues that an organism develops by undergoing a qualitative change and guides its own morphogenesis. Ruyer defines an organism as a primary consciousness, which has the capacity of equipotentiality and self-survey. Equipotentiality refers to an organism's capacity for change and transformation, whereas self-survey is understood as a recursive system of self-organisation which both directs the process of development, or morphogenesis, and maintains the organism's identity. For Ruyer, organic consciousness is primary in relation to secondary cerebral consciousness and to complex psychological consciousness. In this sense, organic consciousness is a characteristic of any living being. Human consciousness thus appears to be not the highest form of organisation, but just a phase in a biological continuum.

Chapter 3, 'Gilles Deleuze and Félix Guattari's Philosophy of Life', traces Simondon's and Ruyer's influence on Deleuze and Guattari's works. In *Difference and Repetition* Deleuze investigates the internal multiplicity within the organism, which appears as a tension between the virtual and the process of actual morphogenesis. The process of morphogenesis is described as intensive 'dramatisation', which ends up in actual differenciation into 'species and parts'. Deleuze argues that the model of actual differenciation allows him to describe physical, biological, psychical, social and linguistic multiplicities, and in this respect he follows the Simondonian method of analogical paradigmatism. However, in his later works, written with Guattari, the distinction between two modes of different/ciation is transformed into an investigation into external multiplicities, made of relations between different organisms, or between organisms and their environments. In *A Thousand Plateaus* Deleuze and Guattari remain hostile to the organicist notion of the organism (understood as an organised whole) and suggest a major reconceptualisation of the organism in terms of an assemblage, which, in contrast to the lines of descent and filiation, is open to symbiosis and 'unnatural participations'. Deleuze and Guattari read symbiosis as a multiplicity that is defined not by biological features but by co-functioning and multiple interactions.

Chapter 4, 'Catherine Malabou: Plasticity of Reason', examines the notion of plasticity which, derived from Hegel's vocabulary, becomes the main characteristic of life from stem cells to the brain and artificial intelligence. If Ruyer distinguishes between preformationism and morphogenetic improvisation, Malabou contrasts the traditional notion of form with her notion of 'plasticity', which refers to qualitative change that takes place both at the level of cells (cell plasticity) and the brain (neuroplasticity), and which can be either creative or destructive. It is destructive plasticity that is the most interesting for neurological and philosophical investigations because it reveals the rupture between the cerebral and the mental, or between cerebral auto-affection and mental auto-affection. In these cases, we discover something that Malabou names as the 'cerebral unconscious' – cerebral activity without consciousness. These discoveries open a gap between the brain and the mind, or between the biological and the logical origin of thinking. Deleuze and Guattari had already started to question the central role of the brain and described it as an interaction between the organism's inside and outside. In a similar tone, Malabou argues that instead of being seen as the proprietor of the brain, the subject is defined by his or her neuronal connectivity, which relates the inside to the outside, the brain to the outside world.

Chapter 5, 'General Organology: Between Organism and Machine', takes the discussion back to Simondon and his reconsideration of technical objects. Simondon creates a quasi-biological notion of the evolution of technical objects, although keeping in mind the difference between technical objects and living beings. Simondon's insights can be traced to Bergson and also to Georges Canguilhem, who proposed the term 'organology'. Organology examines technical invention as 'a universal biological phenomenon' and redefines machines as organs of the human species. Bernard Stiegler significantly elaborated the notion of 'general organology' and asserted that human life can be maintained only through the invention of tools and the organisation of the inorganic. Stiegler explained 'general organology' as a theory encompassing the articulation of bodily, technological and social organs (Stiegler 2010: 34). In this respect, Stiegler's 'general organology' allows us to compare biological, technological and social individuation as different stages of collective ontogenesis. The notion of organology is further elaborated by Hui (2019), who argues that technical objects become organic in the sense that they incorporate organic properties, such as recursivity and contingency. Thus, 'general organology' is a theory which explains technology through the model of the organism and of organic properties characteristic to living beings.

The theory of organology, relating biological, technological and cybernetic beings, poses a more general methodological question – how can these different levels of organisation be combined with each other? Chapter 6, 'Planetary Organism', discusses the attempts to connect all kinds of ontogenetic development into a consistent whole in terms of the Gaia hypothesis. In the 1970s James Lovelock explained Gaia in terms of a cybernetic machine; later, together with Lynn Margulis, they remodelled Gaia in terms of symbiogenesis and explained it as a kind of superorganism. At the same time, when Lovelock and Margulis were trying to conceptualise Gaia theory, Maturana and Varela were working on the theory of autopoiesis. In 1988 Lovelock, Margulis and Varela participated in a Gaia theory symposium in Italy, where Varela argued that Gaia can be characterised as being living-like, and therefore as an autopoietic entity. Margulis took Varela's point further by pointing out that cells and Gaia display a general property of autopoietic entities. The theory of autopoiesis was challenged by Donna J. Haraway's theory of sympoiesis, which helps to define the interaction between organisms and thus to explain how something new might emerge.

This is why chapter 7, 'Hybrid Organism', discusses symbiosis as a specific kind of biological assemblage. Haraway points out the obvious but ignored fact that every living being is dependent on other living beings, such as viruses, bacteria, archaea, etc. Referring to the theory of autopoiesis, Haraway argues that Margulis would have chosen the term 'sympoiesis', but the term had not yet surfaced at that time. The term 'sympoiesis', proposed by M. Beth Dempster, refers to collectively producing systems that do not have self-defined spatial or temporal boundaries. These systems are evolutionary and have the potential for change. Thus, the theory of sympoiesis discredits the notion of the bounded individual and examines living beings as mutually interconnected and interdependent. Similarly, Gilbert argues that there is no such thing as biological individuality; both human and non-human animals are holobionts – organisms coexisting with persistent communities of symbionts (Gilbert et al. 2012; Gilbert 2017). Taking this into account, Haraway suggests sympoiesis as a continuous process of 'becoming-with' which creates new networks of collaboration and gives an increased potency to its collaborators. However, the question that still needs to be answered is whether all forms of coexistence are profitable and welcomed. In this respect, the concept of immunity is central in discussing the theory of sympoiesis: how does one define the limit at which coexistence is collaborative and productive, and beyond which it becomes damaging and lethal?

In the final chapter, 'Conclusion: Organism-Oriented Ontology', I summarise all of the threads coming from these different theories and argue that the concept of an organism-oriented ontology allows us to rethink the differences between living and non-living systems; to explain the tension between the self-referential, homeostatic nature of the organism and its continuous capacity of change and development; and, finally, to reconceptualise the notion of cognition by taking into account the multiplicity of organic processes defining human and non-human living beings. The notion of an organism-oriented ontology helps to reflect different modalities of life, especially the continuity between biological processes taking place in the body and those taking place in the mind. Maturana and Varela's idea that living systems are cognitive systems, and that a living process is nothing other than a process of cognition, radically changes our understanding of cognition and the mind. This means that the brain is not the centre of control and that cognitive processes can take place at different levels of organic organisation. Ruyer's idea about primary consciousness being present in every living being, similar to Deleuze and Guattari's insistence that everywhere there are forces that constitute microbrains, allows us to have a different perspective on the world as rooted in biological cognition. Brian Massumi, influenced by Ruyer and Deleuze, defines this perspective as a 'subjectivity-without-a-subject', while assuming that the word 'subjectivity' might not be the right one (Massumi 2014: 41). In this book I will argue that the notion of 'subjectivity-without-a-subject' has important political and ethical consequences. If organic plasticity is not pre-programmed and does not have to adapt to the environment but rather helps to create it, then it offers a new conceptual tool to rethink resilience and creativity. In this respect, an organism-oriented ontology can be described as an ontology of resistance: if biopolitics operates by creating hierarchies, by making divisions and exclusions, an organism-oriented ontology is all-inclusive and non-hierarchical. To rethink organic plasticity in terms of processuality, multiplicity and potentiality, capable of qualitative change, we need to define organism-oriented ontology, which is the aim of this book.

# 1
# Gilbert Simondon: From Ontology to Ontogenesis

This chapter analyses Gilbert Simondon's theory of ontogenesis, which describes the processes of the individuation of living and non-living beings. Simondon argues that philosophy should be concerned not with substantial, defined and bounded individuals but with the processes of individuation that create these individuals. Thus, Simondon creates a universal theory of individuation, which is understood as a process initiated by the pre-individual state that contains a potential or a charge, and is then accomplished in a series of differentiations that result in creating an individual. In this sense, Simondon argues that ontology is based not on identity but on difference that forces individuals to move from one phase to another and undergo a qualitative change. What is relevant for this book is that Simondon creates a method of analogical paradigmatism that allows one to compare different – physical, biological, psychosocial and technical – systems. Simondon not only defines the unique nature of biological individuation but also reveals that psychical and social individuation, as well as technical invention, are deeply rooted in the biological. The comparison between different kinds of individuations helps Simondon to develop a universal theory of ontogenesis which can explain the continuity between living and non-living, organic and inorganic systems.

Simondon's works are not very numerous: his main ideas are formulated in the doctoral thesis *Individuation in Light of Notions of Form and Information* and the complementary thesis *On the Existence of Technical Objects*, both defended in 1958. The complementary thesis was published immediately after the defence in 1958, whereas his major work on individuation had to wait to become accessible to a wider audience.[1] Nevertheless, Simondon's

---

[1] Simondon's main doctoral thesis, *L'Individuation à la lumière des notions de forme et d'information*, first appeared as two separate works: the first part was published under the title *L'individu et sa genèse physico-biologique* by PUF in 1964, and the second part was published under the title *L'individuation psychique et collective* by Aubier in 1989. The main doctoral thesis was published in its entirety by Jérôme Millon in 2005. It was translated into English quite recently: *Individuation*

works were known to his contemporaries, and his works deeply influenced Gilles Deleuze, who not only wrote a review of Simondon's book, but also incorporated Simondon's ideas into his own work.[2] Simondon's notion of individuation is discussed in Deleuze's *Difference and Repetition*, and his theory of material becoming can be traced throughout Deleuze and Guattari's *A Thousand Plateaus*. Recently Simondon's works have been widely discussed and reconsidered by Bernard Stiegler, Yuk Hui, Elizabeth Grosz, Anne Sauvagnargues, Brian Massumi and others. Several journal issues have been dedicated to Simondon's ideas and their reception in contemporary philosophy.[3] In this chapter I will concentrate on Simondon's theory of ontogenesis, or individuation, which examines the processes of individuation taking place in physical, biological and psychosocial domains. Simondon's theory of technical objects and its influence on the theory of general organology will be discussed in Chapter 5.

## Physical Individuation: Transduction

In defining his philosophical project, Simondon argues that we have to examine being not as something stable and identical to itself, but as something developing or becoming. The most important philosophical question, in Simondon's view, is not 'What is being?' but how being is becoming, what stages or phases it undergoes. Simondon argues that the traditional metaphysical approach to being takes into account only those properties that describe being as a self-identical and substantial entity, whose paradigmatic model is an individual. In the Introduction to his *Individuation* Simondon explains:

> There are two paths according to which the reality of being qua individual can be approached: a substantialist path, which considers the being as consisting in its unity, given to itself, founded on itself, not engendered and as resistant to what is not itself; and then there is a hylomorphic

---

*in Light of Notions of Form and Information*, trans. Taylor Adkins, Minneapolis, MN: University of Minnesota Press, 2020; *Individuation in Light of Notions of Form and Information*, vol. II: *Supplemental Texts*, trans. Taylor Adkins, Minneapolis, MN: University of Minnesota Press, 2020. The complementary thesis, *Du mode d'existence des objets techniques*, was published by Aubier in 1958. It was translated into English as *On the Mode of Existence of Technical Objects*, trans. Cécile Malaspina and John Rogove, Minneapolis, MN: Univocal Publishing, 2017. Some translations of Simondon were published in *Parrhesia* (Simondon 2009a; Simondon 2009b).

[2] There is more about Simondon's influence on Gilles Deleuze in Chapter 3.

[3] *Parrhesia: A Journal of Critical Philosophy* (On Gilbert Simondon), ed. Arne De Boever, Alex Murray, Jonathan Roffe and Ashley Woodward, 7, 2009; *Pli: The Warwick Journal of Philosophy* (special volume: Deleuze and Simondon), 12, 2012; *Deleuze Studies* (Ontologies of Difference: The Philosophies of Gilbert Simondon and Raymond Ruyer), ed. Andrew Iliadis, 11.4, 2017.

path, which considers the individual as generated by the encounter of a form and a matter. (Simondon 2020a: 1)

The substantialist path presumes that there is a principle of individuation which might explain what is an individual. However, the principle of individuation has to be explained itself. The other, hylomorphic path, is also misleading because the principle of individuation is supposed to be contained either in the matter, or in the form. In other words, both substantialist atomism and hylomorphism start from the individual instead of explaining how this individual is created: both approaches presume that, first, there is an individual, and then, secondly, there is individuation or development. By contrast, Simondon suggests that the process of individuation is prior to the emergence of the individual: 'we would try to grasp ontogenesis in the whole unfolding of its reality and *to know the individual through individuation rather than individuation starting from the individual*' (Simondon 2020a: 3, emphasis in original). In other words, philosophical research should focus on the principle of ontogenesis, or individuation, instead of examining an individual as a final and autonomous reality. In this respect, individuation should be considered as an ongoing process, whereas an individual is only a temporary and partial result which emerges by interrupting or arresting the processes of individuation.

Thus, Simondon argues that individuation arises neither from a certain substance, nor from an interaction between a matter and a form, but from a tense and supersaturated system. This system is named as a pre-individual state; in other words, a state that is anterior to unity and identity, because unity and identity can be applied only to being that is individuated (Simondon 2020a: 4). Simondon takes the hypothesis about the pre-individual state from physics, namely, from the thermodynamic notion of metastable equilibrium. A stable equilibrium is achieved when all potential energies are actualised and all transformations achieved; by contrast, a metastable equilibrium is a system that is neither stable nor unstable, but is charged with potentials for becoming, and that contains enough potential to 'produce an abrupt alteration leading to a new, equally metastable structuration' (Simondon 2020a: 369). As one of many examples of metastable equilibrium Simondon discusses the duality of a photon, which can be regarded both as a particle and a wave, or both as a physical individual and as a certain amount of energy, capable of potential change. Thus, a metastable equilibrium, which defines the pre-individual state, can be considered as a reservoir of potential energy, which is the condition for transformation and change, and which engenders the process of individuation.

However, as Simon Mills points out, 'For Simondon potential does not mean the same as possibility or the virtual but something wholly real that is indicative of the potential energy inherent in metastability' (Mills 2016: 36). In other words, the potential is not virtual in the sense that Deleuze gives to the term (we will discuss this point later) but rather designates a physical energy, which has the capacity to undergo a phase shift. For example, under a certain temperature, water can undergo a phase shift and turn into ice or a gas. Hence, as Simondon explains, 'becoming is a dimension of the being and corresponds to the being's capacity to phase-shift with respect to itself, to resolve itself by phase-shifting' (Simondon 2020a: 4). To consider individuation we have to take into account this constant change or flux, which does not allow the application of the categories of unity and identity. The latter can be applied only to the last phase of individuation which creates a completed individual. However, this last phase of individuation exhausts its potential and excludes becoming, therefore no phase shift is possible.

In other words, for Simondon the primary ontological reality is becoming, or the process of individuation, rather than stable and self-identical being. Only by discovering the principle of individuation can we explain being as individuated being. As Simondon points out, *instead of grasping individuation on the basis of the individuated being, the individuated being must be grasped on the basis of individuation and individuation on the basis of pre-individual being*, which is distributed according to several orders of magnitude' (Simondon 2020a: 12, emphasis in original). This methodological shift requires a change in terminology: instead of examining the notions of substance, form and matter, Simondon turns to such terms as information, metastability, internal resonance, energetic potential and orders of magnitude (Simondon 2020a: 12). All these terms imply a relation, but not a relation that is established between two pre-existing terms; it is a relation that is simultaneous with those terms whose existence it guarantees. This relation cannot be explained through the principle of identity and the principle of excluded middle, and it needs a new method – that of transduction.

Transduction appears in the middle of the pre-individual being and expresses the tension, the disparity between a certain problem and its possible solution. It is important to stress that transduction is a process, or a propagation, from which something new emerges – it is simultaneously a transformation, or a change, and a new reality emerging from this change. As Simondon points out,

> By transduction we mean a physical, biological, mental, or social operation through which an activity propagates incrementally within a domain by basing this propagation on a structuration of the domain operated from one region to another: each structural region serves as a principle and model, as an initiator for constituting the following region, such that a modification thereby extends progressively throughout this structuring operation. (Simondon 2020a: 13)

A good example of this structuring activity is the process of crystallisation: the supersaturated mother liquid contains a tension, an excess of potentiality, therefore it is enough to introduce a very small seed – a piece of dust – to resolve this tension and start the process of crystallisation. The crystal starts growing and expanding in all directions, and 'each previously constituted molecular layer serves as the structuring basis for the layer in the process of forming' (Simondon 2020a: 13). As Anne Sauvagnargues points out, 'For Simondon, this term refers to the dephasing or structuring differentiation through which individuation takes place in such a way that each structured region serves as a constitutive principle for the next region' (Sauvagnargues 2012a: 7). Thus, transduction is a method of ontogenetic structuration that explains the genesis of reality and also allows one to compare ontogenetic structuration taking place in different domains.

Simondon argues that the notion of transduction can not only be applied to a physical domain, but also accounts for biological, or vital, and psychical individuation. In the domain of physical operation, transduction expresses the growth and development of a physical structure which is effectuated as progressive iteration (the crystal grows by iterating its own structure), whereas in the domain of the vital operation it can produce heterogeneous domains as a result of the interaction between the living organism and its environment. However, transduction defines not only physical and vital domains, but also the psychical and the domain of knowledge. In the domain of knowledge transduction is related to the discovery of the problematic – an idea that is elaborated in Deleuze's *Difference and Repetition*. This signals that transduction for Simondon is not only a technical term but a new method of thinking: 'Transduction corresponds to this existence of rapports that takes hold when pre-individual being individuates; it expresses individuation and allows for individuation to be thought; it is therefore a notion that is both metaphysical and logical; *it applies to ontogenesis and is ontogenesis itself*' (Simondon 2020a: 14, emphasis in original). In other words, transduction expresses not only the method of dynamic transformation and structuration, but also a different logic, which can account for this transformation in different domains. As Simondon argues, transduction can be used 'as the basis of a new type of analogical paradigmatism in order to pass from physical individuation to organic individuation, from organic individuation to psychical individuation, and from psychical individuation to the subjective and objective transindividual' (Simondon 2020a: 14). Thus, transduction is a new method of thinking which is different from deduction and induction. In contrast to deduction, which searches for a transcendental principle to solve the problem found in the domain, transduction extracts the resolving structure from the domain itself and from its potentials. For example, a supersaturated liquid resolves its tension by using its own potential and starting the process of crystallisation without the help of any external principle or form (Simondon 2020a: 15). On the other hand, transduction is opposed to induction: even if induction extracts the terms from the studied domain, it retains only what is common to all of them and thus eliminates difference and singularity. Transduction, by contrast, retains all differences and disparities and makes them communicate in such a way that it integrates them into a new system or structure.

In this respect, the notion of transduction implies two important consequences. First, transduction is a mental procedure that retains differences and disparities not by negating or reducing them, but by restructuring them into a new system or structure: 'resolving transduction *operates the inversion of the negative into the positive*: that through which the terms are not identical to one another, that through which they are *disparate* [. . .] is integrated into the system of resolution and becomes a condition of signification' (Simondon 2020a: 15, emphasis in original). In this sense, transduction can be compared to Hegelian dialectics, because transduction presupposes a relation between two contradicting or disparate domains. However, in contrast to dialectics, transduction does not seek a resolution to this contradiction, it does not seek a synthesis that could homogenise these disparate domains. 'Where Hegel imagines internal contradiction and difference in the concept, Simondon proposes a real disparity, a heterogeneity between the terms that only the problematic relation puts in tension, and that cannot be put in tension without their heterogeneity being maintained' (Sauvagnargues 2012a: 10). Another important point is that transduction never seeks to overcome differences in a unifying synthesis; instead, 'transductive disparation makes heterogeneity the constitutive condition for the invention of a new solution. Disparation is made possible by this ineradicable difference' (Sauvagnargues 2012a: 10). Transduction maintains difference or disparity between two heterogeneous systems, two orders of magnitude, and forces them to communicate and create a new problematic, full of potentials and capable of new transformations.[4] Deleuze interprets this transductive disparation as the necessary condition of thinking, which he names as the problematic. For Deleuze, 'the problematic replaces the negative' (Deleuze 2004d: 88) and allows for a new categorisation of reality in positive terms.

From this follows the second consequence: the notions of form and matter should be replaced by that of information. As was mentioned before, Simondon criticises both substantialist atomism and the hylomorphic doctrine because both approaches start from the constituted and given individual, and only then examine how this individual is changed in the process of individuation. Substantialist atomism is deceiving because substance is never finished or completed; all elements exist in a relationship with their environment and are defined by it. For example, if we put a crystal into a new supersaturated solution, it will start growing again. The hylomorphic approach is deceiving in a similar way because it presupposes

---

[4] As Elizabeth Grosz points out, 'Transduction can be considered the converse of the dialectic – it analyzes not what must be overcome, negated, and left behind as the detritus of history, as do Hegelian and Marxist dialectical models, but what returns, transforms itself without an unusable residue, and that, if it leaves a remainder, leaves it as dynamic and full of potential, an inexhaustible if changing virtuality' (Grosz 2017: 180).

a passive matter and an active form as two separate and already existing individuals: a form is superimposed upon a matter and moulds it into a certain shape.

By contrast, Simondon argues that instead of examining form and matter as two separate entities, we should think about a form-taking activity that defines what ontogenesis is. For example, a brick can be made by superimposing a mould on to clay: clay is seen as a passive matter that receives its form from the mould. However, as Simondon points out, 'the clay is not just passively deformable; it's actively plastic, because it's colloidal; its capacity to receive a form is not distinct from its capacity to keep it, because keeping and receiving amounts to the same thing' (Simondon 2020a: 24). As Muriel Combes points out, 'The clay can eventually be transformed into bricks because it possesses colloidal properties that render it capable of conducting a deforming energy while maintaining the coherence of molecular chains, because it is in a sense "already in form" in the swampy earth' (Combes 2013: 6). In other words, in order to be moulded, the clay must have a potential for deformation that allows it to transform into a brick.

> The relation between matter and form thus does not take place between inert matter and a form coming from outside: there is a common operation that is on the same level of existence between matter and form; this common level of existence is that of *force* ... [...] Matter and form are brought together as *forces*. (Simondon 2020a: 26–7, emphasis in original)

In other words, the form-taking activity can be accounted for only as a system of an energetic regime where opposite forces are affecting each other.

Thus, the opposition between matter and form (or mould) should be replaced by the notion of modulation, which explains the interaction between form-giving force and form-taking force as a continuous and fluctuating modulation. Therefore, Simondon suggests the replacement of the concept of form by that of information: information is a signification that emerges out of disparity or difference between two orders of magnitude, such as a supersaturated solution and a seed in the process of crystallisation, or as the form-taking activity of clay and the form-giving activity of a mould in brick formation. As Simondon observes,

> in order to think the transductive operation, which is the basis of individuation in its various levels, the notion of form is insufficient [...] *The notion of form must be replaced with that of information*, which supposes the existence of a system in a state of metastable equilibrium that can individuate; unlike form, information is never a single term but the signification that emerges from a disparation. (Simondon 2020a: 16)

As we can understand from this quotation, the notion of information is used here in a non-conventional way:[5] it refers not to the technology of transmission but to signification, which appears from the disparity between two orders of magnitude, or between two different sub-systems. Information here expresses an active communication, an internal resonance between two heterogeneous realities. In this respect, Simondon's notion of information is very different from that which was formulated in cybernetics and information theory, because it cannot be understood in quantitative terms. As Brian Massumi points out, for Simondon, information implies a qualitative change to a new level of existence, a new reality (Massumi 2012: 32). Transduction, modulation and information can be seen as diverse paths to reach a qualitative change enabling the creation of a new ontological reality.

## Biological Individuation: The Membrane

The theory of individuation explains not only the transformation of physical entities but also the development of biological individuals. However, biological individuality is much more complicated than physical: 'in biology it seems that the notion of individuality is applicable to several stages or according to different levels of successive inclusion' (Simondon 2020a: 168). Biological individuation is interpreted as a process of transduction when one biological form is transformed into another. In this sense, both physical individuation and biological individuation involve a kind of transduction. However, some important differences occur between the two: in contrast to physical individuation, which is completed when certain conditions are exhausted, the individuation of a living being is never completed but is an ongoing process; 'it is not merely a result of individuation, like the crystal or molecule, but a theater of individuation' (Simondon 2020a: 7). Moreover, unlike in physical individuation, where heterogeneous transductive characteristics appear at the margins of physical reality, for example at the edges of a crystal, biological individuation requires a transduction that differentiates between the interior and the exterior of a living being. A living being is a system of communication where the interior is always in communication with the exterior and vice versa. In other words, the individuation of a living being cannot be completed in a single stroke, but needs an ongoing transformation. As Simondon observes, 'the living being resolves problems, not just by adapting, i.e. by modifying its relation to the milieu (like a machine is capable of doing), but by modifying itself, by inventing new

---

[5] As Mills points out, 'In the early cybernetic model the notion of information corresponded to the transfer of a message from a sender to a receiver within a system that presumed the pre-establishment of entities between which messages could flow. It is important to understand that in Simondon's conceptualization of information terms do not exist prior to the operation of individuation, therefore this cybernetic model of information exchange is not yet apposite' (Mills 2016: 47).

internal structures, and by completely introducing itself into the axiomatic of vital problems' (Simondon 2020a: 7). The physical being has no real interiority, whereas the living being is constantly transforming itself from within and also keeps track of this continuous transformation.

In other words, physical individuation is finite and it works as a quantum leap that resolves the tension in a single stroke, whereas biological individuation is never completed. It always carries a certain charge of pre-individual potential within itself, which, in its turn, constitutes a new problematic and initiates new phases of individuation. As Simondon points out,

> The living individual is contemporaneous with itself in all its elements, which is not the case for the physical individual, for the latter includes a past that has radically passed, even when it is still in the process of growing. At the interior of itself, the living being is a node of informative communication; it is a system within a system, involving *within itself* a mediation between two orders of magnitude. (Simondon 2020a: 8, emphasis in original)

For example, a crystal, after being formed and completed, becomes inertial and submerges into the past, whereas a living being stretches in two directions at once: it is directed towards the outside, the external milieu, and towards the inside, which is restructured and attuned to this milieu with the help of internal resonance. Thus, the living individual is created by two orders of magnitude: it is constantly restructured according to the external milieu, or environment, which is actual, and, at the same time, it is permanently recharged by its pre-individual potential. As Grosz points out,

> Life remains indebted to the pre-individual to the extent that the resources for all its becomings, all its future individuations, self-actualizations, must be drawn from these singularities which its own must incorporate. The 'phases' of life, from fertilized egg to corpse, are internally structured, organized through the forces that enable life to elaborate itself . . . (Grosz 2012b: 49)

In this sense, a living being, or life in general, can be maintained only if it constantly remains connected to the pre-individual charge and is able to keep a metastable equilibrium. That means that living beings never reach a stable equilibrium because biological individuation proceeds from one metastable condition to another metastable condition, which is seen as the necessary condition of life. As Mills points out, 'in the case of vital individuation the operation does not resolve, for in doing so it would result in the death of the organism. Vital individuation requires an ongoing metastable tension and the need for further problems requiring solution' (Mills 2016: 59). A living being is alive only if it is capable of resolving its problematic by entering into a new phase of metastability.

A metastable equilibrium means that a living being maintains, prolongs and sustains its activity by constantly interacting with its milieu and with the pre-individual potential. In this respect, the theory of individuation, or ontogenesis, challenges the theory of adaptation, as described by Jean-Baptiste Lamarck and Charles Darwin. According to Simondon,

> The notion of adaptation is poorly formed to the extent that it supposes the existence of terms as preceding that of relation; what deserves to be critiqued is not the modality of relation such as the theory of adaptation envisions it; what deserve to be critiqued are the very conditions of this relation coming after the terms. (Simondon 2020a: 234)

The problem here is that such a clear opposition between a living being and its milieu could appear only in a world of stable equilibrium where all potentials have been exhausted and where no transformation is possible. But to account for the activity of the living, one must replace the idea of the stable equilibrium with that of the metastable. Simondon argues that a living being and its milieu are mutually correlative in such a way that their potentials cannot be fully actualised or exhausted but are resolved through integration into the higher dimension.

> According to such a conception, in order to think the living being, life must be thought as a transductive result of operations of individuation or, better yet, as an interlinking of successive resolutions, insofar as each previous resolution can be taken back up and reincorporated in subsequent resolutions. In this sense, we could consider that life in its entirety seems like a progressive construction of increasingly elaborate forms, i.e. forms capable of containing increasingly elevated problems. (Simondon 2020a: 237)

Thus, life is seen as the resolution of problematic, which might not always be successful. Life as a posed problem might not be resolved or might be resolved badly – this is how death comes into life. Death also arrives when the metastable equilibrium is exhausted, deprived of potentials and can no longer enhance new individuations. In this sense, a metastable equilibrium is the necessary condition of life.

And yet some other conditions are required to define life. In the chapter 'Topology and Ontogenesis' Simondon suggests that to define a living being we need a special topology that expresses the relation between a milieu of interiority and a milieu of exteriority. 'Perhaps the space of the living being isn't a Euclidean space . . . [. . .] perhaps the essence of the living being is a certain topological arrangement that cannot be known based on the physics and chemistry that typically use Euclidean space' (Simondon 2020a: 250). But how can we imagine this non-Euclidean space and how does it change our understanding of biological individuation? Simondon argues that a living being requires a special topological arrangement: a membrane. 'The living membrane [. . .] is characterized as what separates a region of interiority from a region of exteriority: the membrane is polarized and therefore allows the passage of some particular body centripetally or centrifugally while blocking the passage of some other particular body' (Simondon 2020a: 251). The membrane functions as a polarising force that differentiates between what is favourable and unfavourable for the organism. Moreover, the membrane not only separates the interiority from the exteriority within the living being but functions as a differentiating force that keeps the organism in a state of metastability. As Sauvagnargues asserts, 'this interiority and exteriority are not absolute but metastable, dynamic, relative to each other, and their interfacing surface is itself in becoming, in relation' (Sauvagnargues 2012b: 67). That means that in a multicellular organism the limit between interiority and exteriority is always relative, depending on its place in the organisation of a living being.

As Simondon explains, in the topology of a living organism we find various levels of interiority and exteriority. For example, the space of the digestive cavities is a space of exteriority in relation to the bloodstream that floods the intestinal walls, but blood is a milieu of exteriority in respect to the endocrine glands that release the products of their activity into the blood (Simondon 2020a: 252). This means that the structure of a complex organism is like a multiple folding where the internal milieu is enfolded into an external milieu, which in its turn becomes the internal milieu to be enfolded into a more complex external milieu. The membrane arranges a transductive mediation between different levels of interiorities and exteriorities. The topological arrangement of living space implies that life is sustained through metastability; in other words, one can never have a final and unifying vision of living systems: 'The totalizing vision and the elementary vision are equally inadequate; we have to start with the basic function that depends on the first topological structure of interiority and exteriority, and then we have to see how this function is mediated by a chain of intermediary interiorities and exteriorities' (Simondon 2020a: 252). This is why vital, or biological, individuation must be interpreted in terms of topological schemata that describe the living being in terms of differentiation and metastability.

The topological arrangement of space is not the only requirement to think the living being. Another requirement is the continuity of time, which virtually condenses all stages of individuation into the lived present. It is this arrangement of time that allows us to draw a line between the living and the non-living. For example, in the individuation of a crystal, the interiority of an already formed crystal has become stable and inert and does not provide any information for its further individuation. A crystal is growing only at the edges, but this growth is not informed by its interiority and its past. As Simondon points out,

> in order for the crystal to individuate, it must continue to grow; this individuation is superficial; the past doesn't serve a purpose in the crystal's

mass ... Conversely, in the living being [...] the whole content of the interior space is topologically in contact with the content of the exterior space at the limits of the living being ... (Simondon 2020a: 253)

The interiority of a living being condenses all forms that have been produced by individuation in the past, and this condensed past is actively related to individuating processes taking place in the exteriority of the living being. This means that topology is a space without distance: the interior space is actively present in the exterior space at the limits of a living being. This reformulation of space is also applicable to time: the chronology of a living being condenses and keeps in the present tense all layers of previous successive individuations. As Simondon argues, 'In the same way that there are no distances in topology, in chronology there is no quantity of time' (Simondon 2020a: 254). Thus, time is not continuous; time is defined as discontinuity, contiguity and envelopment of different time layers, of different moments of the past, which become contiguous in the interiority of a living being. We can argue that the interiority of a living being transforms the quantity of time into the quality of time in the sense that time that has already passed can create the basis for future individuations. Every present moment of a living being is interconnected with the past retained in its interiority, and with the future coming from exteriority. As Simondon points out, 'the present is this metastability of the rapport between interior and exterior, past and future; the exterior is exterior and the interior is interior relative to this mutual allagmatic activity of presence. Topology and chronology coincide in the individuation of the living being' (Simondon 2020a: 254). In other words, Simondon's theory of vital individuation proposes new conceptions of space and time: topology as a theory of space without distance, and chronology as a theory of time without quantity.

In this respect, the individuation of a living being can be compared to a self-organising autopoietic system, discussed by Maturana and Varela in *Autopoiesis and Cognition* (1980). An autopoietic system, for example a cell, is closed on the level of organisation; this condition is known as 'operational closure'. At the same time, an autopoietic unit is energetically open to the environment from which it gets nutrients and energy. Thus, an autopoietic unit is closed and open at the same time: it is closed on the level of organisation, but open to the environment on the level of structure. However, even getting the necessary support from the environment, the autopoietic system remains closed in the respect that it constantly reproduces its internal structure.

In comparison to an autopoietic system, Simondon's theory proposes a more dynamic approach that explains not only the relationship between a living being and its environment, but also its development into a more complex system. As Mills points out,

Simondon's theorization of individuation offers a novel way to think about the openness of systems. Where in the case of autopoiesis the coupling of the system occurs at a single level of magnitude, for Simondon the system maintains an ongoing relation to the broader environment (pre-individual) as a whole. That is to say that the individual 'is sustained by a double relationship' [...] first with its milieu, which exists on the same level of magnitude as it does, and second with the wider metastability of the pre-individual. (Mills 2016: 61–2)

In this respect, Simondon differentiates between the relationship with an environment, which is entirely actual, and the relationship with the pre-individual, which is a potentiality of forces constantly feeding the process of individuation. The pre-individual here can be thought of as the potential or the virtual force of individuation. As Mark B. N. Hansen observes, Maturana and Varela's theory of autopoiesis examines an actual relationship between an individual and the environment, whereas Simondon adds to this a crucial component – 'continuity across the potentiality–actuality divide' (Hansen 2009: 134). In other words, besides the actual relation between a living being and its environment, which occurs within a single level or 'order of magnitude', Simondon adds a relation between an individual and the pre-individual potential, which occurs between two different levels or two 'orders of magnitude' (Hansen 2009: 134). However, Simondon insists that this potential is not virtual but perfectly real; it is a veritable reality. This idea is elaborated further by Deleuze in his theory of the virtual and the actual, as I will demonstrate in Chapter 3.

## Psychical Individuation: The Transindividual

For Simondon, vital individuation is prolonged in psychical individuation: the entrance into the psychical realm manifests itself as a new problematic, charged with pre-individual potentiality. The psychical reality is never enclosed in itself and needs other individuals to resolve its problematic: thus psychical life goes from the pre-individual to the collective. To be more precise, the collective is a transindividual reality that needs to be distinguished from the social and the interindividual. The social expresses the manner in which living beings exist in a society, human or animal; the social encompasses the individuals that are fully formed and do not require new individuations. Similarly, an interindividual relation expresses some reciprocity and exchange between already formed individuals and therefore does not initiate new individuations. By contrast, the transindividual collective puts all individuals in relation to the pre-individual charge, which engenders a new tension, or a new problematic, which, in turn, initiates new individuations. An individuated being always keeps a certain residue of pre-individual reality that allows it to reconnect to the transindividual collective.

Psychical individuation, similar to vital individuation, is organised around a certain polarity: psychical individuals are in contact with their interiority, which is defined as an affect, and also maintain a contact with their exteriority, which is defined as a sensation. Such an explanation of psychical life questions all theories of consciousness and also the psychoanalytic notions of consciousness and the unconscious. As Simondon points out, 'At the limit between consciousness and the unconscious, on the contrary, there is the layer of subconsciousness, which is essentially affectivity and emotivity. This relational layer constitutes the center of individuality' (Simondon 2020a: 273). By placing affectivity and emotivity at the centre of psychical life, Simondon opens a dimension that is common to all living organisms: 'no living being seems to be deprived of affectivo-emotivity, which has a quantum nature for highly complex beings such as humans and also for beings that are only partially organized' (Simondon 2020a: 274). The affectivo-emotive dimension forms the basis of intersubjective communication, which might exist not only between humans but also between animals. Thus, affect refers to non-conscious activity, common to humans and animals, which responds both to the internal disequilibrium within the organism and to the external perturbations coming from the environment. As Mills asserts,

> Affect then is the fundamental way that an organism orients itself within its environment. It operates between two different orders of magnitude and is signified in each of them differently: from the perspective of the organism it is signified as a change in its internal resonance and from an environmental perspective it is signified by a change in the organism's behaviour. (Mills 2016: 74–5)

In this sense, affectivity for Simondon is a more fundamental characteristic than perception: perception always presupposes a certain unity of a perceiving subject, whereas affectivity is a transductive operation, which constantly changes and is changed both by internal impulses and external sensations. Affectivity expresses the organism's metastability, different phase shifts taking place within the living being, which can never be unified: 'it is always *both more and less* than a unity given the metastability internal to the organism that always has the potential for further individuation, but also due to its emergence from and continuing role in the broader individuation of the environment' (Mills 2016: 76, emphasis in original). Similar to the polarising function of the membrane in living beings, affect expresses the dynamic relationships between the organism's interiority and exteriority.

Affective activity keeps the living being in contact with the pre-individual charge and it also relates the living being to the transindividual collective. However, at some point this affective contradiction has to be overcome, and this role is taken by emotion. As Simondon asserts,

> Emotion arises when the integration of the current state into a single affective dimension is impossible, just as perception arises when sensa-

tions call for incompatible tropisms [...] Emotion is a discovery of the unity of the living being, just as perception is a discovery of the unity of the world ... The interior universe is emotive, just as the exterior universe is perceptive. (Simondon 2020a: 289)

Simondon even states that emotion, as much as perception, is 'totalitarian' in the sense that it imposes on affection and sensation a certain form of organisation, which creates a system or a structure. However, even if emotion implies a certain structure, it never results in creating a unified subject. Rather, it attunes the living being with the collective and thus can be seen as a first step towards the transindividual collective. Therefore, the next stage of the structuring activity is perception, which is understood as a transductive operation between the organism and the objective world. For Simondon, perception means not the relationship between a subject and an object, as defined in phenomenology,[6] but a transductive operation that invents and creates this object. As Simondon points out,

Before perception, before the genesis of the form that perception precisely is, the relation of incompatibility between the subject and the milieu only exists as a potential ... Perception is not the grasping of a form but the resolution of a conflict, the discovery of a compatibility, the *invention* of a form. (Simondon 2020a: 259, emphasis in original)

To illustrate this statement, we can turn to Simondon's example of binocular vision: the left retina and the right retina produce different two-dimensional images, which cannot overlap because they represent the world as seen from different perspectives. However, this disparity between two-dimensional images is resolved in a tri-dimensional perception that integrates both images into a higher dimension of vision (Simondon 2020a: 229). In this sense, visual perception is a transductive operation that resolves the disparity by inventing a new form.

In other words, perception is understood not as a subjective experience of an external world, but as a transductive operation that organises both the subject and the world. Following Norbert Wiener, Simondon argues that perception is a struggle against the entropy of a system: 'It is not enough to simply say that perception consists in grasping organized wholes; in fact, perception is the act that organizes wholes' (Simondon 2020a: 269). However, to perceive does not mean to receive the signals of information – neither the quantity nor the quality of information can explain perceptive

---

[6] Simondon was influenced by his doctoral supervisor, Maurice Merleau-Ponty. Both Simondon and Merleau-Ponty were seeking to demonstrate the relationship between the human psyche and the biological body, although in quite different ways. Merleau-Ponty suggested the notion of the lived body (*chair*), whereas Simondon developed his theory of individuation.

activity. Rather it is the intensity, the grasping and organisation of intensities that accounts for the creation of the subject–world system. In this sense, the intensive diversity found in the subject–world system allows it to resemble a supersaturated solution: 'perception is the resolution that transforms the tension that affected this supersaturated system into an organized structure; it could be said that every veritable perception is the resolution of a problem of compatibility' (Simondon 2020a: 270). Similar to Merleau-Ponty, Simondon is attempting to demonstrate that neither the world nor the subject (consciousness) can exist separately from one another, and that every change in the problematic of the vital domain engenders changes in the psychical domain. In other words, the problematic found in biological individuation can be resolved only by entering a higher dimension of psychical individuation.

Thus affect, emotion and perception form the background of psychical activity. However, individual psychical activity never achieves a final resolution of the tensions, differences and disparities that come from vital individuation. These tensions can be resolved only in collective psychical individuation. Simondon argues that within the regime of psychical individuation we can discern two types of relations: the interindividual relation (of affectivity and perception) and the transindividual.

> The interindividual relation goes from individual to individual; it does not penetrate individuals; transindividual action is what makes it such that individuals exist together as the elements of a system that contains potentials and metastability, expectation and tension, then the discovery of a structure and of a functional organization that integrate and resolve this problematic of incorporated immanence. (Simondon 2020a: 339)

Biological individuation does not fully resolve tensions and disparities, neither in humans nor in animals: 'it is precisely based on this position of the unresolved in man, within this not-yet-individuated charge of reality, that man seeks out his fellow man to form a group in which he will find presence through a second individuation' (Simondon 2020a: 340). Thus, the transindividual relation means a passage from one individual carrying a certain pre-individual charge to another individual carrying another pre-individual charge: in this sense, the transindividual is a relation that cannot be associated either with any particular individual, or with the interindividual. In fact, the transindividual relation traverses every individual, and therefore it can be interpreted as the operation of transduction that resolves the problematic that the isolated individual is unable to resolve by itself. The transindividual relation means that individuals are never fully formed and that they are defined only in relation to one another and to the pre-individual potential or charge. The transindividual relation also implies a mediation between individuals through the invention of technical objects (to be discussed in Chapter 5), which in their turn also change and develop.

Thus, the transindividual is a specific form of collective individuation that keeps its members always unfinished and incomplete, in the condition of metastable equilibrium.

As we can see, Simondon creates an original theory of the transindividual that replaces the conventional opposition or conflict between the individual and the social. This opposition is replaced by the process of individuation, which has to resolve a tension between the pre-individual, the individuated individual and the transindividual collective. In this respect, Simondon is critically opposing both psychology, which is concerned only with the individual's interiority, and sociology, which examines individuals as being related to each other by external factors, such as identity or values. By contrast, Simondon defines the psychical individual as a transductive relation between the interiority (the individual and the pre-individual charge) and the exteriority (the transindividual collective). It is important to stress that Simondon regards psychical individuation as a prolongation of biological individuation, and as the extension and elaboration of those tensions that characterise biological existence. Simondon argues that the subject is created by three successive phases: the pre-individual phase, the individuated phase and the transindividual phase, all of which correspond to the concepts of nature, the individual and spirituality (Simondon 2020a: 348–9). In this sense, the individual should be defined not as a substantial being, but as a being which carries within itself something non-human (nature, the pre-individual charge), and which can resolve its tensions only by going beyond itself towards the transindividual collective.

The continuity between the biological and psychical individuation is revealed in Simondon's lecture course *Imagination et invention 1965–1966* (2008). In this course Simondon explains imagination as a cycle of images that develops in the same ontogenetic way as the biological individual. The ontogenetic cycle of images consists of four phases: anticipation, perception, memory-symbolisation and invention. The first phase of the cycle of images refers to the biological domain and expresses the organism's spontaneous reaction to and anticipation of external stimuli. As Daniela Voss points out, 'The first type of image emerges in this interval between external stimuli and endogenic activity: it is an anticipation of possible movements or motor responses – that is, a projection or anticipatory image that flows from the body schema (*schéma corporel*) of the living being' (Voss 2019: 12). This first type of image refers to the spontaneous conduct of anticipation; however, these reactions are virtual and tentative and as such they remain in the interiority of the organism (Simondon 2008: 31). The second type of image belongs to the psychical domain and expresses the perceptive-cognitive interaction between an organism and its milieu. 'At this stage, the living being performs a synthesis of inter-sensory images, identifies objects, receives and selects information' (Voss 2019: 12). This phase is close to what Jakob von Uexküll (2010) described as an *Umwelt* – the relationship between a living being and its milieu. In this phase the organism does not merely anticipate the stimuli, but is actually perceiving information from its environment and is capable of responding to it. The third type of image emerges from an affective-emotive experience and is already organised in a systematic way as a memory image. Simondon argues that memory images are selected and filtered in such a way that certain images are transformed into symbols.[7] These symbols condense opposite and incompatible qualities and thus create the oversaturation of memory images. This oversaturation produces a metastable phase, which is the necessary condition for invention and for the creation of a new system (Simondon 2008: 124). Similar to the oversaturated milieu in a physical domain, which, after being triggered by a seed, initiates the process of crystallisation, the oversaturation of memory images initiates the process of invention, which is the fourth and final phase of image development. Each of the first three phases is related to a specific function (anticipation, perception, memory). However, the third phase is saturated in such a way that it is unable to accept new information; hence a new phase – that of invention – emerges and starts a new cycle where all phases begin anew. Invention produces a new detachable object (an artwork or a technical object), which starts a new cycle of images.

Thus, for Simondon, imagination and invention are specific capacities that define the interaction between an organism and its milieu. The genesis of images clearly demonstrates the ontogenetic continuity between biological, affective and psychical realms. All living beings of different complexity participate in the formation of images and of surrounding milieus. This conceptualisation radically changes the understanding of what imagination is. As Kristupas Sabolius observes, for Simondon, 'imagination is to be discovered within material and biological functions of every living being, not necessarily human' (Sabolius 2019: 44). In this respect, imagination is to be understood not as an exceptional human capacity but as a general function of living organisms that defines their interaction with the milieu. 'This amounts to say that, although we often tend to treat imagination as the most distancing and dissociative function of mind [. . .] for Simondon, it is what signals pre-individual creativity of the world that surpasses any individual mind, be it of human or of any other species' (Sabolius 2019: 44). In other words, imagination as the cycle of images is inevitably connected to the pre-individual potential and expresses the resolution of a certain vital problematic. Human consciousness can be creative and inventive only to the extent that it is able to make use of this pre-individual potentiality.

Simondon's theory of imagination implies that all living beings involved in the creation of images possess a certain kind of cognition – anticipation, perception, memory and invention. Living beings not only adapt to the environment, but they can actively anticipate, perceive, recollect and

---

[7] This type of image refers to the symbolic domain; in this respect Simondon opposes his theory to Jacques Lacan's notions of the Imaginary and the Symbolic, and also to Jean-Paul Sartre's notion of imagination developed in *The Imaginary* (1940).

invent. This insight will be important in discussing a certain kind of organic consciousness espoused in the works of Ruyer in the next chapter. This statement also allows us to extend the capacity of cognition and imagination from humans to all living beings and to reconsider humans as a particular phase in the continuum of living beings.

## Conclusion

To conclude, we can argue that Simondon proposes an original theory of individuation that allows one to compare physical, biological and psychical domains. Simondon also proposes a quasi-biological explanation of technical objects, which will be discussed in Chapter 5. Simondon's theory of individuation, or ontogenesis, is important not only because it allows the comparison of different domains but also because it suggests a major reconceptualisation of the notion of an organism. For Simondon, the ontological reality of an organism is becoming: an organism is examined not as a biological individual, but as a process of individuation, continuous folding and unfolding. The structure of an organism is like a multiple folding of interiorities and exteriorities of different complexity. Thus, an organism is understood as a process of folding and also as a folded multiplicity composed of heterogeneous parts. This biological multiplicity is always in a metastable position, meaning that it always contains potentials and tensions that have to be resolved. A living being is defined as a potentiality, or metastability, which can be resolved by becoming a new structure, a new order of magnitude. By contrast, a stable equilibrium means that the tension is lost and the potential for life is exhausted. In other words, an organism is defined by this metastable condition, which allows it to develop and change. This insight applies both to human and non-human organisms: the human individual is understood not as someone related to itself (as presumed in psychology or psychoanalysis), or to other subjects (as presumed in sociology); rather, it is in constant tension with the pre-individual potential and the transindividual collective. As such, a human individual is always an uncompleted and unfinished entity that is constantly recreated in the process of individuation.

# 2

# Raymond Ruyer: Organic Consciousness

Raymond Ruyer's philosophy of biology takes the notion of an organism as its central theme. As George Canguilhem observed in his 'Note' (1947), the publication of Ruyer's book *Elements de psychobiologie* was an important event which helped to overcome the 'oblivion of life' in French philosophy. In his two most important books, *Neofinalism* (2016) and *The Genesis of Living Forms* (2020),[1] Ruyer defines an organism as a primary consciousness, which has the capacity of self-organisation, self-affection and self-enjoyment. For Ruyer, primary consciousness is a specific phenomenon characteristic both of human beings and all living forms. What defines any living being is the development of forms, or the process of morphogenesis, leading to a certain purpose that is not determined in advance but self-initiated by an organism's 'mnemic themes'. Like Simondon,[2] Ruyer argues against the notion of bounded entities, understood as pre-formed and pre-given, and asserts that morphogenesis is a self-formative activity, which creates without any pre-ordered idea or plan. Ruyer's morphogenesis, similar to Simondonian ontogenesis, is a process that carries within itself the potential for its transformation. Ruyer criticises contemporary theories of embryogenesis as being built on Newtonian physics, which construes living beings as mechanisms placed in a neutral space. In this sense, Ruyer distinguishes between the extensive space of physical entities and the intensive space of living forms. In contrast to physical entities, Ruyer examines living organisms as self-formative and self-surveying beings, which have the properties

---

[1] Originally published as Raymond Ruyer, *Néo-finalisme*, Paris: PUF, 1952; translated into English as *Neofinalism*, trans. Alyosha Edlebi, Minneapolis, MN: University of Minnesota Press, 2016. Raymond Ruyer, *La Genèse des formes vivantes*, Paris: Flammarion, 1958; translated into English as *The Genesis of Living Forms*, trans. Jon Roffe and Nicholas B. de Weydenthal, New York: Rowman and Littlefield, 2020. Some translations of Ruyer were published in *Parrhesia* (Ruyer 2018) and *Angelaki: Journal of the Theoretical Humanities* (Ruyer et al. 2019).

[2] Simondon and Ruyer were working at the same time and knew each other's works; Simondon refers to Ruyer's ideas in his *Sur la psychologie (1956–1967)*, Paris: PUF, 2015.

of primary consciousness. Each living form, from the most primitive organisms to those having a psychological consciousness and a brain, expresses conscious activity and the capacity of maintaining and transforming its form. This insight allows one to reconceptualise the notion of an organism and also to relocate human consciousness from its exceptional position to its place in the continuum of living beings. In this chapter I will concentrate on some specific aspects of Ruyer's theory of morphogenesis and its tension between preformationism and finalism; then I will discuss the notions of equipotentiality and of self-survey, and finally emphasise the uniqueness of his notion of primary consciousness.

## Morphogenesis: Between Preformationism and Finalism

In his account of the development of living forms Ruyer distances himself from earlier theories of both mechanism and vitalism, and refers to the doctrine of organicism as an attempt to overcome the dispute between them: 'Organicism neither seeks to reduce the organism to physicochemical phenomena nor seeks to explain organic specificity by a distinct principle (vital principle or soul), which would intervene *dynamically* in the unfolding of physical phenomena [. . .] To see the organism as a whole is the key' (Ruyer 2016: 190, emphasis in original). However, even if organicists solved the contradiction between mechanism and vitalism by refusing to explain organisms either by alluding to mechanical properties or by acknowledging some vital force, Ruyer does not think that their efforts were successful.[3] Organicists presume that the organism's organisation is a key factor of its unity and regulation. By contrast, Ruyer argues that the notion of organisation cannot account for the development of forms; what is needed is a principle of directed and purposeful activity. Ruyer asserts that Kant's account of organisms is close to that of organicism. However, the principle of final cause or purposiveness that Kant proposes to define organic beings can be applied to nature in general, but it cannot explain the formation and behaviour of living beings. Similar to organicists, Kant explains that a living being is a 'cause and effect of itself', in other words, it is self-organising. For Ruyer, the Kantian explanation of nature is deterministic according to the faculty of understanding, and finalist according to the faculty of reason, and these two faculties are united in the faculty of judgement. As Ruyer points out, 'this faculty is "referred to the supersensible" and the unity arises "in an unknown way". The final cause is not a force; it is merely a legitimate and indispensable point of view, not only on living beings but on the entire world' (Ruyer 2016: 192–3). Ruyer thinks that the concept of finality should be renounced and replaced with the idea of a dynamic force. Such a dynamic force is consciousness, understood not

---

[3] Ruyer turns organicism into a caricature by describing it as 'an empty concept that has no basis in reality; it is a "squared circle"' (Ruyer 2016: 191).

as a transcendental principle but as an absolute form immanent in every living being.

Thus, Ruyer invents the concept of an absolute form, which he distinguishes from molar structures.

> In place of the distinction between the organic and the inorganic, Ruyer proposes a new distinction that cuts across both these domains: a distinction between *absolute forms* (individual beings), on the one hand, and *molar structures* (aggregate or mass phenomena), on the other. Absolute forms include molecules, viruses, cells, embryos, and brains, while molar structures are statistical aggregates of these individual forms, such as clouds, gases, crowds, or geological formations. (Smith 2017: 117–18, emphasis in original)

Similar to organicism, Ruyer is concerned with the nature of organisation, or bonding, which for him is of two different types: absolute forms are involved in constant formation that establishes an irreducible unity between their parts, whereas the functioning of molar structures is a result of external forces. For example, a rock or a cloud is a molar structure, or an aggregate, because it is shaped by mechanical external forces and does not produce any internal bonds; by contrast, absolute forms, such as molecules or organisms, produce internal bonds that are maintained throughout all changes. In other words, Ruyer establishes a fundamental distinction between *functioning* and *formation*: functioning is merely mechanical and it cannot explain the self-organising activities of living beings; by contrast, formation is an incessant activity characteristic to individuals which can create, maintain and repair themselves. As Smith points out, 'This distinction in turn entails a new distribution of the sciences: the primary sciences are those that focus on absolute forms, while the secondary sciences are those that only study individuals from their molar or statistical side' (Smith 2017: 119). Thus, for Ruyer, the main problem is not the distinction between the organic and the inorganic, but that between self-individuating forms and forms that are individuated by other forces (to use Simondon's vocabulary). The central philosophical problem is to explain absolute form as a self-formative force.

So what is an absolute form? And how can we explain its persistence? How can we explain the obvious fact that, according to the theory of embryogenesis, an organism may have different forms, from a fertilised egg to a fully developed adult, and still be the same individual? Ruyer describes this self-organising activity as a process of morphogenesis, and, in this sense, he reinterprets the traditional opposition between matter and form that has guided philosophy since Plato and Aristotle. Ruyer's theory of morphogenesis breaks with the metaphysical definition of form as something pre-given and already structured. In order to develop and change, a living being should be independent both from a pre-existent model and a pre-defined goal. As Jon Roffe points out, Ruyer conceives form not 'in terms of a fixed model, an *eidos* whose outline is given secondary material content in being incarnated, but in terms of non-determining developmental *themes*. These themes, rather than preforming the individual in genesis, are non-material hinges or hooks around which improvisation takes place' (Roffe 2017: 585, emphasis in original). Form is understood as a formative activity which creates connections and bonds between different parts of an individual, and also between different phases or shapes of the same individual. In this respect, form is understood not as something existing separately from matter but as an active force that is always already embodied in matter. As Ruyer points out,

> form is inseparable from matter. Living matter only ever appears as formed, just as the benzene molecule only ever appears, as matter, in its well-known hexagonal shape. Benzene is not an amorphous matter that comes to be 'informed' by the shape of the hexagon, produced like an Aristotelian form. It is this form itself, which is in turn derived from the modes of bonding of carbon and hydrogen. In the same way, biological forms arise without hiatus from molecular morphology. (Ruyer 2020: 31)

In other words, both inorganic and organic entities carry their forms in themselves and actively participate in their own self-forming. Matter and form cannot be clearly separated, because matter is forming itself and invents its own forms in the process of morphogenetic development.

Another important feature of absolute form is that Ruyer defines it in terms of consciousness. 'Consciousness *is* any active formation in its absolute activity, and all formation *is* consciousness' (Ruyer 2020: 162, emphasis in original). This reference to consciousness does not imply a return to any kind of vitalism, because consciousness is not a transcendent substance but a form embodied in material forces. 'Every form, from atoms to molecules, viruses, bacteria and more complex organisms, is a self-sustaining configuration of forces of connection. Each of these forms, according to Ruyer, is a consciousness' (Bogue 2009: 304). The notion of consciousness also has to be separated from panpsychism, which expresses the attitude that human consciousness can be extended to explain the existence of other entities. Rather, Ruyer is trying to assert that consciousness is an organising activity or force that can account for the organisation of absolute forms (from molecules to organisms). In contrast to molar structures, which are observable and definable from the outside, absolute forms have their organising principle in themselves, and also have the capacity of surveying their own development. It is this capacity of self-survey that helps form-consciousness to follow the individual's internal state and to maintain its integrity throughout all stages of its development.

To account for the process of morphogenesis, Ruyer introduces the notion of a formative theme, which can be imagined as the main theme of a melody. A melody can operate in two modes: the musical theme can exist as an 'ideal', which is trans-temporal and trans-spatial, existing outside the coordinates of time and space; and it can be actually performed in real time and space while being open to improvisation and adjustments.[4] In a similar way, such an ideal melody can direct the morphogenesis of an organism; however, its actual performance, or embodiment, is open to improvisations and changes according to its environment and other factors. As Ruyer points out, 'morphogenesis can only be understood by invoking a non-mechanical model, by thinking of an individualised melodic theme which can both be integrally repeated and distribute itself in variations through which the initial, repeated theme serves as its own "development" (in the musical sense of the term)' (Ruyer 2020: 61). Thus, the ideal melody can be understood as a potential or virtual idea in the Deleuzian sense, whereas its performance can be understood as the actual process of differentiation.

At this point we have to ask: what is the ontological status of these trans-temporal and trans-spatial themes in Ruyer's theory? As we know, Ruyer condemned mechanism, vitalism and organicism as incapable of explaining the formative activity of living beings. However, this 'ideal' theme seems to be very similar to a transcendent principle that is guiding any actual development. As Bogue explains, 'Ruyer's concept of the developmental theme does not imply a conventional idealism, for the theme, though "trans-spatial", is always immanent within the material world' (Bogue 2017: 524). For example, an embryo contains all potential themes, which become more and more restricted when an organism develops and takes some specific form. However, this developmental theme is embodied within the organism and disappears only when the organism exhausts its potential and vanishes. Elizabeth Grosz also observes that even if the melodic theme pre-exists its development, it is to be understood not as a transcendent idea but as a phenomenon immanent to the processes of development. The melodic theme is like a score, a virtual whole that can be actualised in many different ways in an actual performance:

> The trans-spatial theme pervades all of time, to the extent that it constitutes the melody, the rhythm, through which each thing forms itself. Primary form appropriates themes that have already been laid out for it in advance, not a priori like a command, but more like the musical performance of a score, which preexists and to some extent directs but does not determine each performance. (Grosz 2017: 226)

---

[4] As Ruyer points out, 'truly epigenetic appearance in space and time and specific complex structures all lead us to admit a non-geometric "dimension" – a "non-spatial" region in which the "ideals" of specific forms subsist in a "semantic" state ... At the same time, these ideals act dynamically on that which actualises them and are actively realised by it; in turn, these are adopted as *its* ideas' (Ruyer 2020: 162, emphasis in original).

Thus the organism's developmental theme is never separated from an actual organism and is always immanent in all forms of its development.

Thus, the original notion of absolute form allows Ruyer to avoid the danger of being trapped either in preformationism or in finalism. He distances himself from any form of preformationism, asserting that it is 'the biological form of the theory of functioning' (Ruyer 2020: 157). This presumes that biological forms are given in advance and later develop only in quantities. In contrast to this assumption, morphogenesis is understood as a formative activity that creates and invents qualitatively new forms of organisation. In this respect, genetics, or 'gene-centrism', is also seen as a certain kind of preformationism because it explains organic development as an activation of commands coded in the genome.

> We cannot claim today that the egg, with its genes and protoplasm, contains – like a kind of 'written plan', or like the record that only needs to be played – all the future forms of the adult organism and its nervous system. The whole of experimental embryology, and all the studies of instinct, prove that formational dynamic themes are truly formational and organisational. They do not simply deploy structures, make structures 'speak', since these structures do not yet exist, and since it is precisely the formational themes that give birth to them. (Ruyer 2020: 167)

In other words, absolute forms, or formational themes, are the only agents of morphogenetic invention.

On the other hand, the creativity of the formative theme allows Ruyer to avoid the trap of finalism. As Smith points out, 'Ruyer is not a traditional "finalist," presuming a teleology or purpose throughout nature or for nature as a whole. Rather, he defends a "*neofinalism*"' (Smith 2017: 122). The development of absolute forms is neofinalist in the sense that it implies creativity, freedom and consciousness, and is not pre-programmed in advance. As Hansen explains, 'in calling his finalism a "neofinalism," Ruyer does not simply mean to emphasize its rejuvenation of traditional commitments. Rather, he seeks to highlight its fundamental relocalization of the operation of finalism – from individual organisms and biological entities to the entire system of biological operationality' (Hansen 2016: xix). As Ruyer himself explains in a text 'Raymond Ruyer par lui-même' (2007), his attempts to explain the formation of living beings in terms of finalism led him not only to teleology but also to theology.[5] Looking retrospectively at his own work,

---

[5] 'In the end, this conception of consciousness-activities in participation implies a new finalism, not only at the level of individual activities, but in the system that is itself comprised of all the individual activities. It is necessary, finally, to postulate a region beyond the transspatial domain; in its dimension of "nature", obedient to non-mechanical and non-geometric laws that nonetheless remain natural, this region can only be called theologic, since it was the source of all

Ruyer had to admit that a theological explanation at some point appeared to be futile and insufficient to explain the formation of living beings.[6] Ruyer himself came to the conclusion that a teleological and theological explanation contradicts his theory of morphogenesis, according to which living beings are self-forming and self-maintaining entities.

To avoid the limitations of both preformationism and finalism, Ruyer asserts the autonomy and self-organisation of any living being: 'The living being is at once the agent and the "material" of its own action [. . .] The living being forms itself directly in accordance with a theme, without the theme first having to become an idea-image or represented model' (Ruyer 2020: 175). In this respect, Ruyer's idea of a formative theme is very close to Simondon's thesis that 'the living being is an agent and theatre of individuation' (Simondon 2020a: 9). Actually, Ruyer's formative theme can be compared to Simondon's notion of transduction: transduction is both the process that differentiates and the new reality of what has been differentiated. Similarly, for Ruyer, 'organic morphogenesis [. . .] results not only in the transformation of an initial form, and not only a brute increase in complexity [. . .] but in an increase in complexity in a self-sustaining, consistent, unified totality capable of serving as the basis for a new formation in its turn' (Ruyer 2020: 2). The idea of a formative theme means that an organism carries within itself the themes of its own formation and organisation, and, in this sense, serves as an immanent cause of its own development.

## Equipotentiality

As we can see, the notion of finalism posed for Ruyer a certain kind of theoretical impasse. Even after reformulating his project in terms of 'neofinalism', he still had to account for the formation of living beings and to find the source of their creativity. If neither a predetermined form nor a final cause can explain the process of morphogenesis, what is the driving force of this formation? The embryologist Étienne Wolff, who was Ruyer's companion in wartime captivity,[7] argued that one could avoid these difficulties by replacing the notion of 'final cause' with the notion of 'potentiality' (Favre et al. 1988). The notion of potentiality (or, more precisely, equipotentiality) is an important term in Ruyer's works, where it is used in several

individualized activities, of all forms and all laws' (Ruyer 2007: 10; cited from Hansen 2016: xix).
[6] As Ruyer observes, in trying to understand this 'theology', which he was attempting to elaborate until 1946, he discovered – although it was not a pleasant discovery – that his attempts were futile and insufficient. This is why his research conducted after 1946 – on neofinalism, values, morphogenesis – is dissociated from his theological works (Ruyer 2007: 10).
[7] Ruyer and Wolff were prisoners of war in a camp in Austria during the Second World War. In this camp they founded the Université en captivité, where Wolff gave a course on biology that Ruyer attended for a year (Colonna 2007: 10–11).

different aspects. First, equipotentiality means that a part can stand for the whole in the same organism. As Ruyer points out, 'There is an ordinary "equipotentiality" in countless adult tissues: we can live with a single lung, a single kidney, and even with a fragment of a lung, which is in this sense equivalent to the whole' (Ruyer 2016: 60–1). The part takes on the role of the whole, and continues to play the formative theme in the organism's development. However, as Ruyer observes, this type of equipotentiality is purely quantitative or measurable: for example, the equipotentiality of the pulmonary or renal tissue is quantitative in comparison to the qualitative equipotentiality of the brain.

The second aspect of equipotentiality is related to the development of the embryo and also to the development of the brain, which both imply a qualitative change. Ruyer observes that in the early stage of organisation embryonic cells are unspecified in their function and are capable of developing in multiple ways. Today this phenomenon is known as the pluripotentiality of stem cells. Ruyer suggests that embryonic equipotentiality expresses a certain kind of organic consciousness that organises the embryo's development. In this respect, Ruyer establishes a parallelism between the equipotentiality in the embryo and the equipotentiality of the brain because both of them presume a 'conscious' and self-forming activity. He observes that

> we are forced to treat cerebral equipotentiality and embryonic equipotentiality in the same way [. . .] Numerous signs indicate that these two 'inobservable' domains are one. The organic memory that guides the differentiations of the embryo, the organic inventions that perfect the species in the course of successive ontogeneses, closely resemble psychological and individual memory, consciousness, and the faculty of invention. (Ruyer 2016: 69)

In other words, both the embryo and the brain are saturated with potentiality, which guides their development. And they both possess a certain organic consciousness that orchestrates their material becoming: 'The brain is an embryo that has not finished its growth; the embryo is a brain that begins to organize itself before organizing the external world' (Ruyer 2016: 69).

However, some important differences appear: first, the brain continues to grow and differentiate even when its organic development is finished; second, the differentiation of the brain is reversible, whereas the development of the organism is irreversible. In other words, cerebral equipotentiality is inexhaustible and persists during the entire process of an organism's development. Cerebral equipotentiality might be captured in the provisional closure of the cortical network's synaptic connections, but physiologically it remains open (Ruyer 2016: 69). In other words, the cortical network oscillates between a provisional closure (at the moment of a definite perception or action) and a physiological openness towards new perceptions. In contrast to the quantitative or measurable equipotentiality that defines the development of pulmonary or renal tissue, which forms closed and final structures, the equipotentiality of the brain is always involved in a new thematic system and, in this sense, remains open: 'Ever-new thematic systems [...] alter at every instant the "closures" of the neural network, and this amounts to transforming the network into an organ with a new structure' (Ruyer 2016: 70). Thus, even if the brain's activity can be captured by a certain perception or an idea and form a provisional closure, it still remains open for further differentiations. The neural network functions like an operationally open system which permanently reorganises itself through circular causality. By contrast, embryonic equipotentiality disappears progressively: 'The theme of organs, by taking shape, ceases to be a theme to become a structure' (Ruyer 2016: 70). When organic development is finished, its potentiality vanishes and gives place to the closed structures that it has established.

Another aspect of equipotentiality is related to the interaction between different organisms. Ruyer refers to the early experiments in embryogenesis, which proved that a certain degree of equipotentiality prevailed in cells that were grafted into other embryos. Ruyer refers to the works of German embryologist Hans Spemann, who experimented by transplanting certain parts of an embryo into a specific region of another embryo. Spemann was building his experiments on the premises of his predecessors, Wilhelm Roux and Hans Driesch. Roux took two blastomeres of a frog's egg after the full accomplishment of its first cleavage, and killed one with a hot needle. The remaining cell continued to develop but formed only half of an embryo. Roux's results were published in 1888; three years later Driesch tried to repeat the experiment with sea urchin cells. He shook the germs during their two-cell stage and managed to separate the two blastomeres from one another. He expected that the next morning he would see the half-organisation of his subject; however, he observed a typically whole gastrula differing only by its small size from a normal one. Thus, in contrast to Roux's mechanistic explanation that a half would develop only into a half, Driesch found that a half can also develop into a whole organism by a simple process of rearrangement of its material (Driesch 2020: 41–3). Driesch believed that there is a vital force in the organism that cannot be exhausted by mechanical explanation. Thus, the same experiment ended with different results, which Roux explained in terms of mechanism, and Driesch interpreted in terms of vitalism.

Following the work of his predecessors, Spemann conducted a series of experiments in which a selected part of one embryo was transplanted into a specific region of another embryo. Together with Hilde Mangold he conducted an experiment known as 'the organiser experiment'. Mangold took the tissue from the dorsal lip of the blastopore and grafted it into a host embryo, which induced the formation of a secondary embryo. The new embryo was composed of a mosaic of host and donor cells. 'Therefore, the transplanted dorsal lip and the host embryo both participated in the formation of the secondary embryo. Because the tiny amount of tissue from the donor embryo was powerful enough to cause the formation of a new embryo, the dorsal lip was called the "organizer region"' (Magner n.d.). Repeating this experiment, Spemann discovered other organiser regions. In 1935 he was awarded the Nobel Prize for his discovery of the 'organiser effect' in embryonic development (Spemann 1935). The outline of his ideas was later published in his *Embryonic Development and Induction* (1938).

Ruyer interprets Spemann's experiments as an affirmation that embryonic development has a thematic character. As Grosz explains, 'The transplanted blastopores were still living elements or fragments that invoke a mnemic theme other than that which regulates the host species, bringing into being a chimera that nevertheless obeys the overall form of the host' (Grosz 2017: 233). The grafted cells still retain their equipotentiality and develop according to the specific site where they are grafted on.

> The embryonic host performs its melodic theme: the graft, while now located in the embryonic host, continues to play its own melody, create its own form according to its theme, even as the embryo continues to play its own mnemic theme, with which the graft must now, in its own way and through its own inventiveness, harmonize. (Grosz 2017: 234)

Thus, Ruyer takes Spemann's experiments as proof that embryonic equipotentiality is bound up with the thematic character of development. Embryonic cells are self-organising and 'conscious' in the sense that they operate as an autopoietic system, capable of maintaining its organisation and, at the same time, reacting to the environment (even if this environment is another organism). The embryonic cells react to this environment in such a way that they manage to incorporate these contingent elements into the system and produce a new hybrid embryo. In this sense, a living form can be interpreted as an organic consciousness that is able to maintain its form and to transform this form by incorporating otherness.

## Types of Forms, Types of Consciousnesses

As we have seen, Ruyer makes a comparison between embryonic equipotentiality and cerebral equipotentiality: both the embryo's and the brain's capacity of self-organisation is seen as a certain form of consciousness. Ruyer explains morphogenesis as a theory of forms, which derive from each other and which relate to different types of consciousness. Form I, primary consciousness, is the characteristic of all material entities at the scale of atoms or molecules, and also of the most elementary organisms. Even at this level, primary consciousness expresses a structuring activity. Form II, secondary consciousness, is characteristic of all beings with motor schema, which leads to becoming a perceptive or schematising consciousness in humans and animals. Finally, there is Form III, human self-reflective consciousness, which develops thanks to the techniques of language and symbolisation. What is important for Ruyer is that these three types of consciousness derive from each other: 'It is indeed necessary to grasp that Form I is fundamental, and that forms II and III would be inconceivable if they were not based on Form I, of which they are only particular cases. The three types are distinct, but each is united with the one preceding it' (Ruyer 2020: 150). In other words, there is a certain continuity between the primary, secondary and self-reflective human consciousness: the physiology of the organism and its specific psychological and reflective phenomena are interrelated by internal and external circuits.

Ruyer describes Form I, or primary consciousness, as a 'consciousness of transformation': for example, a hormone exercises a chemical action on the relevant tissue and deforms or transforms it in a certain manner. Thus, primary consciousness already works as an 'organiser-effect' inducing a certain transformation into the organism: 'for the organism, being an absolute form in spatio-temporal self-possession, *trans-formation* is given in itself, it is subjectivity and primary consciousness as much as it is primitive form trans-formed' (Ruyer 2020: 153, emphasis in original). Thus, Form I is a self-organising system that has the potential for qualitative change and internal transformation. Besides that, the organism is not only in possession of itself, but in relation to its vital domain: for example, an animal organises its domain as a den, a burrow, as hunting terrain or terrain of refuge (Ruyer 2020: 154). Following Jakob von Uexküll (2010), Ruyer argues that an animal has at its disposal not the whole of the objective space but a piece of subjective time and space that is called the *Umwelt*. The constitution of this subjective milieu is characteristic of Form II, which expresses the emergence of perceptual consciousness in higher animals. At this point there appears a certain differentiation between an organism and its vital domain and the exchange of information circulating between them. Thus, in Form II, the consciousness of transformation is replaced by the consciousness of information (Ruyer 2020: 154). At this stage an organism projects itself into the environment in such a way that its organic morphology is prolonged into the external morphogenesis of the vital domain: for example, a burrow presupposes specific organs suitable for digging, and a spider's web presupposes certain glands for excreting silk. In other words, an organism and its milieu are interconnected in an informational network, which is 'like a morpho-genetic theme ordering both the organic and extra-organic, internal and external circuits, biotope and psychotope, and which is to the interior what the skin is to the exterior' (Ruyer 2020: 155). If Form I is actively transforming the organism's internal space, Form II is actively projecting the organism towards its environment, orchestrating the organism's externalisation towards the vital domain.

In its turn, Form III, which is self-reflective human consciousness, presupposes a higher level of externalisation which is mediated by the techniques of language and symbolisation. If animal life was guided by a signal or an index, then human life is guided by a symbol that can be detached from a vital domain. Vocal gestures become words, emotional gestures become ritualised gestures, the expressivity of perceived forms becomes the free creation of artistic forms. In this respect, symbolisation allows Form III, or self-reflective consciousness, to detach itself both from its primary organic morphology and from its vital domain. As Roffe points out, 'symbolisation at once projects the primary activity of the being into the world and separates it from the need – in the social(ised) part of the environment – for unrestricted direct engagement' (Roffe 2017: 587). In other words, the passage from Form II to Form III can be seen as increased externalisation of morphogenetic themes. As Bogue observes, 'The simpler the form, the smaller its domain of space-time control. The movement from Form I to Form III is one of increasing mastery of space-time, increasing flexibility and increasing autonomy' (Bogue 2009: 312). This increased exteriorisation of Form III presupposes not only the mastery of symbols and language, but also the use of tools and technologies.

As has already been established, the invention of tools is not something specific only to human consciousness. According to Ruyer, 'It is impossible not to recognize that instinctive technology prolongs organogenesis: the spider's art of weaving clearly extends the formation of his silk glands . . . But what is true for instinctive behavior is equally true for intelligent behavior' (Ruyer 2016: 19). Humans also prolong their bodies through the invention of clothing, weaving and the use of furs. In this respect, Ruyer differentiates between three levels of exteriorisation: it is organogenesis, instinctive behaviour and intelligent activity. Organogenesis produces organs within the organism; instinctive behaviour produces the extension of organs (for example, a spider's web as the extension of silk glands); and intelligent activity creates tools and technologies that are detachable and extended towards the world. For Ruyer, internal organs in some sense already serve as tools: for example, the teeth are grinding tools, and the stomach is an automatic mixer. Therefore, technological tools are seen as an extension of bodily organs. Referring to André Leroi-Gourhan, Ruyer argues that technological invention should be regarded as an extension of instinctual behaviour by which living beings strive to control the world: 'It is because the tool and the machine extend organic activity that they always remain subordinate to it and have no persistence of their own' (Ruyer 2016: 21). As Smith concludes, 'Ruyer thus distinguishes three levels of technicity: bodily organs as an originary technicity; externalized organs as an extended phenotype (webs, dams, nests); and the detachable artifacts that enter into a circuit external to the body' (Smith 2017: 122).

Thus, technical invention is understood as a continuation of organic invention, and they are both seen as manifestations of different types of consciousness.

Long before we had formulated a definition of cybernetics, we had come to realise that organic techniques could inspire industrial techniques, and that the progress of industrial techniques could allow for a better comprehension of organic techniques. All forms, whether of type I, II or III, appear to depend on the same Reason. (Ruyer 2020: 171)

Usually we think that technological invention is achieved by human intelligence and knowledge; however, what gets lost in this assumption is that the human brain itself is an organic invention. Thus, human reflective consciousness can define itself only because it is derived from primary organic consciousness:

> This is to simply forget that the human brain which invents itself is first of all only an organic tissue, a network of cells, and that *every human and social deployment of invention is only auxiliary and accessory* [. . .] The human is only conscious, intelligent and inventive because all living individuality is conscious, intelligent and inventive. (Ruyer 2020: 171, emphasis in original)

Our brain has the capacity of perception and cognition only because it is made of organic tissue and possesses the characteristics of primary consciousness.

In this respect, Ruyer creates an original conception of consciousness which is understood as a forming activity driving the process of morphogenesis. As Ruyer points out,

> Consciousness is not a passive knowledge but the active unity of a behaviour or a perception. Consciousness *is* always a forming activity. It is always a dynamic effort of unification [. . .] This hypothesis, we must underline, does not consist in saying that consciousness *explains* morphogenesis; it rather asserts that consciousness and morphogenesis are one and the same. (Ruyer 2020: 160)

Consciousness is nothing other than a form, an active principle, which refers neither to a transcendent realm, nor to a subjective consciousness of any particular subject. However, what keeps the unity of this consciousness throughout the process of morphogenesis? To answer this question we have to explain the notion of self-survey.

## Self-Survey without a Self

Ruyer explains the notion of self-survey in chapter 9 of *Neofinalism*, where he reveals that primary consciousness is capable of surveying itself without any distance or mediation. As Smith points out, 'It is not an exaggeration to say that the pages where Ruyer develops his concept of absolute survey are among the most original passages in twentieth-century philosophy' (Smith 2017: 123). In this chapter, Ruyer asserts that consciousness knows itself without making itself an object of external observation. Ruyer gives an example of himself sitting at a table with a chequerboard surface. In order to capture the entire surface, the 'eye' or a camera (a 'mythical' third eye, usually used in photography or in cinematography) has to be in a supplementary dimension (n+1), from which it can observe and perceive; however, this act of perception requires another supplementary dimension from which it can be perceived, so these supplements go on ad infinitum. Another thing is that in this geometrical space the table's chequerboard squares are perceived as contiguous to each other, they are *partes extra partes*, or parts that are external to each other. However, as Ruyer observes, the laws of physics, which can be applied to perception operating in the geometrical Cartesian space, cannot be applied to the visual sensation as a state of consciousness. As he asserts, in his internal sensation the perceived object and its perception form a single whole that is indivisible and in no need of any supplementary dimension. For Ruyer, consciousness simultaneously perceives the object, the act of this perception, and itself; hence all these components merge into one sensation of self-survey.[8] This internal sensation does not obey the laws of physics; thus the chequerboard squares are perceived not as contiguous to each other, but given all at once, so that the distance between them 'is not a true distance that would require physical means and energy to be overcome' (Ruyer 2016: 94). There is no true distance and no real distinction between the perceiver and the perceived object; therefore all sensations are 'absolute', non-dimensional and indivisible, merged in self-enjoyment.[9] Self-enjoyment in this context means not pleasure but rather an internal immediacy without recourse to objective geometrical space where it could be observed from the outside. According to Ruyer,

> My visual field necessarily sees itself through an 'absolute' or 'nondimensional survey.' It surveys itself without positioning itself at a distance and in a perpendicular dimension. It is therefore a gross error to imagine the visual field in the occipital area as a kind of photograph, or as those cinematographic montages in which a three-dimensional scene suddenly becomes an album page that begins to turn before us on the screen. Between the 'I-unity' and the visual field, there is only a purely symbolic 'distance'. (Ruyer 2016: 97)

---

[8] The term 'survey' (in French *survol*, which derives from *survoler*) literally means 'to fly over' or 'to skim or rapidly run one's eyes over something'. *Survol* is sometimes translated into English as 'survey' (Ruyer 2016; Deleuze and Guattari 1994) and sometimes as 'overflight' (Bogue 2017; Grosz 2017).

[9] As Ruyer points out, the term 'self-enjoyment' is taken from the philosophy of Samuel Alexander, *Space, Time, and Deity: The Gifford Lectures 1916–1918*, London: Macmillan, 1927. Alexander opposes 'enjoyment' to 'contemplation' (Ruyer 2016: 266, n. 2).

In other words, the notion of absolute survey means that internal (visual) perception doesn't need any external observer and that a living system can survey itself in self-referential circuits. This 'inner vision' can be compared with the self-reflective circuits of I-consciousness as described in idealistic philosophy. However, what makes Ruyer's insight so interesting is that he ascribes this capacity not only to self-reflective human consciousness but also to the primary consciousness of simple organisms.

In this respect, the notion of self-survey can be interpreted as a certain kind of non-human cognition, which is characteristic of consciousness of any kind. As Ruyer points out, 'why couldn't the protozoan "see" itself directly just as much as our cortical tissue? The protozoan has neither eyes nor mirror; but neither does our cortex have an eye or a mirror to see what the eyes have already brought it' (Ruyer 2016: 97). In 'seeing' itself, the protozoan cannot see external forms but is capable of seeing its 'unity' in recursive self-referential loops. This isomorphism between different kinds of living systems allows Ruyer to conclude that 'there is at bottom only a single mode of consciousness: primary consciousness, form-in-itself of every organism and at one with life' (Ruyer 2016: 98). Secondary cerebral or perceptual consciousness presents external objects to our consciousness, but 'this particular content does not represent an essential trait of consciousness and life. There is no reason to deny subjectivity, primary consciousness, self-survey, and the self-enjoyment of their own form to our noncortical or even nonneural cells or to our organism in general' (Ruyer 2016: 98). In this respect, self-survey collects the different layers of biological multiplicity into a 'unity' that might look very similar to the ways in which psychological or self-reflective consciousness maintains the unity of the human individual.[10] However, what is important for Ruyer is to demonstrate that consciousness, or absolute form, is present in any organic being that is capable of organising itself without an external mind or observer.

In this respect, Ruyer distinguishes between an external perception taking place in a geometrical space and an internal sensation as a self-survey. An external (visual) perception is based on the extensive qualities of composites and their parts (*partes extra partes*), which can be divided, measured, etc., whereas a sensation as a self-survey is indivisible and thus 'absolute'. It is a unity of forces, a structuring activity, which forms and directs everything from atoms to complex organisms. This structuring activity is consciousness, which, for Ruyer, is defined by the capacities of self-survey, self-enjoyment and self-proximity. In this respect, consciousness first of all is 'conscious' of its own form in self-survey, and only then is it 'conscious' of anything else.

---

[10] In *Sur la psychologie (1956–1967)*, Simondon makes an interesting remark regarding Ruyer's *La conscience et le corps*: 'Biology itself allows itself to be absorbed by psychology; the intelligence of the amoeba is of the same type as that of man; and it is from ours that we know it. Intelligence is one with life' (Simondon 2015b: 127–8).

As Ruyer points out,

> The fundamental paradox, which is the origin of all the others, is that a domain of primary consciousness is in 'absolute survey' – that is to say without any need of an external scanning – that it possesses a kind of *autovision without gaze* [...] It is very difficult to admit that a protoplasm, a molecular edifice, an embryo, an organic tissue or a cortex, are conscious of themselves (possess their own form) before becoming, by added modulation, conscious of the form of other beings, and without being obliged to pass by this detour. (Ruyer 1966: 167; cited in Grosz 2017: 224)

This 'autovision without a gaze', characteristic of atoms, molecules, simple organisms and also embryos and brains, is nothing other than the capacity to create their form, maintain their internal bonds and connections. These bonds are 'non-localisable', because they are not stable structures but activities and forces maintaining a given form. Here again, Ruyer makes a distinction between structures and patterns, found in Cartesian space, and the absolute forms, made of non-localisable and non-dimensional bonds.

From this we can conclude that Ruyer's notion of consciousness is very original: consciousness is not a property of any subject, and it is not directed towards any object. Ruyer explicitly opposes his notion of consciousness to the phenomenological notion of consciousness:

> Contrary to those theories inspired by [...] Husserlian ideas, consciousness is neither always nor essentially 'consciousness of ...', consciousness of a real or ideal object [...] Primary consciousness is neither consciousness *of* a perceiving Mind-subject nor the consciousness *of* an Object, whether real or ideal. Consciousness *is* any active formation in its absolute activity, and all formation *is* consciousness. (Ruyer 2020: 161–2, emphasis in original)

The distinction between subject and object disappears and is replaced here by the self-reference of self-observing systems. Consciousness (the observer) is not beside or above the phenomena to be observed but acts itself as the observing system. In this respect, Ruyer's notion of self-survey functions like a self-observing model of recursive cognition found in second-order cybernetic systems. What is original in Ruyer's theory is that this capacity of self-survey, or self-observation, is not only characteristic of the self-reflective consciousness of humans, but is extended to all organic forms. As Ruyer observes,

> Consciousness, intelligence, invention, memory, and active finality are tied to the organic form in general. The brain's 'superiority' or its distinctive character is that it is an incomplete organ, an always-open network, which thus retains equipotentiality, the active embryonic consciousness, and applies it to the organization of the world. (Ruyer 2016: 75)

In other words, organic form can be defined as a self-referential system, which constantly changes through the interactions with the external world but still maintains its organisation through self-referential circuits.

Ruyer's theory of consciousness not only questions conventional notions of cognition and the brain but also redefines the notion of subjectivity. If consciousness is defined not by someone's capacity to perceive the world (or self) as an external object but by immediate self-survey and self-enjoyment, then the notion of subjectivity could be dramatically extended. What is important to understand here is that the capacity of self-survey is a kind of recursive cognition characteristic of second-order systems. In other words, recursive cognition is the property of the system's self-referential process, and therefore it has no need of a brain behind the brain or subject behind the subject. As Grosz points out, this kind of consciousness is without a 'subject-individual who would be the proprietor of the consciousness' (Grosz 2012a: 6). Primary consciousness is not appropriated by any subject or any individual, therefore it expresses a certain kind of 'subjectless subjectivity' (Bains 2002). This 'subjectless subjectivity' embraces all living beings capable of self-referential organisation. Human consciousness thus appears to be not the highest form of organisation but a transition phase in the continuum of absolute forms. As Bogue points out,

> Ruyer's object is not to attribute all aspects of human consciousness to other living forms, but instead to situate human consciousness within a continuum of living forms from atoms to humans, such that human consciousness is seen as a complex, highly specialised self-aware version of the consciousness evident in varying degrees of complexity throughout the world of living forms. (Bogue 2017: 522)

In this sense, every living being is seen as an absolute form, capable of self-formative and self-organising activity.

It is important to note that Ruyer is not trying to ascribe human consciousness to all living beings and is aware of the 'risk of naive anthropomorphism'. As he observes, the researcher's aim is 'not to define the atom, the molecule, and the physical individuality as organisms or as psychological consciousnesses, but instead to seek what is schematically common to the molecule, the organism, and consciousness. In all these cases, the common schema is a domain of absolute survey and activity' (Ruyer 2016: 162). In other words, what defines primary consciousness is self-organisation, a dynamic activity that has the power to change and to evolve using its force of equipotentiality, and to harmonise these changes through the unity of self-survey. In this respect, the features of equipotentiality and self-survey define any consciousness (or absolute form) regardless of its complexity. Ruyer asserts that the human brain has no monopoly over consciousness but is rather immersed in general organic activity, which the brain might appropriate only in some circumstances.

Ruyer's theory of primary consciousness is very close to Maturana and Varela's theory of autopoiesis, also known as the Santiago theory. The central insight of the theory of autopoiesis is that cognition is identical to the process of life. '*Living systems are cognitive systems, and living as a process is a process of cognition.* This statement is valid for all organisms, with and without a nervous system' (Maturana and Varela 1980: 13, emphasis in original). All living beings are manipulating their environments to create preferable conditions for their existence. This means that even the simplest organisms, such as a bacterium or a plant, are capable of cognition and perception, even if they do not have brains or minds. The notion of cognition implies self-awareness, perception, emotion and organic activity. It may also include specific characteristics of human cognition, such as language and conceptual thinking, but the notion of cognition is much broader and doesn't necessarily include thinking. Thus, the notion of cognition, similar to Ruyer's idea of primary consciousness, creates a kind of isomorphism between living systems of different complexity, and, in this sense, asserts the continuity of life forms.

Another point that allows us to compare Ruyer's theory of primary consciousness with the Santiago theory is the reconceptualisation of the mind and body divide. Ruyer establishes a certain continuity between primary organic consciousness, secondary cerebral consciousness and psychological consciousness. Similarly, Maturana and Varela argue that cognition not only operates in the brain but is embodied in the entire process of organic activity. Their research indicates that in the human organism the nervous system, the immune system and the endocrine system form a single cognitive network (Capra 1997: 171). This insight allows one to conclude, first, that cognition and knowledge are rooted in organic activity, and, second, that there is a certain continuity between different levels of cognitive systems or different forms of consciousness. According to the Santiago theory, primary organic activity and human consciousness are two sides of the same phenomenon of life.

## Conclusion

This overview cannot reveal the entire richness of Ruyer's work. However, Ruyer gives many important insights for organism-oriented ontology. He distinguishes between a structure and an absolute form: structures are organised by external forces, whereas the absolute form is a forming activity, capable of creating and maintaining itself. In this sense, the absolute form is consciousness, capable of engendering changes using its potentiality and of unifying these changes through self-survey. Thus, not only organisms but also atoms and molecules are interpreted as living forms in so far as they can self-organise and maintain their form. Simondon compares physical and biological individuations in terms of analogy (he used the term 'analogical paradigmatism'), whereas Ruyer is looking for a homology of forms between organic and inorganic beings. If we agree that different entities – from atoms and molecules to complex organisms – are homologous in respect to form, that they are forming activity, then we can formulate a new understanding of cognition. It is a non-human cognition, to use N. Katherine Hayles's term, which blurs the distinction between human and non-human, and also between organic and inorganic. Of course, we understand that atoms are not conscious of their forms in the same way as humans are. The theory of forms doesn't mean that differences do not exist; rather it demonstrates the ways in which these different forms, or consciousnesses, are interconnected. These different forms create various kinds of multiplicities, which leads us to the discussion of Deleuze and Guattari's works.

# 3
# Gilles Deleuze and Félix Guattari's Philosophy of Life

Simondon's and Ruyer's philosophy influenced Gilles Deleuze and helped him to formulate his original theory of life. The traces of Simondon's philosophy can be felt in Deleuze's *Difference and Repetition*, where the interaction between the pre-individual state and individuation is transformed into the interplay between the virtual and the actual. Simondon's ideas are also present in Deleuze and Guattari's book *A Thousand Plateaus*, where they directly refer to Simondon while discussing the *machinic phylum*, an energetic power of materiality. Ruyer's works also appear in the footnotes of *A Thousand Plateaus* and have a more visible presence in Deleuze's book *The Fold*.[1] Ruyer's concept of self-survey becomes an important theme in Deleuze and Guattari's *What Is Philosophy?*, where it is applied to describe the functioning of the brain. Thus, Simondon's and Ruyer's ideas are creatively employed in Deleuze's (and Guattari's) philosophical project where they develop, evolve and create something new. In this chapter I will discuss those aspects of Deleuze's (and Guattari's) philosophy that are related to the notion of an organism as follows: individuation as differentiation in Deleuze's *Difference and Repetition*, the reconceptualisation of the notion of an organism in *A Thousand Plateaus*, and the notion of the brain in *What is Philosophy?* Deleuze and Guattari take into account different theories of development, such as individuation and morphogenesis, to create a processual philosophy of life, where all living beings share the same formative materiality.

---

[1] In *The Fold: Leibniz and the Baroque* Deleuze introduces Ruyer as one of 'Leibniz's great disciples' and then gives one of his 'monstrous' interpretations in which Ruyer's living forms are described as monads (Deleuze 2006b: 116–18). As Bogue points out, this interpretation is far-fetched, because 'Ruyer, though inspired by Leibniz, formulates a much different monadology, one in which monads are nothing but doors and windows, nothing but *liaisons* actively forming themselves' (Bogue 2017: 534, emphasis in original). For this reason I will leave this interpretation aside.

## Individuation as Differentiation

Simondon's theory of individuation had a significant influence on Deleuze, who wrote a review of Simondon's book *L'individu et sa genèse physico-biologique* in 1966.[2] As Deleuze points out, Simondon creates a profoundly original theory of individuation that presumes the existence of a metastable system. This metastable system, named as the pre-individual state, contains the disparation of at least two orders of magnitude, two disparate scales of reality. This disparation, or difference, exists as potential energy, a potentiality that structures and individuates reality. In this sense, Deleuze reads Simondon's theory of individuation as being methodologically close to his own philosophical project: 'It seems to us that Simondon's perspective can be reconciled with a theory of intensive quantities, since each intensive quantity is a difference in itself [. . .] Like any metastable system, it is a structure (not yet a synthesis) of the heterogeneous' (Deleuze 2001: 44). For Simondon, the pre-individual state is the place of tension that is resolved by initiating the process of individuation. Similarly, Deleuze argues that difference is prior to identity, that it is difference that engenders change or becoming. Difference appears between two orders of magnitude, between different potentials, which create a tension or a 'problem'. This tension is solved by shifting into another system, which is now seen as different from the previous one. In this sense, difference refers both to the difference existing in the pre-individual state and to that difference which appears between different phases of individuation. As Deleuze points out, 'What Simondon elaborates is an entire ontology, one in which Being is never One: as pre-individual, it is a metastable more-than-one, superimposed and simultaneous to itself; as individuated, it is again multiple because it is "multiphasic", it is a "phase of becoming that will lead to new operations"' (Deleuze 2001: 49). Thus, according to Deleuze, Simondon defines being as potentially multiple in its pre-individual state and actually multiple or 'multiphasic' in the process of its individuation. Seen from a Deleuzian perspective, Simondon conceives of 'a new moment of Being, the moment of *phased being*, being coupled to itself' (Deleuze 2001: 46, emphasis in original).

The tension between the pre-individual state and the process of individuation is the main focus of *Difference and Repetition*,[3] where it is rephrased as

[2] Gilles Deleuze, 'Gilbert Simondon, *L'individu et sa genèse physico-biologique.* Paris: PUF, 1964', *Review Philosophique de la France et de l'Étranger*, 156, 1966, pp. 115–18. Translated into English as 'Review of Gilbert Simondon's *L'individu et sa genèse physico-biologique (1966)*', *Pli: The Warwick Journal of Philosophy*, 12, 2001, pp. 43–9. Another translation into English is 'On Gilbert Simondon', in Gilles Deleuze, *Desert Islands and Other Texts 1953–1974*, ed. David Lapoujade, trans. Michael Taormina, Los Angeles: Semiotext(e), 2004, pp. 86–9.

[3] Originally published as Gilles Deleuze, *Différence et répétition*, Paris: PUF, 1968. Translated into English as *Difference and Repetition*, trans. Paul Patton, London: Continuum, 2004.

the tension between the virtual and the actual. Deleuze finds these tensions not merely in the physical world of thermodynamics (as Simondon did), but in what he calls 'multiplicities' – a term that comes from mathematician Bernhard Riemann and was later adopted by Husserl and Bergson. A multiplicity is neither the one, nor the many, but rather it is a special form of organisation. 'The art of multiplicities', as Deleuze defines it, is 'the art of grasping the Ideas and the problems they incarnate in things, and of grasping things as incarnations, as cases of solution for the problems of Ideas' (Deleuze 2004a: 230). Thus, multiplicity is a special form of organisation that encompasses both Ideas or problems, which in their turn relate to potentials or powers, and the solutions of these problems, which incarnate these potentials and powers into real things (or living beings).

As Deleuze points out, multiplicities imply three conditions. First, multiplicities are indeterminable in the sense that they have no prior identity that could determine them in advance. Multiplicities are made of a potential or a virtuality: it is a difference freed from all subordination and open to all kinds of actualisation. Second, multiplicities are made not of bounded identities but of intrinsic relations. 'In all cases the multiplicity is intrinsically defined, without external reference or recourse to a uniform space in which it would be submerged' (Deleuze 2004a: 231). In other words, a multiplicity excludes identity as a prior condition: a multiplicity is made not of an inter-relation between finite and bounded identities (or individuals, in Simondon's terms) but of intra-relations of incomplete entities that are reciprocally determining each other. Third, multiplicities are defined by the coupling of a virtual structure and an actual genesis:

> the genesis takes place in time not between one actual term, however small, and another actual term, but between the virtual and its actualisation – in other words, it goes from the structure to its incarnation, from the conditions of a problem to the cases of solution, from the differential elements and their ideal connections to actual terms and diverse real relations which constitute at each moment the actuality of time. (Deleuze 2004a: 231–2)

In this sense, the actualisation of a virtual idea corresponds to the Simondonian notion of individuation, which at some point results in creating a bounded individual. However, the actualisation of the virtual is much more complicated than the individualisation of the pre-individual, as I will demonstrate later.

What is important for Deleuze is that multiplicities or Ideas correspond to different regions of being; this multi-dimensionality in some sense echoes Simondon's method of analogical paradigmatism. As Deleuze points out, 'There are Ideas which correspond to mathematical relations and realities, others which correspond to physical laws and facts. There are others which, according to their order, correspond to organisms, psychic structures, languages and societies: these correspondences without resemblance are of a structural-genetic nature' (Deleuze 2004a: 232). These correspondences are not resemblances but analogies, which allow us to examine different regions of knowledge. Deleuze refers to a linguistic multiplicity, which contains both a virtual system of reciprocal relations between phonemes and their actual incarnations in language; he also refers to a biological multiplicity of genes, which, taken as a whole, constitutes an organism's potential, and which can be incarnated in actual organisms and determine their species. As Deleuze points out, the same can be said about other multiplicities: 'the psychic multiplicities of imagination and phantasy, the biological multiplicities of vitality and "monstrosity", the physical multiplicities of sensibility and sign' (Deleuze 2004a: 243). In other words, the notion of multiplicity is a special form of organisation that allows Deleuze to compare physical, biological, psychic and social systems.

For Simondon, the pre-individual, or metastable, system is charged with potential, which is defined as a disparity between two orders of magnitude. This disparity, or tension, is solved by entering into a new phase, which initiates the process of individuation. In *Difference and Repetition* Deleuze creates a similar dynamic model: he refers to the virtual mode of differentiation, charged with internal differences, and the actual process of genesis, which incarnates these differential traits into actual beings.[4] Thus the virtual mode of differentiation – called differentiation – can be defined as a differential relation taking place in a structure, where elements are in their 'embryonic' form. 'The elements, varieties of relations and singular points coexist in the work or the object [...] without it being possible to designate a point of view privileged over others' (Deleuze 2004a: 260). The actual mode of differentiation – called differenciation – can be imagined as a process, or genesis, creating a series of qualities and extensions. 'Whereas differentiation determines the virtual content of the Idea as problem, differenciation expresses the actualisation of this virtual and the constitution of solutions (by local integrations)' (Deleuze 2004a: 261). Thus, for Deleuze, the double model of different/ciation combines the two aspects of individuation: that of a virtual structure and an actual genesis.

However, the question is how this virtual Idea incarnates itself into different qualities and extensities? What forces those differential relations that coexist within the virtual structure to differentiate themselves into actual entities? Or, as Levi R. Bryant has asked, 'why the virtual actualizes itself

---

[4] The virtual has to be distinguished from the possible. As Deleuze points out, 'The possible is opposed to the real; the process undergone by the possible is therefore a "realisation". By contrast, the virtual is not opposed to the real; it possesses a full reality by itself. The process it undergoes is that of actualisation [...] the real is supposed to resemble the possible [...] The actualisation of the virtual, on the contrary, always takes place by difference, divergence or differenciation' (Deleuze 2004a: 263–4).

at all?' (Bryant 2011: 104). For Deleuze, the answer lies in the intensive quantities: 'Intensity is the determinant in the process of actualisation. It is intensity which *dramatises*. It is intensity which is immediately expressed in the basic spatio-temporal dynamisms and determines an "indistinct" differential relation in the Idea to incarnate itself in a distinct quality and a distinguished extensity' (Deleuze 2004a: 306–7, emphasis in original). In this respect, Deleuze defines three ontological domains, which can be described as the virtual, the intensive and the actual.

How does intensity fulfil this determining role? It is interesting that to explain the role of intensification Deleuze refers back to Simondon and explains intensification in terms of individuation:

> The essential process of intensive quantities is individuation. Intensity is individuating, and intensive quantities are individuating factors [. . .] Gilbert Simondon has shown recently that individuation presupposes a prior metastable state – in other words, the existence of a 'disparateness' such as at least two orders of magnitude or two scales of heterogeneous reality between which potentials are distributed [. . .] Individuation emerges like the act of solving such a problem, or – what amounts to the same thing – like the actualisation of a potential and the establishing of communication between disparates [. . .] In all these respects, we believe that individuation is essentially intensive, and that the pre-individual field is a virtual-ideal field, made up of differential relations. (Deleuze 2004a: 307–8)

In other words, Simondon's notion of the pre-individual potential is reinterpreted by Deleuze in terms of a virtual-ideal field, and the notion of individuation is reinterpreted as an intensive quantity, which incites the process of actualisation, leading to the creation of actual individuals (Bowden 2012: 144–9). However, we can notice that, for Simondon, the pre-individual expresses the potential that is given in advance and only waits to be realised (for example, the supersaturated mother liquid waits to meet the piece of dust to start the process of crystallisation), whereas for Deleuze the virtual means a kind of potentiality that may or may not come into existence. It seems that the metastable pre-individual, as described by Simondon, has to resolve the tension by necessity, whereas the virtual may or may not come to actualisation, hence it comes into being by contingency.

Thus, to the question 'why the virtual actualizes itself at all?' Deleuze has an answer: the virtual incarnates itself in things because of a specific agent, which *differentiates the differential*. The virtual is fully differential in itself (as in the case of mathematical differential relations, or as in the case of genes creating a system of differential relations), before differentiating itself in the actual. These differential relations are differentiated through intensities, which are nothing other than the difference of difference, or a second degree of difference. This intensification which is the driving force of individuation is called 'dramatisation', whereas the agent behind this drama is named as a dark precursor. As Deleuze points out, 'Thunderbolts explode between different intensities, but they are preceded by an invisible, imperceptible *dark precursor*, which determines their path in advance but in reverse, as though intagliated. Likewise, every system contains its dark precursor which ensures the communication of peripheral series' (Deleuze 2004a: 145–6, emphasis in original).[5]

The dark precursor, being invisible itself, incites the dramatisation of spatio-temporal dynamisms, which form different sequences or series within the system. These series start communicating under the impulse of some force, which relates different series to one another and thus creates differences of differences, or second-degree differences. 'This state of affairs is adequately expressed by certain physical concepts: *coupling* between heterogeneous systems, from which is derived an *internal resonance* within the system, and from which in turn is derived a *forced movement* the amplitude of which exceeds that of the basic series themselves' (Deleuze 2004a: 143–4, emphasis in original). Although Deleuze is using a vocabulary of physical systems, he points out that such intensification, or spatio-temporal dynamisms, are characteristic to physical, biological, psychic, social, aesthetic and philosophical systems. For example, embryology demonstrates that there is a certain spatio-temporal dynamism in the morphogenesis of an egg: 'the augmentation of free surfaces, stretching of cellular layers, invagination by folding, regional displacement of groups' (Deleuze 2004a: 266). The spatio-temporal dynamisms appear only at the edges of the living being, because only developing and plastic forms can sustain these dramatic vital movements.

It is interesting that, in discussing these spatio-temporal dynamisms, Deleuze invokes Ruyer and his notion of a morphogenetic 'role'.

> When a cellular migration takes place, as Raymond Ruyer shows, it is the requirements of a 'role' in so far as this follows from a structural 'theme' to be actualised which determines the situation, not the other way round. The world is an egg, but the egg itself is a theatre: a staged theatre in which the roles dominate the actors, the spaces dominate the roles and the Ideas dominate the spaces. (Deleuze 2004a: 269)

As was discussed in the previous chapter, Ruyer explains morphogenesis as a musical theme, or a 'role', which is ideal, trans-temporal and trans-spatial, and, at the same time, is an actual performance open to improvisations and

---

[5] We can find a very similar description in Deleuze's 'Method of Dramatization', where a dark precursor is translated as an 'obscure precursor': 'A lightning bolt flashes between different intensities, but it is preceded by an *obscure precursor*, invisible, imperceptible, which determines in advance the inverted path as in negative relief, because this path is first the agent of communication between series of differences' (Deleuze 2004c: 97, emphasis in original).

adjustments. Similarly, Deleuze describes differentiation as a virtual system of differential relations and also as a series of actual differenciations which are incited by spatio-temporal dynamisms and a dark precursor. According to Deleuze, 'Ruyer, no less than Bergson, profoundly analysed the notions of the virtual and actualisation. His entire biological philosophy rests upon them along with the idea of the "thematic"' (Deleuze 2004a: 279, n. 28). Like Ruyer, who differentiated between an 'ideal' virtual or potential theme and its actual performance, Deleuze differentiates between virtual multiplicity as an internal structure and actual multiplicity as a process of morphogenesis.

Deleuze suggests that actualisation proceeds in the following way: 1) the depth or spatium in which intensities are organised; 2) intensities form disparate series and fields of individuation (individuating factors); 3) the 'dark precursor' which causes them to communicate; 4) the linkages, internal resonances and forced movements which result; 5) the constitution of passive selves and larval subjects in the system and the formation of pure spatio-temporal dynamisms (Deleuze 2004a: 347–8). But what are these 'passive selves' and 'larval subjects'? The passive selves are the perceivers or 'contemplators' of these dynamic changes, whereas larval subjects are 'the patients' of dynamisms. In other words, the morphogenetic process implies a certain form of consciousness, or cognition, which designates not 'a substantial, completed and well-constituted subject, such as the Cartesian Cogito' (Deleuze 2004a: 145), but rather, an incomplete and undefined subject, which is a patient of dynamisms. As Deleuze explains, vital dynamisms would destroy any well-constituted subject, hence only an embryo can sustain them: 'These are movements for which one can only be a patient, but the patient in turn can only be a larva' (Deleuze 2004a: 145). This larval subjectivity resonates with Ruyer's idea of primary or organic consciousness, which is in the background of all formative activities. The notion of a larval subject can also be compared to Varela's notion of 'selfless selves' (Varela 1991), and more generally to the notion of an embodied self in the theory of autopoietic systems. In this context the Deleuzian notion of 'larval subject' might be interpreted as a recursive cognition immanent in self-organising systems that do not need any external observer or 'mind'.

And yet, even if the notion of a larval subject does not lead us to the conventional notion of subjectivity, another term, that of a dark precursor, looks like a conventional notion of cause.[6] Thus, one can have the impression that the process of differentiation is not sufficient in itself, but needs a quasi-cause to be initiated. As Alberto Toscano points out,

---

[6] Deleuze points out that the dark precursor 'has no place other than that from which it is "missing", no identity other than that which it lacks: it is precisely the object = x, the one which "is lacking in its place" as it lacks its own identity' (Deleuze 2004a: 146).

it is quite difficult to see how this 'differenciator', albeit deprived of any self-identity, can refrain from constituting a totalizing structural principal upon which differences themselves would in turn depend. In other words, once the communication between series demands a paradoxical intermediary, how is one to stop the slide towards an ultimate Differenciator, a pure *principle* of anarchic production? (Toscano 2006: 173, emphasis in original)

It seems that, by introducing the notion of a dark precursor as a quasi-cause, Deleuze compromises the notion of multiplicity. However, we can argue that the notion of a dark precursor functions not as a cause of production, as Toscano suggests, but as a set of conditions that force individuation to happen. As Manuel DeLanda points out, the dark precursor functions as a 'quasi-causal operator', which breaks the determinism linking causes and effects by necessity (DeLanda 2002: 52, n. 54; 101, n. 62). This new kind of determination is named by Deleuze as 'destiny', meaning that connections are 'non-localisable', therefore not necessary. Also it is important to point out that the process of actualisation may be accompanied by a process of counter-actualisation, which extracts virtual events from actual states of affairs. In this respect, the Deleuzian notion of the virtual can be differentiated from the Simondonian notion of the pre-individual: for Simondon the shift from the pre-individual to the process of individuation is necessary, one-directional and irreversible, whereas for Deleuze the transition from the virtual to the actual is quasi-causal, multiple, and can be followed by counter-actualisation (Deleuze 2004b). This double relationship between the virtual and the actual organises the whole theoretical structure of Deleuze and Guattari's *A Thousand Plateaus*.

## The Deconstruction of an Organism

In *Difference and Repetition* Deleuze describes the conditions that make individuation happen, whereas in *A Thousand Plateaus*[7] Deleuze and Guattari concentrate on the interaction between different systems. As Toscano points out,

> The individuations that Deleuze and Guattari foreground in *A Thousand Plateaus* are not of the sort that engender individuals; rather, they traverse already constituted individuals, drawing them towards impersonal becomings, compositions of one multiplicity with another ... It is as if, rather than reconfiguring the domain of transcendental production from

[7] Originally published as Gilles Deleuze and Félix Guattari, *Capitalisme et schizophrénie 2. Mille plateaux*, Paris: Les Éditions de Minuit, 1980. Translated into English as *A Thousand Plateaus: Capitalism and Schizophrenia*, vol. 2, trans. Brian Massumi, London: Continuum, 2004.

the inside, by revealing the anomaly and heterogeneity lying *beneath* the individuated, Deleuze and Guattari were opening out a dimension *beside* that of constituted beings, a fugitive world of pure intensities, alliances, and transformations . . . (Toscano 2006: 176, emphasis in original)

In other words, in *Difference and Repetition* Deleuze was trying to answer the question 'why the virtual actualizes itself at all?', whereas in *A Thousand Plateaus* Deleuze and Guattari ask how the actual and the virtual are interrelated. These two ontological modalities have many names, such as the plane of organisation and the plane of consistency, the arborescent and the rhizomatic, the molar and the molecular, the striated and the smooth, and – what is more relevant to our discussion – an organism and the body without organs. It seems that Deleuze and Guattari remain hostile to the notion of an organism and try to replace it with what they name the body without organs. However, after a closer examination, it becomes clear that Deleuze and Guattari are trying to question the conventional understanding of an organism as an organised whole (as it was defined by Kant) and to reconceptualise it in terms of an assemblage. As Bennett and Posteraro observe,

> The organism might be understood as an assemblage in just this sense: it consists of a coordination among various parts sourced from elsewhere, acquired both vertically, by heredity, and horizontally, through its integration in an environmental haecceity; and it is structured on the basis of an abstract diagram that outlines possible parts and the functions that would enlist them. (Bennett and Posteraro 2019: 12)

Redefined in this way, the organism as an assemblage opens many productive ways to examine complex phenomena, such as symbiosis or the holobiont, and helps to contextualise the philosophical notion of an organism within recent developments in biology, such as complexity theory, developmental systems theory or the theory of symbiosis.

Thus, what do these two notions – an organism and the body without organs – mean for Deleuze and Guattari? As they explain in *A Thousand Plateaus*, an organism is the result of a more general procedure of stratification, which means organisation, coding and territorialisation (named as 'the judgments of God'). Deleuze and Guattari distinguish three major strata: physicochemical (geological), organic and anthropomorphic. Every stratification proceeds by double articulation: for example, in geological stratification the first articulation is the process of sedimentation, which is followed by a second articulation, such as folding. Organic stratification is also implemented by a double articulation:

> First, on the level of morphogenesis: on the one hand, realities of the molecular type with aleatory relations are caught up in crowd phenomena or statistical aggregates determining an order [. . .] on the other hand,

these aggregates themselves are taken up into stable structures that 'elect' stereoscopic compounds, form organs, functions, and regulations, organize molar mechanisms . . . (Deleuze and Guattari 2004: 47)

The organism appears as the result of active formation, organisation and stratification; these procedures make obvious the fact that an organism is not something 'natural' or 'given' but is artificially and forcefully imposed. As such, an organism is seen as a certain limitation of life: 'not all Life is confined to the organic strata: rather, the organism is that which life sets against itself in order to limit itself, and there is a life all the more intense, all the more powerful for being anorganic' (Deleuze and Guattari 2004: 554). In a similar vein, anthropomorphic stratification imposes on the human body forms, functions, bonds, as well as dominant and hierarchised organisations.

At the same time, stratification is opposed by another tendency, that of destratification, which takes place in the plane of consistency, or the body without organs, and which refers to 'the unformed, unorganized, nonstratified, or destratified body and all its flows: subatomic and submolecular particles, pure intensities, prevital and prephysical free singularities' (Deleuze and Guattari 2004: 49). This plane creates the body without organs, which does not refer to any actual organism or body but, rather, is a virtual state in which organisms and bodies can be rearranged and rearticulated. For example, an organism might return to a more powerful inorganic Life, or an anthropomorphic body might return to non-human becomings.

Thus, in contrast to morphogenetic development, discussed in *Difference and Repetition*, Deleuze and Guattari argue that there are two planes, or two ontological modalities: the plane of organisation and the plane of consistency. The plane of organisation follows the lines of structural or genetic development, creating organic forms and subjects. By contrast, the plane of consistency, or the body without organs, produces neither forms nor subjects, but the interrelations between unformed elements and particles of all kinds (Deleuze and Guattari 2004: 293–4). Structural or genetic development is here replaced by assemblage-like connections: 'There are only haecceities, affects, subjectless individuations that constitute collective assemblages. Nothing develops, but things arrive late or early, and form this or that assemblage depending on their compositions of speed' (Deleuze and Guattari 2004: 294). It is precisely the plane of consistency, or composition, where the distinction between the natural and the artificial vanishes and where organisms and bodies can be rearranged in new assemblages.

In this respect, the body without organs is a virtual tendency, which haunts every actual body and organism. As Keith Ansell Pearson points out, we can think of a body without organs not as an opposition to the rigid organisation of organs, but as a tendency or a phase that an organism might take on:

there is a body without organs *of the organism that belongs to its stratum*. The aim is not, therefore, to negate the organism but to arrive at a more comprehensive understanding of it by situating it within the wider field of forces, intensities, and durations that give rise to it and which do not cease to involve a play between nonorganic and stratified life. Creative processes inform *both* the body without organs and processes of stratification. (Ansell Pearson 1999: 154, emphasis in original)

In other words, an organism might tend to become the body without organs and vice versa: the body without organs might be captured and become an organised organism. As Ansell Pearson observes, 'The organism that Deleuze and Guattari are attacking [. . .] is not a neutral entity but rather the organism construed as a given hierarchized and transcendent organization. It can only be represented in such terms by being abstracted from its molecular and rhizomatic conditions of possibility' (Ansell Pearson 1999: 154). To become the body without organs would mean to open the body to its virtual potentiality, to abandon the rigid forms of organisation, signification and subjectification. However, that doesn't mean that the body as an organism should be dismantled. As Deleuze and Guattari observe, 'Dismantling the organism has never meant killing yourself, but rather opening the body to connections that presuppose an entire assemblage, circuits, conjunctions, levels and thresholds' (Deleuze and Guattari 2004: 177). Thus, tearing the body away from the organism would simply lead to death. Even Artaud was aware that the body without organs should not lead to a suicidal collapse but has to enhance those effects and intensities that are profitable for the body. To create a body without organs is to open the body to new assemblage-like connections and increase its potentiality.

Thus, stratification and destratification, or the plane of organisation and the plane of consistency, express two tendencies, which run over organisms and bodies. As Deleuze and Guattari point out,

The plane of organization is constantly working away at the plane of consistency, always trying to plug the lines of flight, stop or interrupt the movements of deterritorialization, weigh them down, restratify them, reconstitute forms and subjects in a dimension of depth. Conversely, the plane of consistency is constantly extricating itself from the plane of organization [. . .] breaking down functions by means of assemblages or microassemblages. (Deleuze and Guattari 2004: 297–8)

Thus the body without organs is a tendency that expresses the very vitality of life, whereas the organism expresses a still life, devoid of change and potentiality. As Smith points out, 'the body without organs is the model of Life itself, a powerful non-organic and intensive vitality that traverses the organism; by contrast, the organism, with its forms and functions, is not life, but rather that which imprisons life' (Smith 2012: 209). Thus, the notion of the body without organs can be interpreted as the model of Life, a certain organic potentiality, which is liberated from the constraints of evolutionary development. Deleuze and Guattari suggest the novel notion of 'involution', which implies that an organism might develop not according to the lines of filiation but in creative and non-predetermined ways.[8] However, involution does not mean a regression or a desire to vanish in an undifferentiated primordial soup. Rather, it means that the relationships between organic forms are established not according to lines of descent or filiation but through assemblage-like connections between heterogeneous elements.

In this respect, Deleuze and Guattari's notion of the body without organs resonates with Lynn Margulis's theory of symbiosis. Margulis argued that biological innovation cannot be explained in terms of Darwinian evolution and must have another origin – it is the symbiotic interaction between heterogeneous organic forms. For example, cellular mitochondria originated from different bacteria that symbiotically merged about two billion years ago. New alliances and cooperation between different living forms created functional novelty, which isolated individuals would never have had. As Barry Allen points out,

> Microbial symbionts carry out many chemical reactions otherwise impossible for their hosts to perform. Collectively they photosynthesise, fix nitrogen, metabolise sulphur, synthesise amino acids, provide vitamins and growth factors, and ward off pathogens [. . .] Virtually all mammalian and insect herbivores would starve without cellulose-digesting bacterial symbionts. (Allen 2019: 27)

Margulis described many examples of such symbiotic cooperation, but her favourite creature was *Mixotricha paradoxica*, a composite organism which consists of a protist and four different types of bacteria, and which lives in the gut of a termite (Margulis and Sagan 2001).[9] This example questions the notion of a biological individual and demonstrates that symbiosis creates heterogeneous assemblages.

It seems that Deleuze and Guattari tend to generalise the notion of symbiosis, which they understand not only as biological cooperation but as a certain form of 'unnatural participations' which are not merely biological but also anthropomorphic: 'what interests us are modes of expansion, propagation, occupation, contagion, peopling. I am legion' (Deleuze and

---

[8] 'It is thus a plane of proliferation, peopling, contagion; but this proliferation of material has nothing to do with an evolution, the development of a form or the filiation of forms. Still less is it a regression leading back to a principle. It is on the contrary an *involution*, in which form is constantly being dissolved, freeing times and speeds' (Deleuze and Guattari 2004: 294, emphasis in original).

[9] The biological notion of symbiosis will be discussed in Chapter 7.

Guattari 2004: 264). This is a kind of multiplicity which is created not by development, but by the co-functioning characteristic of machinic systems. In a similar manner, living systems can be defined not only by their descent, filiation or heredity (by their biological relations), but by assemblage-like connections.

> We oppose epidemic to filiation, contagion to heredity, peopling by contagion to sexual reproduction, sexual production. Bands, human or animal, proliferate by contagion, epidemics, battlefields, and catastrophes [. . .] Unnatural participations or nuptials are the true Nature spanning the kingdom of nature' (Deleuze and Guattari 2004: 266)

Filiation connects more or less homogeneous beings, while symbiosis or contagion occurs between beings that are entirely heterogeneous: they can be a human being, an animal, a bacterium, a virus, a molecule. Heterogeneous becomings imply a multiplicity, which, in its turn, implies a symbiosis: 'Each multiplicity is symbiotic; its becoming ties together animals, plants, microorganisms, mad particles, a whole galaxy' (Deleuze and Guattari 2004: 275). However, it is important to ask if every symbiosis is profitable, increasing the partner's vital potential, or is lethally dangerous, as in the case of contagion.

For Deleuze and Guattari, symbiosis is one of these 'unnatural participations', in which living beings affect each other in such a way that it increases the partner's potential and hence is seen as profitable and wanted. As Allen points out, 'The basic idea of symbiosis is an assemblage of heterogeneous organic forms that persists for a long period relative to the generation times of the interacting organisms, and which typically leads to the emergence of novel metabolic capabilities in at least one of the partners' (Allen 2019: 26). Allen argues that there is a difference between machinic assemblages connecting humans and tools, and symbiotic assemblages connecting two living beings:

> Tools remain as they are unless we change them. Symbionts struggle together, cooperatively, to become all that they can be. When I enrol a tool, I become more effective at what I already am. When I form a symbiotic relation with a second centre of life I enhance my potential, acquiring qualitatively new tendencies. (Allen 2019: 34)

And yet this distinction seems much more complicated. First, we should ask, does symbiosis always work to increase the partner's potential? Here we can evoke parasitism, when the symbiotic relationship is partial and profitable only to one partner, and also epidemics and contagion which lead not to potentiality but to impotentiality, the deprivation of vital power. Writing in the days of the COVID-19 pandemic, it is obvious that certain heterogeneous assemblages, such as between humans and viruses, might be dangerous and lethal. It seems that the question of heterogeneous symbiotic assemblages necessarily leads to the notion of immunity, which will be discussed in the final chapter.

Second, machinic assemblages are not just mechanical and repetitive, as Allen presents. Deleuze and Guattari's understanding of technicity is informed by Leroi-Gourhan, who interprets technological artefacts as biological phenomena. For example, in *Gesture and Speech* (1993), Leroi-Gourhan defines the hand–tool and mouth–speech poles as two important directions in technological evolution. He interprets technology as an externalisation of human organs: the hand itself might be used as a tool for producing different operations; at the same time the hand can be used as a motor force for externalised tools, such as forks or hammers. Similarly, the mouth can be used as a tool for different operations, and, at the same time, it becomes the force that allows the invention of language as an externalised technology. In this sense, technology can be seen as an externalisation of living beings and their body organs; in other words, biological evolution is prolonged and extended in technological evolution. Ruyer is saying the same thing when he distinguishes between three levels of technicity: bodily organs as an originary technicity or proto-technicity, externalised organs as an extended phenotype (webs, dams, nests), and detachable artefacts or technologies. However, Deleuze and Guattari are not completely satisfied with the theories of exteriorisation, presuming that the body itself is constituted by its proto-technicity. This is why they suggest replacing the notion of exteriorisation with their original notion of assemblage. As Smith points out,

> Deleuze and Guattari created the concept of an assemblage as a corrective to Leroi-Gourhan's analyses ... The hand–tool pole is generalised into the concept of a *machinic assemblage of bodies*, or form of content, and the mouth–language pole is generalised into the concept of a *collective assemblage of enunciation* (regime of signs), or form of expression ... (Smith 2019: 268)

In other words, Deleuze and Guattari complicate the theory of exteriorisation by opposing technological lineage and the notion of an assemblage.

Thus, Deleuze and Guattari suggest a twofold schema, which consists of a machinic phylum (phylum meaning a major taxonomic division of living organisms) and technological assemblages. A machinic phylum is a continuum, the flow of matter in continuous variation, as much artificial as natural. This flow is cut by technological assemblages which are selected, organised, stratified constellations (Deleuze and Guattari 2004: 448). 'The assemblages cut the phylum up into distinct, differentiated lineages, at the same time as the machinic phylum cuts across them all [. . .] Leroi-Gourhan has gone the farthest toward a technological vitalism taking biological evolution in general as the model for technical evolution' (Deleuze and

Guattari 2004: 449). Deleuze and Guattari evoke Simondon's critique of hylomorphism and support this critique by asserting that, instead of thinking form and matter as separate entities and imposing form upon a passive matter, we should think the interaction between operations and materiality, or between assemblages and machinic phylum. The machinic phylum is a flow of materiality, 'a vital state of matter as such, a material vitalism[10] that doubtless exists everywhere but is ordinarily hidden or covered, rendered unrecognizable, dissociated by the hylomorphic model' (Deleuze and Guattari 2004: 454).

The machinic phylum is the vital power of technology, which is caught or stratified into distinct technological assemblages, in a similar way as organic processes of individuation are stratified into distinct organisms. In this respect, assemblages relate to the machinic phylum in the same way as the organism relates to the body without organs. A body without organs designates the same flow of materiality, both natural and artificial. It is a life proper to matter, an inorganic life, which now is dissociated from organic metaphors and associated with metallurgy and metal: 'Metal is neither a thing nor an organism but a *body* without organs' (Deleuze and Guattari 2004: 454, emphasis in original). However, it is the same materiality that makes the corporeality of every organism. In this respect, we can argue that all assemblages, natural or artificial, symbiotic or technological, are temporary constellations of this corporeality, which interrupt the flow of vital materiality but are unable to stop it.

## The Brain: Between the Mental and the Cerebral

The theme of vital activity reappears in Deleuze and Guattari's *What Is Philosophy?*,[11] where they attempt to rethink philosophy, science and art. What these three planes have in common is that they all relate to the brain: '*The brain is the junction* – not the unity – *of the three planes*' (Deleuze and Guattari 1994: 208, emphasis in original). Philosophy creates concepts, science creates prospects and functions, and art percepts and affects – and yet all these activities are related not to mind or consciousness but to the cerebral materiality of the brain. 'If the mental objects of philosophy, art, and science (that is to say, vital ideas) have a place, it will be in the deepest of the synaptic fissures, in the hiatuses, intervals, and meantimes of a

---

[10] Deleuze and Guattari's 'material vitalism' is very close to Jane Bennett's 'vital materialism'. As Bennett points out, 'when Deleuze and Guattari speak of a material vitality, they do not mean simply to draw attention to a "Hobbesian" movement of bodies in space [...] The aim is to articulate the elusive idea of a materiality that is *itself* heterogeneous, itself a differential of intensities, itself *a* life' (Bennett 2010: 56–7, emphasis in the original).

[11] Originally published as Gilles Deleuze and Félix Guattari, *Qu'est-ce que la philosophie?*, Paris: Les Éditions de Minuit, 1991. Translated into English as *What Is Philosophy?*, trans. Hugh Tomlinson and Barbara Burchill, London: Verso, 1994.

nonobjectifiable brain' (Deleuze and Guattari 1994: 209). The originality of this statement should be discussed in the context of the mind and brain divide: conventionally, mental activity is always related to the idealist notion of the mind, whereas the brain is seen as a cerebral material object existing among other objects. By contrast, Deleuze and Guattari suggest that mental activity should be related to the brain, which, in its turn, should be regarded not as an object, but as a subject. 'It is the brain that thinks and not man – the latter being only a cerebral crystallization [. . .] Philosophy, art, and science are not the mental objects of an objectified brain but the three aspects under which the brain becomes subject' (Deleuze and Guattari 1994: 210). In this respect, Deleuze and Guattari create a connection between the mind and the brain, the mental and the cerebral, and reassert the biological roots of any conceptual or cognitive activity.

One of the important arguments that allows them to abandon the notion of the objectified brain and assert the theory of the brain-subject is the brain's capacity of self-survey. As was already discussed in Chapter 2, for Ruyer the notion of self-survey is an essential characteristic of every living being, which allows it to stay in immediate proximity to itself. The principle of auto-affectivity allows an organism to survey all of its components and to maintain its smooth functioning. Deleuze and Guattari take the concept of self-survey from Ruyer's theory of primary consciousness and apply it to the functioning of the brain and, as a consequence of this, to any intellectual activity.

> What are the characteristics of this brain, which is no longer defined by connections and secondary integrations? It is not a brain behind the brain but, first of all, a state of survey without distance, at ground level, a self-survey that no chasm, fold, or hiatus escapes. It is a primary, 'true form' as Ruyer defined it: neither a Gestalt nor a perceived form but a *form in itself* that does not refer to any external point of view . . . (Deleuze and Guattari 1994: 210, emphasis in original)

This means that to account for the functioning of the brain we do not need another brain, a brain of higher dimension, such as 'cogito', or psychological and reflective consciousness. The brain surveys itself without the help of any supplementary dimension. Thus, the brain functions like a self-organising system which is self-referential and self-maintaining, and, in this sense, it functions like any conceptual activity: 'The concept is in a state of *survey* [*survol*] in relation to its components, endlessly traversing them according to an order without distance. It is immediately co-present to all its components or variations, at no distance from them, passing back and forth through them' (Deleuze and Guattari 1994: 20–1). It is important to stress that concepts and brains are different aspects of the same cognitive process: every concept presupposes the brain and the brain is the faculty of concepts. In this respect, the brain is an absolute consistent form that surveys *itself* independently of any supplementary dimension, which does not appeal therefore to any transcendence, which has only a single side whatever the number of its dimensions [...] and which makes of them so many *inseparable variations* on which it confers an equipotentiality without confusion. (Deleuze and Guattari 1994: 210, emphasis in original)

This means that concepts and brains develop and create themselves in the same manner as living beings, using their capacity of equipotentiality and self-survey.

In other words, Deleuze and Guattari assert a new type of cerebral conceptuality, or cerebral cognition, which is defined immanently, through equipotentiality and self-survey, and without any recourse to transcendent ideas, and without reference to a global embedding space. In this respect, we can make a clear opposition between cerebral cognition, described by Deleuze and Guattari, and the conventional understanding of brain activity as perception. Cerebral cognition is immanent, in proximity with itself and equipotential, whereas perception always needs an external space where the objects of perception can be measured and quantified. As Grosz points out, 'Perception requires an external perspective, and in many cases, it requires actual physical distance, as in the case of seeing and hearing; it addresses objects that can be positioned side-by-side; and it requires a delimitable field within which these objects are positioned' (Grosz 2012a: 6). As such, perception needs a geometrical space which is measurable and divisible, whereas cerebral cognition takes place in the inner space of self-survey and is defined by internal connections that relate to each other in such a way that the nature of these relations is always changing. In other words, these connections are not quantitative but qualitative: 'The plurivocity of the concept depends solely upon neighborhood (one concept can have several neighborhoods). Concepts are flat surfaces without levels, orderings without hierarchy' (Deleuze and Guattari 1994: 90). Thus, cerebral cognition is organised in recursive circuits which refer either to the system's internal structure (self-surveying) or to other neighbouring regions. Cerebral activity of the brain is described as a self-organising system maintaining both its internal coherence and its openness towards neighbouring systems.

Understood in this way, cerebral cognition is not an exceptional human activity but a general characteristic of living and non-living beings. Deleuze and Guattari assert that cerebral activity can be extended to organic and inorganic beings at different scales:

> Of course, plants and rocks do not possess a nervous system. But, if nerve connections and cerebral integrations presuppose a brain-force as faculty of feeling coexistent with the tissues, it is reasonable to suppose also a faculty of feeling that coexists with embryonic tissues and that appears in the Species as a collective brain ... [...] Not every organism has a brain,

and not all life is organic, but everywhere there are forces that constitute microbrains, or an inorganic life of things. (Deleuze and Guattari 1994: 212–13)

Hence, the brain is not the locus of subjectivity and consciousness, but a form-taking force, present in all life forms capable of self-survey and equipotentiality. The brain-force establishes the brain's relationship with itself, its self-awareness, and its capacity to follow its own development; and, at the same time, it establishes the brain's relationship with the outside world, its capacity to affect and to be affected.

The brain-force can be imagined as pure potentiality which resides in every organic and inorganic being. Deleuze and Guattari discuss this point when they refer to the concept of 'vitalism' and its two possible interpretations: 'that of an Idea that acts, but is not – that acts therefore only from the point of view of an external cerebral knowledge (from Kant to Claude Bernard); or that of a force that is but does not act – that is therefore a pure internal Awareness (from Leibniz to Ruyer)' (Deleuze and Guattari 1994: 213). It is the second interpretation that seems to them imperative. The 'force that is but does not act' can be imagined as pure contemplation without knowledge, as a cerebral activity that can retain certain habits but restrain itself from knowledge or action. Can this awareness without knowledge still be attributed to Ruyer? Bogue is quite critical about this possibility and points out that for Ruyer,

> organic processes are always active, and the self-enjoyment of living forms is never associated with beatitude or contemplation, but only with the autonomy and completeness of each living form [. . .] Living forms are agents pursuing goals [. . .] Hence [. . .] Ruyer's vitalism cannot be described as that of a force that is but does not act. (Bogue 2017: 533)

It seems that by describing cerebral activity as a 'force that is but does not act', Deleuze and Guattari want to assert the virtual, indeterminate character of cerebral cognition. The virtual might be actualised in different bodies and states of affairs, but it might go in an opposite direction – from states of affairs to the virtual plane of immanence, the plane of the body without organs. This indeterminate character of virtual conceptuality is what sets apart Ruyer's neofinalism and Deleuze and Guattari's ontology.[12]

[12] As Bogue points out, 'Ultimately, it is Ruyer's finalism that sets him apart from Deleuze and from Deleuze and Guattari. Ruyer's trans-spatial is virtual, but it is never without a purposive developmental theme. A living form is a consciousness-agent working through memory and creativity towards a goal [. . .] By contrast, Deleuze and Guattari's philosophy-brain is a superject mind/spirit (*esprit*) in absolute overflight at infinite speed, and their arts-brain is an inject soul (*âme*) of contraction and contemplation. Philosophy's plane of immanence is without direction or orientation' (Bogue 2017: 534).

For Deleuze and Guattari, actual morphogenesis is only one direction of becoming; another direction moves towards indeterminate virtuality: 'It is the virtual that is distinct from the actual, but a virtual that is no longer chaotic, that has become consistent or real on the plane of immanence that wrests it from the chaos' (Deleuze and Guattari 1994: 156). Although Deleuze and Guattari relate these two directions to science and philosophy (science moving towards the states of affairs, and philosophy towards the virtual), we can presume that they allude to different tendencies of conceptuality. The oscillation between the virtual and actual can be seen as the main character of cerebral activity. It might be related to the brain's plasticity or potentiality, which, according to Catherine Malabou, designates the brain's capacity to receive form, to give form, or to destroy form. This virtual indeterminacy of the brain will be discussed in the next chapter.

## Conclusion

To conclude, we can observe that Deleuze's notion of life undergoes a certain 'evolution'. In *Difference and Repetition* Deleuze seeks to account for the ontogenetic dimension of life and to explain the passage from the virtual to the intensive and the actual. In *A Thousand Plateaus*, Deleuze and Guattari create a different ontological mapping, where the virtual and the actual are described as the plane of consistency and the plane of organisation, cutting across each other. In *What Is Philosophy?* they assert the same ontological scheme, which is now related to the functioning of cerebral activity that has a different field of application: the plane of consistency is the field of philosophy and art, whereas the plane of organisation is the field of science. The field of conceptuality, and of cerebral cognition, might navigate through these fields and proceed from the virtual to the actual and from the actual to the virtual.

However, what makes Deleuze and Guattari's theory so exceptional, and also so different from Ruyer's, is that they value the undetermined, virtual character of life. In one of his latest texts, 'Immanence: A Life',[13] Deleuze introduces the notion of indeterminate life, a life which is freed from the restraints of individuality and subjectivity. 'A life contains only virtuals. It is made up of virtualities, events, singularities. What we call virtual is not something that lacks reality but something that is engaged in a process of actualization following the plane that gives it its particular reality' (Deleuze 2005: 31). A virtual life might do without any individuality; it also might actualise itself into a certain individual, but it can also deindividualise itself and become the body without organs or a machinic phylum. Following

---

[13] Originally published as Gilles Deleuze, 'L'Immanence: une vie', *Philosophie*, 47, 1995, pp. 4–7. Translated into English as 'Immanence: A Life', in Gilles Deleuze, *Pure Immanence: Essays on Life*, trans. Anna Boyman, New York: Zone Books, 2005, pp. 25–33.

Deleuze, Agamben interprets 'a life' as a principle of virtual indetermination, which is all inclusive:

> *a life* ... marks the radical impossibility of establishing hierarchies and separations. The plane of immanence thus functions as a principle of virtual indetermination, in which the vegetative and the animal, the inside and the outside and even the organic and the inorganic, in passing through one another, cannot be told apart. (Agamben 1999: 233, emphasis in original)

'A life' is defined not by its capacity to take form to become an organism or an individual, but by its undetermined potentiality and impotentiality.

# 4
# Catherine Malabou: Plasticity of Reason

The tension between preformationism and the freedom of morphogenetic development, which we observed in examining Ruyer's work, also guides Catherine Malabou's philosophy. Malabou examines this tension through the notion of 'plasticity', which means the capacity of the living being to receive form and to give form, and also the capacity to explode form. Plasticity refers to the qualitative change that takes place both at the level of cells (cell plasticity) and the brain (neuroplasticity), and that can be either creative or destructive. It is destructive plasticity that is the most interesting for neurological and philosophical investigations, because it reveals the rupture between the cerebral and the mental, or between cerebral auto-affection and mental auto-affection. In these cases, we discover something that Malabou names the 'cerebral unconscious' – cerebral activity without consciousness. These discoveries open a gap between the brain and the mind, or between the biological and the transcendental origins of thinking. Deleuze and Guattari already started questioning the central role of the mind and asserted the importance of cerebral cognition. In a similar tone, Malabou argues that reason, or the field of the transcendental, is not something pre-formed and pre-given but is subject to epigenetic development. Reason is evolving, developing and changing in the same way as a living being is. In this sense, Malabou refers to the 'epigenesis of reason', which allows us to question the universal and necessary nature of transcendental reason.

## Plasticity and Potentiality

The notion of plasticity first appears in Malabou's doctoral thesis on Hegel, which was later published under the title *The Future of Hegel*.[1] Although originating from a close reading of Hegelian dialectics, the notion of plasticity

---

[1] Catherine Malabou, *L'Avenir de Hegel*, Paris: Libraire Philosophique J. Vrin, 1996. Translated into English as *The Future of Hegel: Plasticity, Temporality and Dialectic*, trans. Lisabeth During, London: Routledge, 2005.

is detached from the Hegelian vocabulary and, as Jacques Derrida pointed out in his 'Preface', extended to the realm of the living in general (Malabou 2005: xxiii). Malabou discusses plasticity as a general characteristic of life that defines the living being as capable of receiving form and also of giving form to its environment. However, to exercise its vital functions, an organism has to transform the reservoir of energy into something else; in other words, it has to make this energy explode to acquire new vital qualities. Here the word 'plasticity' acquires a third meaning, that of explosive substance (deriving from the French words *plastiquer* or *plastiquage*). In this sense, plasticity means both the creation of forms and the annihilation of forms, which is necessary for future transformations: 'life is responsible for the donation of the vital forms, but [. . .] each of these forms, to the degree that it is made of a concentrated energy, provokes an explosion' (Malabou 2005: 61). In this sense, plasticity refers to the potentiality of any living being, and its capacity to trigger a change, to transform reservoirs of energy into substances required for an organism's development. In *Philosophy of Nature* Hegel argues that an organism possesses a certain *Bildungstrieb*, a 'plastic instinct', which allows it to transform its environment through active power. Thus, the concept of plasticity encompasses three different aspects of organic life: an organism takes form to become what it is; it gives form to its environment and reshapes it according to its needs; and it explodes form to transform the reservoirs of energy into the substances it needs for its further development.

The notion of plasticity acquires slightly different connotations in Malabou's other books, where she relates the concept of plasticity to the synaptic activity of the brain. In *What Should We Do with Our Brain?*[2] Malabou examines the plasticity of the brain, which in some sense is similar to the plasticity of an organism: it receives form in the sense that it is a self-organising system and gives form in the sense that it shapes and organises the environment around itself. As Malabou points out,

> It is precisely because [. . .] the brain is not already made that we must ask what we should do with it, what we should do with this plasticity that makes us, precisely in the sense of a work: sculpture, modelling, architecture. What should we do with this plastic organic art? (Malabou 2008: 7)

What should we do with this living brain which appears at the most elementary levels of life and is one of the fundamental characteristics of living beings? Because the brain is *in us*, how do these new discoveries about the plasticity of the brain correlate with our personality?

---

[2] Catherine Malabou, *Que faire de notre cerveau?*, Paris: Bayard, 2004. Translated into English as *What Should We Do with Our Brain?*, trans. Sebastian Rand, New York: Fordham University Press, 2008.

Malabou points out that the new discoveries in neuroscience are very rarely confronted with our philosophical knowledge of personhood and subjectivity. Instead, one should ask what is the relationship between the neuronal and the mental, or between the biological and the transcendental origins of thought. The divide between different approaches became obvious in the discussion 'What Makes Us Think?', which took place between neuroscientist Jean-Pierre Changeux and philosopher Paul Ricoeur in 1998.[3] The discussion demonstrated the untranslatability of neuroscientific discourse into philosophical discourse and vice versa. 'Changeux's position is emblematic of the reductive "cognitivists" who "seek to elaborate a natural philosophy of mind by exposing the neuronal substrates of our mental activities", and Ricoeur exemplifies the "Continentals", for whom contemporary neuroscience is quite simply a crude determinist threat to freedom of thought and action' (Watkin 2017: 95). Malabou critically deconstructs both sides of this debate. On the one hand, she questions the unproblematic continuity and linearity between the neuronal and the mental, which is presupposed in neuroscience; on the other hand, she questions the unproblematic 'forgetfulness' of continental philosophy, which does not bother to take into account neuroscientific discoveries. We cannot deny the neuronal substrate of our mind and think that our mind is rooted exclusively in the transcendental. The neuronal patterns might be invisible to us when they run smoothly and take the form of a habit, but they certainly become visible in some specific cases when this smooth functioning is interrupted, as in the case of neurodegenerative disease or brain damage. In these cases, the plasticity of the brain acquires a third meaning, that of an explosion: the continuity between the neuronal and the mental is interrupted, and the damaged brain cannot reconnect with its previous form of personhood. It is this rupture or discontinuity that is the main focus of Malabou's philosophy.

In *What Should We Do with Our Brain?* Malabou discusses plasticity in two respects: as cell plasticity and neuronal plasticity. In relation to cell plasticity Malabou distinguishes between different types of stem cells: totipotent (omnipotent) stem cells, which can give rise to any of the 220 cell types found in an embryo as well as extra-embryonic cells (placenta); pluripotent stem cells, which can give rise to all the cell types of the body; and multipotent stem cells, which can develop into a limited number of cell types in a particular lineage. Thus, if totipotent stem cells express the potential to produce any type of cells found in embryos, pluripotent and multipotent stem cells express the potential to replicate and differentiate in adults. The stem cells' capacity to replicate and differentiate themselves is called stem-cell plasticity. As Malabou observes, 'In the first case – the capacity to differenti-

---

[3] The discussion was published as Jean-Pierre Changeux and Paul Ricoeur, *What Makes Us Think? A Neuroscientist and a Philosopher Argue about Ethics, Human Nature, and the Brain*, trans. M. B. DeBevoise, Princeton, NJ: Princeton University Press, 2002.

ate themselves into cells of the same tissue – stem cells are called *multipotent*. In the second case – the capacity to develop themselves into types of cells specific to other tissues – stem cells are called *pluripotent*' (Malabou 2008: 16, emphasis in original). Having in mind these different levels of potentiality, Malabou argues that stem-cell plasticity embraces both meanings, 'closed' and 'open': it is determination (to produce cells of the same type of tissue) and freedom (the ability to differentiate and produce cells of other tissues). 'According to this meaning, plasticity designates generally the ability to change one's destiny, to inflect one's trajectory, to navigate differently, to reform one's form and not solely to constitute that form as in the "closed" meaning' (Malabou 2008: 17). Stem cell plasticity allows the living being to acquire and maintain its proper form, and, on the other hand, it allows it to change and improvise.

The same kind of plasticity that is characteristic of an organism at the level of stem cells can be detected in the operation of synaptic connections taking place in the brain. Malabou observes that the brain's plasticity operates on three levels: first, it is developmental plasticity, which appears in the brain of the embryo, and which begins by establishing the neuronal connections and then multiplying and modelling them. In this regard the brain is not something that is given from birth in its finished form; rather it is undergoing a process of sculpting, which eliminates useless connections and strengthens those that are useful. The elimination of useless connections taking place in the brain reminds us of the biological phenomenon called apoptosis, or 'cell death'. As Claude Ameisen points out, 'Cell death is . . . a tool allowing the embryo to work out its form in its becoming, by eliminative procedure that allies it with sculpture' (Ameisen 1999: 30; cited in Malabou 2008: 19). When neuronal sculpting is completed, the next phase of the modelling of the brain depends on contacts with the external world: it is the relationship with the environment that becomes crucial for the brain's development. This means that apoptotic sculpting is replaced by epigenetic sculpting, which now takes the role of neuronal morphogenesis. 'In both cases, the brain appears at once as something that gets formed – progressively sculpted, stabilized, and divided into different regions – and as something formative: little by little, to the extent that the volume of connections grows, the identity of an individual begins to outline itself' (Malabou 2008: 20). At this point developmental plasticity is replaced by modulational plasticity, which works through the brain's connections with the external world.

Thus, the second level of neuronal plasticity is modulational plasticity, which refers to the modification of neuronal connections in the adult brain. The brain's synaptic efficiency can dramatically increase (a long-term potentiation) or diminish (a long-term depression). External stimuli, such as learning, experience and imagination, can activate and increase the number of synaptic connections. This capacity is characteristic not only of humans, but also of animals: for example, birds' behaviour, such as stockpiling food, can significantly increase their neuronal connections. Similarly, human animals have the capacity to potentiate their brain activity during the processes required for perception and learning. The idea of modulational plasticity questions the old assumption that the brain of an adult is incapable of changes; on the contrary, it is open to constant morphogenetic modulations. In this respect, neuronal plasticity can be compared with stem-cell plasticity: 'one could claim that neuronal connections, because of their own plasticity, are always capable of *changing difference*, receiving or losing an imprint, or transforming their program' (Malabou 2008: 24). Malabou argues that our brain literally is what we do with it: by activating our brain, we can escape biological determination and increase the potential for improvisation.

The third level of plasticity is so-called reparative plasticity, which encompasses both neuronal renewal and the brain's capacity to repair itself after being damaged. Neuronal renewal or secondary neurogenesis refers to the modification of synaptic connections in the adult brain and in this respect is similar to the modulational plasticity discussed above. Reparative plasticity refers to the brain's capacity to recreate or invent new connections after particular damage, such as a stroke or an amputation. Thus, reparative plasticity reveals the brain's capacity to create a 'natural prosthesis', to invent new forms of self-repair, which were not foreseen or pre-formed in advance. For example, certain neuronal connections that are responsible for movement or cognition might be lost or destroyed after a stroke. However, this loss can be compensated by activating different parts of the brain which take on the role of damaged neuronal connections. As Marc Jeannerod points out, 'The patient, by himself or through rehabilitation, has learned to use nerve pathways that would not be there in the normal state. This reorganization of motor function testifies once more to the plasticity of brain mechanisms' (Jeannerod 2002: 69; cited in Malabou 2008: 28). Another example that Malabou gives to prove the brain's reparative function is in a hand transplant operation: even if it is possible to re-establish the anatomical continuity between the donor's hand and the recipient's forearm, there still remains the question whether it is possible to re-establish the neuronal connections between the transplanted hand and the brain. However, the brain manages to restore the representation of the hand in such a way that the transplanted hand is recognised as its own. These examples demonstrate that the brain has the potentiality for creation and invention, and can be modified in many different ways.

Thus, both the plasticity of stem cells and the plasticity of brain connections express potentiality as one of the most important characteristics of every living being. It is important to stress that plasticity as potentiality is not actualised according to a certain pre-existing plan or form, but is open to change, improvisation and even accidents. Similarly to Ruyer, who argued that the living form initiates its own morphogenetic development, Malabou's philosophy reconceptualises developmental, modulational and reparative plasticity as potentiality, which appears not only in the embryo but also in adult individuals. Plasticity as potentiality allows one to interpret the organism and the brain not as something that is actually given and finite, but as an open system, virtually carrying within itself its future transformations. In this respect, Malabou's idea of plasticity as potentiality has an affinity to the Deleuzian notion of the virtual, which in *What Is Philosophy?* was used to describe the undetermined character of the brain. The virtual or potential character of the brain implies not only the potential to be (or to form), but also the potential not to be (or to deform). In other words, beside the three types of plasticity that increase the number of synaptic connections, there is a fourth type of plasticity that appears as an explosion, or a rupture. It is an intermediary type of plasticity – never discussed by neuroscientists – which is situated between cellular plasticity and neuronal plasticity. In contrast to neuroscientists, who believe in the smooth continuity between the neuronal and the mental, Malabou argues that in this case there is a certain incommensurability, or rupture, which interrupts the smooth functioning of the brain.

## Damasio: From the Neuronal to the Mental

Malabou formulates her position taking into account recent research in neuroscience, and especially referring to the works of Antonio Damasio. Damasio is a strong proponent of the univocity of life, asserting the continuity between different levels of organic organisation. In his latest book *The Strange Order of Things* (2018), Damasio observes that all living beings, from unicellular organisms to complex organisms with a central nervous system, follow the fundamental principle of homeostasis: 'Homeostasis is the powerful, unthought, unspoken imperative, whose discharge implies, for every living organism, small or large, nothing less than enduring and prevailing' (Damasio 2018: 25). Homeostasis is not only responsible for the organism's endurance and survival, but also establishes '*a projection of life into the future of an organism or a species*' (Damasio 2018: 25, emphasis in original). In this sense, homeostasis works as a principle of potentiality, which not only maintains the present condition, but also projects it towards future developments. Both un-minded bacteria and complex organisms such as human beings, having their senses and feelings, seek for the flourishing of life. Between the pure organic state and the mental state there is an intermediary level of feelings, which, according to Damasio, are 'the mental deputies of homeostasis': negative feelings express deficient homeostasis, whereas positive feelings express the appropriate levels of homeostasis. However, the notion of feeling here refers not to a mental state, but to the non-conscious biological or chemical processes taking place in our bodies. As Damasio points out, 'the term "homeostasis" refers to a nonconscious form of physiological control that operates automatically without subjectivity or deliberation on the part of the organism. Obviously [. . .] it can even operate well in organisms without a nervous system' (Damasio 2018: 47). For example, most organisms automatically control the level of sugar, temperature or water balance by alerting the compensatory mechanisms. Hence, it is important to stress that homeostasis leads not to a perfect equilibrium (that would lead to death), but to a state of flourishing and well-being.

Thus, Damasio creates a strong analogy between unicellular organisms and complex organisms with a central nervous system, as they are both striving for homeostasis in a similar way; however, he observes that this principle of homeostasis cannot be interpreted as a certain kind of 'consciousness'. In contrast to Ruyer, who argued that there is an organic, or primary, consciousness characteristic of all living beings, even the most simple ones, Damasio is reluctant to name homeostatic activity as 'consciousness'. He asserts that simple living beings respond to their environment; for example, plants respond to temperature, hydration and sunlight, but this response is not conscious.

> All of these creatures continually *sense* the presence of other living creatures or of the environment. But I resist calling them conscious, in the traditional meaning of the word, because that traditional meaning is tied to the notions of mind and feeling, and in turn I have linked mind and feeling to the presence of nervous systems. (Damasio 2018: 157, emphasis in original)

Obviously, bacteria and protozoa have no nervous system and cannot experience mental states. However, Damasio argues that between basic biological processes, such as cellular sensing, and mental states there is an intermediary level of feelings. 'Feelings are core mental states, perhaps *the* core mental states, those that correspond to a specific, foundational content: *the internal state of the body within which consciousness inheres*' (Damasio 2018: 158, emphasis in original). Feelings express the intimate relationship between the body and the brain, which together with the network of the nervous system form an organismic single unit. In other words, neither the nervous system nor the brain can provide and produce mental phenomena if they work separately, and only their permanent interaction creates a continuity between the organism and the brain. As Damasio points out, 'brains and bodies are in the same mind-enabling soup' (Damasio 2018: 240), which creates a kind of cerebral organism.

In his earlier book *The Feeling of What Happens* (1999), Damasio gives a more detailed analysis of feeling and a more nuanced explanation of different levels of consciousness. His basic insight is that feelings express a certain type of organic consciousness, which exists 'before' subjective consciousness. Damasio asserts that our brain, which is undoubtedly conscious, contains some kind of non-conscious mechanisms, which inform the brain about the state of our organism. 'These devices continually represent, *nonconsciously*, the state of the living body, along its many dimensions. I call the state of activity within the ensemble of such devices the *proto-self*, the nonconscious forerunner for the levels of self which appear in our minds as the conscious protagonists of consciousness: core self and autobiographical self' (Damasio

1999: 22, emphasis in original). In other words, the proto-self is a collection of neural patterns which represent the state of the organism at multiple levels of the brain, but represent that non-consciously. These representations create feelings, sensory patterns or images, which inform the brain about the state of the organism and also help to create a 'core self', which collects these feelings into a second-order pattern and is conscious of them. This 'core self' is encapsulated in the 'autobiographical self', which includes both past experiences and future anticipations. The 'autobiographical self' is an archive of imaginary representations or storytellings through which the 'self' is endlessly presenting itself to itself. 'The entire construction of knowledge, from simple to complex, from nonverbal imagetic to verbal literary, depends on the ability to map what happens over time, *inside* our organism, *around* our organism, *to* and *with* our organism, one thing followed by another thing, causing another thing, endlessly' (Damasio 1999: 189, emphasis in original).

In this sense, Damasio asserts that there is a neural continuity between the organism and the brain:

> the relationship between organism and nervous system is incestuous. The nervous system is, after all, inside the organism ... The nervous system *interacts* with varied parts of the body thanks to neural pathways, which are distributed in all body structures, and thanks, in the reverse direction, to chemical molecules, which travel in the circulating blood and can gain direct access to the nervous system ... (Damasio 2018: 126–7, emphasis in original)

In other words, the body and the brain interact and form an organismic single unit, which expresses itself as a feeling: a feeling is a perception not of some object, but of body-as-subject; it is a feeling of what happens within the body. The discovery of the continuity between the body and the brain reveals 'the strange order of things': it appears that feeling and the sense of 'self' depend on the prior emergence of a nervous system and not on the existence of the cerebral cortex. This discovery might change the common-sense idea about human exceptionalism, because humans are not the only species that possess feelings and self-awareness. As Damasio asserts,

> the emergence of feeling and subjectivity is not recent at all, let alone exclusively human [. . .] Not only are all vertebrates likely to be conscious experiencers of a variety of feelings but so are a number of invertebrates whose central nervous system design resembles that of humans as far as spinal cord and brain stem are concerned. Social insects are likely to qualify, and so do charming octopuses drawing on a very different brain design. (Damasio 2018: 238)

Human exceptionalism is based on the presumption that subjectivity is determined by the cerebral cortex of upper vertebrates, whereas Damasio highlights that subjectivity depends on the auto-affective capacities of the cerebral organism, which inform the organism about ongoing life processes. This auto-affectivity is the precursor of feelings and subjectivity: 'The fact that we can find so much in common in the social and affective behaviors of single-celled organisms, sponges and hydras, cephalopods, and mammals suggests a common root for the problems of life regulation in different creatures and also a shared solution: obeying the homeostatic imperative' (Damasio 2018: 239). Nervous systems are only servants to this primary homeostatic imperative, which is the basis of any organic activity. This insight helps to assert the continuity between all forms of life and to question the exceptional place of human beings.

## Malabou: Between the Neuronal and the Mental

Malabou is quite critical of this harmonious passage from the body as organism to the complexity of the brain. She argues that between the 'proto-self' and the 'conscious self' there should be an intermediary plasticity, which would represent the transition from the neuronal to the mental in terms of negation and resistance. 'There is no simple and limpid continuity from the one to the other, but rather transformation of the one into the other out of their mutual conflict' (Malabou 2008: 72). Malabou argues that the transition from the neuronal to the mental is more like a rupture, or an explosion, than a continuum.

> Only an ontological explosion could permit the transition from one order to another, from one organization to another, from one given to another. The neuronal and the mental resist each other and themselves, and it is because of this that they can be linked to one another, precisely because – *contra* Damasio – they do not speak the same language. (Malabou 2008: 72, emphasis in original)

In the same way that an organism has to destroy certain cells in order to change and develop (the phenomenon of apoptosis), the neuronal network also has to destroy itself to remain creative. Here is actualised the third meaning of plasticity, which means destruction and explosion. In this sense, there is a contradiction between the maintenance system, or homeostasis, and the potential for change. Homeostasis has to be exploded if the system is to change. As Malabou points out, 'if we didn't explode at each transition, if we didn't destroy ourselves a bit, we could not live' (Malabou 2008: 74). Thus explosion is seen as the necessary condition for creativity and freedom. However, this explosion does not necessarily lead to positive changes, but might take a destructive turn: in some specific cases, such as brain lesion or neurodegenerative disease, the neuronal and the mental break apart.

Malabou discusses this rupture in *The New Wounded*,[4] where she re-examines Damasio's thesis about the continuity between the neuronal and the mental. What is problematic in Damasio's work is the question of representation: if the 'proto-self' is collecting data about the state of the organism, why is this activity described as non-conscious? Damasio asserts that the 'proto-self' consists of a multiplicity of neuronal patterns, which map the state of the body at different levels. However, this mapping is not collected in the brain, but appears at different levels, from the brain stem to the cerebral cortex. In other words, according to Damasio, the organism is both being sensed and sensing at the same time: 'These structures are intimately involved in the process of regulating the state of the organism. The operations of acting on the organism and of sensing the state of the organism are closely tied' (Damasio 1999: 154). The signals coming from neuronal patterns produce certain images or a kind of internal representation, which should not be confused with our conscious feeling of self. '*We are not conscious of the proto-self* [. . .] The proto-self has no powers of perception and holds no knowledge. Nor is the proto-self to be confused with the rigid homunculus of old neurology' (Damasio 1999: 154, emphasis in original). Thus, the 'proto-self' is a cerebral auto-affection, or, in Ruyer's terms, a kind of self-survey, which expresses an immediate proximity of an organism to itself. Both for Ruyer and Damasio, this auto-affection exists before perception and knowledge, and does not presuppose any 'subject' behind it.

Malabou makes an interesting theoretical intervention here by suggesting a relation between non-conscious activity, taking place via neural patterns and feelings, and the Freudian notion of the unconscious. Malabou suggests the term 'cerebral unconscious', which would cover the entirety of these cerebral processes that both inform the brain about ongoing organic activities taking place in the organism, and translate this information into affects. As Malabou points out,

> The autorepresentative activity of the brain, ceaselessly mapped out within psychosomatic states, thus scrutinizes its own inside, translates it into images and affects itself with this activity, of which, we see, it is both sender and receiver. The 'cerebral unconscious', then, designates less the entirety of nonconscious processes than *the auto-affection of the brain itself in its entirety*. (Malabou 2012a: 41, emphasis in original)

However, the notion of auto-affection does not mean that the brain is 'conscious' of itself, or 'perceives' itself directly. Malabou makes a distinction between subjective auto-affection and cerebral auto-affection. Subjective

---

[4] Catherine Malabou, *Les nouveaux blessés*, Paris: Bayard, 2007. Translated into English as *The New Wounded: From Neurosis to Brain Damage*, trans. Steven Miller, New York: Fordham University Press, 2012.

auto-affection in a traditional sense means that the subject is capable of experiencing itself as self-identical, of creating its subjectivity and identity with the help of inner mental space. Cerebral auto-affection means something different: it is the brain's capacity to track organic processes taking place within the organism. As Malabou points out,

> Cerebral auto-affection, which designates the set of homeostatic processes, thus characterizes *the brain's capacity to experience the altering character of contact with itself*. Emotion plays a fundamental role within the constitution of this cerebral psyche: the brain affects itself – that is, modifies itself – within the constant flow of vital regulation. (Malabou 2012a: 42, emphasis in original)

However, the question is who is the holder of these affects and what kind of representation does this cerebral auto-affection presuppose? If the organism is both the sender and the receiver of these affects, how can this auto-affectivity be translated into the language of mental states?

Malabou argues that this is a kind of blind spot: our psyche cannot directly access the unconscious, and, in a similar way, our subjective consciousness cannot access our organic consciousness or the 'proto-self'. Thus, cerebral auto-affectivity does not create any kind of identity or self-reflectivity, and in this respect it should be distinguished from subjective auto-affectivity, which is the essence of our subjective identity. In the structure of subjective auto-affectivity the subject reflects itself as being identical to itself, whereas in the structure of cerebral auto-affectivity the feeling of 'what happens' does not lead to subjective identity or self. As Malabou points out,

> *No one can feel his or her own brain; nor can he or she speak of it, hear it speak, nor hear himself or herself speak within it.* Cerebral auto-affection is necessarily and paradoxically accompanied by a blindness, *an inability of the subject to feel anything as far as it is concerned* [. . .] *Cerebral auto-affection is the unconscious of subjectivity.* (Malabou 2012a: 42–3, emphasis in original)

In other words, the 'cerebral self' remains unconscious and is not fully represented in the subjective self.

And yet we might ask if this recourse to psychoanalysis is justified and if the term 'unconscious' is the right one, because the 'cerebral self' is quite 'conscious' and well informed about its own activity. We can agree with Malabou that the 'cerebral self' does not represent itself in the sense that it has no language, but this does not mean that it is deprived of representation. Malabou admits this by pointing out that cerebral auto-affection is not verbal but of specular nature: 'To speak of cerebral auto-affection, therefore, is to admit that the brain is capable of looking at itself, touching itself as it constitutes its own image. Homeostatic regulation has a specular structure; it operates as a kind of mirror within which the brain sees itself live' (Malabou 2012a: 42). The brain sees itself but does not speak to itself; in other words, it functions in a different register than the unconscious, which, according to Lacanian psychoanalysis, is structured like a language. For this reason, we can argue that Malabou's suggestion of naming it the 'cerebral unconscious' might not be the right one, because the cerebral and the mental are not translatable one into the other. As Damasio points out, any organism, and the brain as a kind of cerebral organism, is capable of mapping and image-making, which provides information about the current state of affairs. The cerebral organism is always busy with making a 'movie-in-the-brain' (Damasio 2018: 146), which provides the internal representation of 'what happens'. This idea is very close to Ruyer's insight about self-survey as an organism's sort of inner cinematography, as a vision without a gaze, which creates the condition of immediate self-proximity. This inner representation can be imagined as 'cerebral cinematography', which does not need any actual observer in the sense of a bounded individual. The cerebral organism is both the film that is screened and the observer who is watching this film. As Damasio points out, it expresses 'the never-ending background music of life, the continuous execution of life's score, complete with changes of pace and rhythm and key, not to mention volume' (Damasio 2018: 107). Thus there is a clear disparity between cerebral auto-affectivity as the inner representation of life processes and subjective auto-affectivity, which creates the sense of the individual self.

This incommensurability between the neuronal and the mental is disclosed in such cases as brain lesions or neurodegenerative diseases – dementia, Parkinson's or Alzheimer's. Malabou is interested in these cases because here the 'cerebral self' and the 'subjective self' break apart: the importance of cerebral auto-affectivity reveals itself only in a negative and destructive way and exposes the fragility of every subjective identity.

> Cerebral auto-affection is a process that becomes all the more fragile and all the more exposed to the extent that *the event of its destruction constitutes the only proof of its existence for the subject*. The importance of this auto-affection can be revealed only negatively, through an accident – a wound, damage, or trauma – that happens to interrupt or disrupt its functioning. (Malabou 2012a: 46, emphasis in original)

In these cases, the 'cerebral self' is undergoing a radical change and cannot reconnect to its former subjective personality. Although change is a necessary component of the notion of plasticity, this time we have a different kind of plasticity – destructive plasticity. In *Ontology of the Accident*[5] Malabou

---

[5] Catherine Malabou, *Ontologie de l'accident*, Paris: Éditions Léo Scheer, 2009. Translated into English as *Ontology of the Accident: An Essay on Destructive Plasticity*, trans. Carolyn Shread, Cambridge: Polity, 2012.

defines destructive plasticity as a phenomenon that appears only through a negation or rupture:

> Something *shows itself* when there is damage, a cut, something to which normal, creative plasticity gives neither access nor body: the deserting of subjectivity, the distancing of the individual who becomes a stranger to herself, who no longer recognizes anyone, who no longer recognizes herself, who no longer remembers her self. (Malabou 2012b: 6, emphasis in original)

Destructive plasticity tears apart the 'cerebral self' and the 'subjective self' and presents itself as a scar, a radical change that is irreversible, and whose effects are unrepairable.

However, as was discussed above, this destruction is a necessary component of plasticity and change. To get a new form, to acquire a different identity, we have to undergo a change, to destroy our old forms and identities. As Malabou points out, 'The fact that all creation can only occur at the price of a destructive counterpart is a fundamental law of life. It does not contradict life; it makes life possible' (Malabou 2012b: 4). This imperative for destruction is obvious even at a cellular level: in order to develop and acquire a new organic form, an organism has to destroy its previous form. Malabou refers again to the biologist Ameisen, who notes that 'the sculpting of the self assumes cellular annihilation or apoptosis, the phenomena of programmed cellular suicide: in order for fingers to form, a separation between the fingers must also form. It is apoptosis that produces the interstitial void that enables fingers to detach themselves from one another' (Malabou 2012b: 4–5). In this respect, destruction is a necessary part of any creation. However, the annihilation of cerebral connections looks much more horrifying because it destroys the 'feeling of what happens' and disconnects the 'cerebral self' from the 'subjective self'. Damasio gives many examples of such disconnections referring to his experience in treating neurological cases, and also interpreting some fictional examples, such as Samuel Beckett's character from *Happy Days*. He refers to the character of Winnie as expressing a certain wakefulness and purposeful activity, which seems to be running automatically (Damasio 1999: 92). And yet, even while demonstrating a certain attention and purposefulness, this activity lacks core consciousness which could collect her reactions into a coherent unity of 'subjective self'. Similarly, patients with neurological diseases can express a certain purposeful behaviour, physical and affective activity, but this cerebral activity is not related to the subjective self.

Having these examples in mind, we can redefine the meaning of positive and destructive plasticity. It seems clear that change is the necessary condition of plasticity: in order to change and evolve, we have to destroy ourselves to some extent, to deform in order to get another form. However, this deformation might be irreversible and might not lead to another form, as in cases of neurodegenerative diseases or brain lesions. In these cases the change is permanent, and the potential for plasticity is lost. Destructive plasticity is reductive because it exhausts the virtuality or potentiality of what might happen. However, without engaging in destructive plasticity, we could not open the potential for creative plasticity and transform ourselves into something new. In this sense, the notion of plasticity is involved in a certain kind of Hegelian dialectic (from which it actually originated) because it is constantly torn between the necessity to maintain homeostasis and the potentiality to develop into new forms.

## Epigenesis and Reason

The notion of plasticity brings into light another dialectical contradiction – that between preformationism and epigenesis. This dialectic is the central theme in Malabou's *Before Tomorrow: Epigenesis and Rationality*,[6] where she discusses the divide between the transcendental and the biological, or between the laws of rationality, or reason, and the laws of biological development, or epigenesis. 'Epigenesis' is an Aristotelian term referring to the process of development through which cells differentiate and organs are formed. British biologist Conrad Waddington coined the term 'epigenetics' in 1940 to refer to a branch of molecular biology that studies the relations between genes and the individual features they produce, or between genotype and phenotype (Malabou 2016a: 78–9). Genotype marks the genetic constitution of an organism, whereas phenotype is the sum of characteristics, which appear as a consequence of the organism's interaction with the environment. In this sense, epigenetics is a theoretical model, which explains the development of an organism not in relation to its genetic determination but through its interaction with external factors throughout life. In this respect, the theory of epigenetics undermines preformationism, the belief that a living being is pre-programmed by its genetic features, and expresses the dialectic between determinism and freedom.

What makes Malabou's approach so interesting is that she takes a biological theory of epigenetics and applies it to reason itself. Is the transcendental innate or is it acquired? In other words, can we speak about the 'preformationism of reason', or, by contrast, should we insist on the 'epigenesis of reason'? As a starting point for these questions Malabou takes the 27th paragraph of Kant's *Critique of Pure Reason*, where Kant uses the term 'epigenesis' to describe the agreement between a priori categories and the objects of experience. There are two ways in which the agreement is possible: either the experience makes these concepts possible or these concepts make the experience possible. The first way is negated because a priori concepts cannot be

[6] Catherine Malabou, *Avant demain. Épigenèse et rationalité*, Paris: PUF, 2014. Translated into English as *Before Tomorrow: Epigenesis and Rationality*, trans. Carolyn Shread, Cambridge: Polity, 2016.

generated from experience: 'The first is not the case with the categories (nor with pure sensible intuition); for they are *a priori* concepts, hence independent of experience (the assertion of an empirical origin would be a sort of *generatio aequivoca*)' (Kant 1998: 264, B 167, emphasis in original). Thus, only the second way remains – that the condition of possibility of our experience lies in pure concepts, 'as it were a system of the *epigenesis* of pure reason' (Kant 1998: 265, B 167, emphasis in original). In other words, in describing the two ways of necessary agreement, Kant uses two biological concepts: *generatio aequivoca* and *epigenesis*. Referring to the conflict between these two ways, and prioritising the second, Kant contrasts it with a 'middle way', that of a '*preformation-system* of pure reason' – in this case the categories 'were rather subjective predispositions for thinking, implanted in us along with our experience by our author in such a way that their use would agree exactly with the laws of nature along which experience runs' (Kant 1998: 265, B 167, emphasis in original); however, 'in such a case the categories would lack the *necessity* that is essential to their concept' (Kant 1998: 265, B 168, emphasis in original). Thus, in defining the agreement between the categories and the objects of experience, Kant examines three biological categories – *generatio aequivoca*, *preformation* and *epigenesis* – which all relate to biological theories of generation (equivocal generation, preformationism and epigenesis).

As Malabou points out, *generatio aequivoca*, or equivocal generation, is a biological theory that explains the generation of life through the spontaneous differentiation of inorganic matter. This is a kind of miraculous transformation whereby a being made of organic matter originates from inorganic matter. This model of generation is dismissed as an instance of occasionalism. The categories, and the agreement between the categories and the objects of experience, cannot arise out of nothing. As Malabou observes,

> This approach postulates the existence of a birth foreign to its source, offspring born of nothing. By contrast, the categories are well and truly the categories *of* the understanding, born of it and belonging wholly to it. Equivocal generation, which contradicts the very idea of generation, is a theoretical monstrosity that warrants no further consideration. (Malabou 2016a: 22, emphasis in original)

In a similar way, Kant dismisses a 'middle way' of preformation, according to which there is an ideal correspondence between our categories and the objects of experience, presuming that this correspondence is innate to our mind. Preformationism in biology presupposes that the form of an organism is given in advance, and that in the course of its development it changes only in quantity following the pre-given plan. The 'preformation-system of pure reason' would imply that

> the pure elements of cognition are innate logical tendencies, placed in us by God and arranged in such a way that their use corresponds exactly

to their objects [. . .] Following this 'middle way' produces the assertion that the mind is originally 'predisposed', according to the economy of a relation settled in advance . . . (Malabou 2016a: 22)

To accept this theory would mean that our understanding is pre-formed by God, in other words, that our understanding is devoid of any spontaneity and freedom. The laws of nature and causality would be imposed on us in advance, and that would make our subjective decision a mere illusion.

This is why Kant supports the theory of epigenesis as the only possible way to reflect the transcendental. The biological theory of epigenesis dismisses preformationism and emphasises the role of the unforeseeable in the generation of living beings. In a similar way, the agreement between the categories and the objects of experience has to be reflected not as something originating from matter of a different nature (as in equivocal generation), or as given by God in advance (as in preformationism), but as something which has the principle of differentiation and development in itself. As Malabou points out, 'the agreement must be thought by analogy with an embryo developing *by itself*, through the process of gradual cellular differentiation and complexification' (Malabou 2016a: 25, emphasis in original). In this respect, the theory of epigenesis allows Kant to reject both the theory of equivocal generation and preformationism, and to argue that pure reason is driven by self-generating and self-differentiating vital force.

> The agreement between the categories and objects can only be thought as the product of a dynamic, creative, and self-forming relation. It can come neither from a prior accord (preformationism) nor from a magical animation of the inorganic (equivocal generation). The understanding imposes, of itself, a form on the given and thereby constitutes knowledge as the product of its own activity. (Malabou 2016a: 25–6)

This allows us to assert that Kant introduces the principle of self-generation into the core of reason.

However, the question is what is the relationship between Kantian epigenesis and the recent developments of epigenetics? Is the Kantian reference to epigenesis just an analogy, a figure of thought, or is there a deeper link between the transcendental and the biological? Malabou argues that recent debates between genetics and epigenetics are reminiscent of the debates in the Kantian era. In the second half of the twentieth century the field of biology was dominated by genetics, which presumed that all features of the organism are pre-formed in the genetic code. In this sense, genetics can be seen as the 'resurgence of preformationism' (Malabou 2016a: 80). The genetic approach is questioned by epigenetics, which presumes that, despite its genetic determination, the organism is changing through its interaction with the environment. In this sense, 'the debate between preformationism and epigenetism has shifted and now occurs between genetic determinism and epigenetic shaping' (Malabou 2016a: 82). Recent research in biology, such as Mary-Jane West-Eberhard's (2003) theory of developmental plasticity, provides strong evidence that developmental and external factors play a crucial role in the passage from the genotype to the phenotype.

Malabou seeks to create a kind of 'critique of neurobiological reason', which would take into account both recent research in neurobiology and the transcendental notion of rationality. Neuroscientist Jean-Pierre Changeux pointed out that the brain's complexity is much greater than genetic complexity: the brain's complexity is always increasing, whereas the DNA content is quite limited. This discontinuity is accounted for in Changeux's theory of the epigenesis of neuronal networks (Changeux et al. 1973), which interprets the brain's activity as a process of selection and stabilisation. According to this theory, the brain develops in three stages: the first stage is growth, when the brain produces multiple neurons and synapses; the second is the transient redundancy stage, when the most efficient synaptic connections are selected, and others are eliminated; and the third is the stage of selective stabilisation, when the connections that are most frequently used are stabilised. The theory asserts that the brain is constantly changing through its relations with the external world, such as experience and learning, and, in this sense, it becomes the principle of its self-generation.

However, Malabou is quite critical towards this neurobiological approach because it fails to make a connection between the biological question of neurological development and the transcendental nature of reason: 'the problem is that the neurobiological viewpoint simply erases the transcendental. A bridge is thrown directly between epigenesis, understood as organic growth, and brain epigenetics, understood as a selection-stabilization process of neuronal connections, without going through the transcendental question of the formation of reason and rationality' (Malabou 2016a: 152). Even if neuroscientists can explain the formation of a synaptic network, they cannot account for the transcendental nature of rationality. The philosophical or the transcendental aspect of the brain is always omitted. Therefore, Malabou argues for the need to create an epigenetic philosophy, or an epigenetic paradigm of rationality, which could reconcile 'the biological and the transcendental without granting either one the supremacy of a proper meaning' (Malabou 2016a: 160).

Malabou asserts that the Kantian attempt to explain the transcendental through the biological notion of epigenesis already anticipates an epigenetic philosophy. She points out that to explain the transcendental in §27 of *Critique of Pure Reason*, Kant addresses the three examples of generation and prioritises epigenesis as the best analogy to explain the agreement between the categories and objects of experience. It is important to point out that the same theories of generation appear in §81 of Kant's *Critique of the Power of Judgement*: this time they appear not as mere analogy, but as laws which can explain the growth of a living being. For Kant, there are two theories explaining the generation of a living being – 'occasionalism' and 'prestabilism'. According to 'occasionalism', 'the supreme world-cause, in accordance with its idea, would immediately provide the organic formation to the matter comingling in every impregnation'. However, 'If one assumes the occasionalism of the production of organic beings, then everything that is natural is entirely lost, and with that is also lost all use of reason for judging the possibility of such a product' (Kant 2000: 291, 5:422). Therefore, Kant turns to 'prestabilism', according to which 'an organic being produces more of its kind and constantly preserves the species itself' (Kant 2000: 291, 5:422). Kant explains 'prestabilism' in two ways:

> it considers each organic being generated from its own kind as either the *educt* or the *product* of the latter. The system of generatings as mere educts is called that of *individual preformation*, or the *theory of evolution*; the system of generatings as products is called the system of *epigenesis*. (Kant 2000: 291, 5:423, emphasis in original)

Kant argues that the theory of epigenesis has a great advantage over other theories, 'because it considers nature, at least as far as propagation is concerned, as itself producing rather than merely developing those things that can initially be represented as possible only in accordance with the causality of ends' (Kant 2000: 292, 5:424). Thus, if in the first *Critique* the biological principle of epigenesis appears as a mere analogy, then in the third *Critique* epigenesis is introduced as the biological principle of life and living beings. In other words, the relationship between the transcendental and the biological undergoes a transformation from the first to the third *Critique*: 'The meaning of the epigenesis of and in critical philosophy derives from the long rational maturation of the relation between the transcendental and that which appears to do without it, to resist it: the living organism, which self-forms and has no need for categories' (Malabou 2016a: 161). This dialectical link between the transcendental and the biological allows Malabou to conceptualise the epigenesis of neurobiological reason, in other words, to state the self-generative and self-organising power of rationality.

By asserting the self-organising power of reason and rationality, Malabou also redefines the nature of causality: if the transcendental field is subject to the epigenesis common to all living beings, then it is freed from the laws of logical necessity and is opened to contingency. In contrast to Quentin Meillassoux, who asserted in *After Finitude* (2008) that contingency can be explained only mathematically, Malabou argues that contingency can be explained biologically. 'Kant allows us, from finitude, to discover a meaning of contingency that is more innovative and radical than the one that Meillassoux proposes' (Malabou 2016a: 172). The epigenesis of reason not only allows us to embrace the contingency characteristic of the organic world but also clarifies the durational, gradual and processual nature of reason: we can observe and follow 'the gestation and embryogenesis of reason itself'

(Malabou 2016a: 173). As Jennifer Mensch argues in *Kant's Organicism*, 'Kant found epigenesis to be attractive for thinking about reason because it opened up possibilities for thinking about reason as an organic system, as something that was self-developing and operating according to an organic logic' (Mensch 2013: 144). The theory of epigenesis allowed Kant to think of reason as 'cause and effect of itself', as a self-organising creature open for change and contingency.

## Conclusion

The epigenetic approach to reason, or, more generally, the biologisation of reason, might have important biopolitical consequences. Following Foucault, Malabou argues that the epigenesis of reason allows us to question the universal and necessary nature of transcendental reason and to replace it with the plastic, contingent and arbitrary character of 'biological reason'. The biologisation of reason allows one to think beyond formal structures and universal values and, as Malabou writes, 'authorizes subjects to shape and form themselves as such' (Malabou 2019: 131). In this respect, the biologisation of reason might be seen as a successful strategy of resistance to biopolitical power. Both Foucault and Deleuze argued that when biopolitical power takes life as its object, it is the vital power of life that allows us to resist power. In a similar vein, Malabou argues that recent developments in biology, such as epigenetics, cloning or gene editing, demonstrate that the biological dimension of our lives should be understood not as determination but as a potential for freedom and change.

In her text 'One Life Only: Biological Resistance, Political Resistance', Malabou points out that 'a resistance to what is known today as biopower [. . .] might emerge from possibilities written into the structure of the living being itself, not from the philosophical concepts that tower over it; that there might be a biological resistance to the biopolitical' (Malabou 2016b: 429). This is what can be inferred from the notion of plasticity: plasticity refers to biological creativity and the capacity of a living being to receive form and give form, to change and develop. Living beings are not predetermined in advance but rather constitute formative activity which carries its forms within itself. As Malabou points out, 'Plasticity is in a way genetically programmed to develop and operate without program, plan, determinism, schedule, design, or preschematization. Neural plasticity allows the shaping, repairing, and remodelling of connections and in consequence a certain amount of self-transformation of the living being' (Malabou 2015: 43–4). In this sense, the divide between the transcendental and the biological is undermined, because the biological does not follow any transcendental law but develops according to its own immanent potentiality. Biological plasticity allows us to imagine different forms of life and subjectivity, free to take any shape or form and to avoid the pressure of normativity. Where plasticity deserts, biopolitics takes over.

# 5
# General Organology: Between Organism and Machine

In this chapter I will discuss the theory of organology, which examines the interaction between an organism and a machine. We can argue that organology appears as an attempt to overcome the opposition between mechanism and vitalism: mechanism explains living beings according to the laws of physics and chemistry, whereas vitalists argue that to understand living beings we have to presume the existence of some non-physical force. In the first part of the twentieth century we can see an attempt to overcome this opposition – this is the theory of organicism. Both vitalists and organicists stress the teleological behaviour of organisms; however, they differ in how they explain the organising principle of organisms: vitalists assert some non-physical entity, a vital force, whereas organicists insist that wholeness and organisation can be explained without such notions (Haraway 2004: 34). Organismic biologists assert that to understand the phenomenon of life we have to explain its 'organisation' or 'organising relations'. These organising relations are immanent in the physical structure of the organism, therefore living beings can be defined in terms of 'self-organisation' (Capra 1997: 25). This attention to the patterns of organisation, which was implicit in living beings, became the main question of cybernetics, which examines the self-organising functioning of a new generation of machines. Norbert Wiener defined cybernetics as the science of 'control and communication in the animal and the machine' (Wiener 1985). Cybernetics overcomes the opposition between mechanism and vitalism by analysing both living and non-living beings as self-organising structures supported by information and feedback.

Besides these influential theoretical stances, we can discern another current named 'organology'. The term 'organology' was proposed by Georges Canguilhem in his text 'Machine and Organism'.[1] Canguilhem traces the

---

[1] Published in Georges Canguilhem, *La connaisance de la vie*, Paris: Librairie Philosophique J. Vrin, 1965. Translated into English as *Knowledge of Life*, trans. Stefanos Geroulanos and Daniela Ginsburg, New York: Fordham University Press, 2008. The same idea appears in Canguilhem's 'Note' where he argues

term to Bergson's *Creative Evolution*, saying that it is a treatise on organology, although Bergson never used the term. Thus, organology not only examines the relationships between machines and organisms, but also treats machines as an extension of the human organism and its organs. Referring to his predecessors, such as Ernst Kapp, Alfred Espinas and André Leroi-Gourhan,[2] Canguilhem argues that tools and technologies can be understood as extensions of biological organisms.

As Canguilhem points out, 'machines can be considered organs of the human species. A tool or a machine is an organ, and organs are tools or machines' (Canguilhem 2008: 87). Thus, explaining organs or organisms through mechanical models can be considered tautological. In contrast to machines, which are quantitatively measurable and have a defined purpose, organisms are self-organised and develop according to their internal transformations. The most important thing is that no machine can create another machine or replace itself (as was already asserted by Kant), hence the invention of any machine should be inscribed into the history of human beings and life in general. As Canguilhem points out, 'it seems legitimate to hold that biological organization must necessarily precede the existence and meaning of mechanical constructions' (Canguilhem 2008: 91). This insight allows Canguilhem to examine machines through the model of biological organisation.

In a similar way, Simondon discusses technical objects as belonging to general ontogenesis, which encompasses both living and non-living beings. Later this idea is significantly elaborated by Bernard Stiegler, who creates his own theory of 'general organology' and asserts that human life can be maintained only through the invention of tools and the organisation of the inorganic. The notion of organology is further re-examined by Yuk Hui, who argues that technical objects are becoming organic in the sense that they incorporate organic properties, such as recursivity and contingency. Thus, 'general organology' can be seen as a theory which explains technology through the model of the organism and inscribes technology into the continuum of living beings.

## Simondon on Technical Objects

Simondon used the word 'organology' occasionally in *Communication et information* (Simondon 2015a: 167), without giving much attention to the term. However, as Guillaume le Blanc has suggested, organological thought

---

that the Bergsonian motif of an 'organology' should 'inscribe the mechanical within the organic', to 'return mechanism to its place in life and for life' and 'to reinsert the history of mechanism into the history of life'. See Canguilhem 1947.

[2] Ernst Kapp, *Grundlinien einer Philosophie der Technik*, Braunschweig: Georg Westermann, 1877; Alfred Espinas, *Les origines de la technologie*, Paris: Alcan, 1897; André Leroi-Gourhan, *Milieu et techniques*, Paris: Albin Michel, 1945.

stretches from Bergson to Simondon, passing by Canguilhem (Le Blanc 2010: 203, n. 2; cited in Hui 2019: 148). Canguilhem was the supervisor of Simondon's supplementary thesis *On the Mode of Existence of Technical Objects*, published immediately after its defence in 1958. In this supplementary thesis Simondon attempts to describe the ontogenesis of technical objects and explain the relation between technical objects and living beings. Simondon examines technical objects as a part of general ontogenesis, which includes physical, biological and psychosocial phenomena. The development of technical objects is compared to an evolution of living beings as described by Jean-Baptiste Lamarck (Simondon 2008: 173), including simple as well as complex organisms, such as humans. A technical object is seen as a mediator between a human and a machine, between the biological and the artificial. As Simondon points out, 'The opposition drawn between culture and technics, between man and machine, is false and has no foundation . . . Behind a facile humanism, it masks a reality rich in human efforts and natural forces, and which constitutes a world of technical objects as mediators between man and nature' (Simondon 2017: 15). Simondon argues that there is something inherently human inside technics – a human thought or an invention – and that human thinking itself contains something technical or machinic – this idea is later taken up and elaborated by such thinkers as Derrida and Stiegler.

Simondon was influenced by cyberneticians of his time, especially Norbert Wiener and his notion of feedback. However, he criticises cybernetics and its general idea that there is an identity between a technical object and a natural object, or, more specifically, a living being. For Simondon, cybernetics is inefficient in postulating the identity between living beings and self-regulating technical objects (Simondon 2017: 51). This relationship is much more complicated with regard to their general tendencies: living beings tend towards individuation, whereas technical objects tend towards concretisation. The genesis of technical objects moves from the abstract to the concrete by resolving disparities and 'tending toward internal coherence, toward a closure of the system of causes and effects that exert themselves in a circular fashion within its bounds' (Simondon 2017: 49). Both biological individuation and technical concretisation imply a process that resolves disparities between different systems. As Mills points out, similar to the process of individuation of living beings, 'the development of the technical lineage is the progressive resolution of problems through concretization. As such the concretization of the technical object is also, in a sense, its naturalization' (Mills 2016: 109). However, technical objects can become more concrete but they never become individuals because they need an inventor to be completed. In other words, Simondon defines concretisation as an invention, which needs a human being to intervene, and which appears as a leap from one technical system to another. A good example of concretisation is the invention of the Guimbal turbine: this is a turbine that uses a river both as a driving force and as a cooling agent to reduce overheating caused by the Joule effect, which might otherwise burn out the engine (Hui 2019: 191). In this example concretisation refers to a technical invention that resolves the specific problem of overheating. It is important to point out that this invention not only resolves technical problems but also connects a technical object and a natural milieu.

This issue needs special consideration because, in the process of concretisation, the technical object not only evolves into a new invented object, but, according to Simondon, creates an 'associated milieu': 'This simultaneously technical and natural milieu can be called an associated milieu. It is that through which the technical object conditions itself in its functioning' (Simondon 2017: 59). In other words, to become viable, a technical object needs to resolve disparities and also to invent a new milieu which is a condition of its functioning. *The technical object is thus its own condition, as a condition of existence of this mixed milieu* which is simultaneously both technical and geographical' (Simondon 2017: 58, emphasis in original). Simondon argues that technical objects and their natural milieus get into a relation of recurrent causality, which implies that, once constituted, technical objects are open to new processes of concretisation. The term 'recurrent causality' here means 'a causality that comes back to itself to act on itself'; in other words, it is a feedback, or, in Simondon's terms, an internal resonance (Hui 2019: 190). The capacity to come back to itself defines a technical object as a self-organising system that supports and conditions its own existence. In this sense, a technical object can be compared to a living being: 'The reason the living being can invent is because it is an individual being that carries its associated milieu with it; this capacity for conditioning itself lies at the root of the capacity to produce objects that condition themselves' (Simondon 2017: 60). Both living beings and technical objects are self-determining and self-referential systems which define themselves through interaction with an associated milieu.

This leads us to the question of invention, which means both the interaction between an organism and its milieu, and the interaction between a technical object and its inventor (or human mind). For Simondon, invention can occur only through recourse to pre-individual potentiality which, as was discussed in Chapter 1, is an indefinite origin of every process of individuation. According to Simondon, 'what is determinant and plays an energetic role are not forms but that which carries the forms, which is to say their ground; the ground [. . .] is what harbors the dynamisms' (Simondon 2017: 60). The notions of form and ground refer to Gestalt psychology,[3] which is considered to be insufficient to explain the process of imagination.

---

[3] Simondon is using the notions of *fond* and *forme* taken from Gestalt psychology: *forme* (form or figure) acquires meaning only in relation to a certain *fond* (background). Simondon modifies the meaning of *fond*: it refers not to the background but to the system of virtualities and potentials.

As Simondon points out,

> the ground is the system of virtualities, of potentials, forces that carve out their path, whereas forms are the system of actuality [...] Forms are passive in so far as they represent actuality; they become active when they organize in relation to this ground, thereby bringing prior virtualities into actuality. (Simondon 2017: 61)

Thus, the ground can be related to the pre-individual state, which harbours virtualities and potentialities, and which can acquire an actual form through the interaction with a milieu. Similar to a living being, which acquires its actual form through interaction with its pre-individual potential and the potentialities found in its milieu, a technical object acquires an actual form through interaction with the potentiality of the inventor's imagination and the potentialities arising from the natural milieu. In both cases invention belongs to the living being (human or non-human inventor) who has access to the potentialities of the pre-individual and transforms them into actual forms.

The question of invention is also discussed in Simondon's lecture course *Imagination and Invention 1965–1966*. As was demonstrated in Chapter 1, Simondon creates an original theory of imagination and invention that relates to a wide range of biological phenomena, from simple organisms to humans. What is original in Simondon's theory is that creativity is explained through the cycle of images, which reaches its resolution by creating an artefact or a technical object. Technical objects are understood as a part of general ontogenesis because they develop and evolve as if they were living beings. The most interesting thing here is that the impulse for the invention of new forms is found not in the inventor's mind or consciousness (there is no preformationism of technical objects), but in the metastable equilibrium of living beings. Simondon describes this as the third phase of the cycle, when memory images reach a certain oversaturation by condensing opposite and incompatible qualities. This oversaturation produces a metastable phase which is the necessary condition for invention and structural change, allowing the recreation of these qualities within a new system (Simondon 2008: 124). The oversaturation of memory images is transformed into a symbol image which at some point cannot accept any information, and therefore the cycle starts anew. Similar to a living being which develops through interaction with the potentiality found in its milieu, a technical object develops through the interaction between the oversaturated field of imagination and the potentiality of the associated milieu. Human invention can be successful only to the extent to which it participates in a general process of ontogenesis.

Another important point is that both living beings and technical objects develop through recursive causality; in other words, they constantly return to themselves in order to enter a different level of organisation. This means that a technical object – in a paradoxical way – is liberated from the Cartesian model of linear causality which used to be the essential trait of technicity. The principle of recursive causality incorporates contingency, usually associated with the natural, or organic, world. As Hui points out, 'Recursivity is not only a mechanism that can effectively "domesticate" contingency . . .; it is also a mechanism that allows novelty to occur, not simply as something coming from outside but also as an internal transformation' (Hui 2019: 138). Thus, the principle of recursivity allows contingency to be integrated within the system; in this respect, both living beings and technical objects can effectively use contingency in order to produce something new (Hui 2019: 138). The machine, similarly to a living being, is able to fight against entropy:

> the machine, being a work of organization and information, is, like life itself and together with life, that which is opposed to disorder, to the leveling of all things tending to deprive the universe of the power of change. The machine is that through which man fights against the death of the universe; it slows down the degradation of energy, as life does, and becomes a stabilizer of the world. (Simondon 2017: 21)

By integrating contingency and fighting entropy, technical objects belong to the realm of life.

However, writing in 1958, Simondon didn't anticipate second-order cybernetics and could not have been acquainted with self-organising machines. Therefore, he outlines some important differences between machines and living beings: a living being can solve its vital problems by taking recourse to virtuality. And yet, 'There is no true virtuality in a machine; the machine cannot reform its forms in order to solve a problem' (Simondon 2017: 156). The functioning of a machine is always actual, whereas a living being has the faculty to modify itself according to the virtual: 'this faculty is the sense of time, which the machine does not have because it does not live' (Simondon 2017: 157). A living being has the faculty to change itself according to the virtuality or potentiality found in the milieu, whereas a machine can act upon itself only in its actuality. An animal, or a living being in general, is a transducer as far as it stores chemical substances and then transforms them into something else during the course of vital operations. A living being intervenes between the potential energy and actual energy and acts as a transducer: 'the living thing is *that which modulates*' (Simondon 2017: 156, emphasis in original). Similarly, a human, or an inventor, acts as a transducer in relation to machines, converting the potential energy into actual functioning. The true analogy between human and machine is not on the level of corporeality (the machine neither nourishes itself nor perceives) but between the mental functioning of the human and the physical functioning of the machine. 'To invent is to make one's thought function as a machine might function, neither according to causality, which is too fragmentary, nor according to finality, which is too unitary, but according to the dynamism of lived functioning, grasped because it is produced, accompanied in its genesis' (Simondon 2017: 151). The functioning of an inventor's mind and the functioning of a machine are analogous in the sense that they are dynamisms producing new forms.

This intervention into the realm of technical objects changes the nature of the human subject – both individual and collective. Simondon argues that the relation between an inventor (a subject) and a technical object creates a special mode of relationship which he calls transindividual: 'the technical object insofar as it has been invented, thought and willed, and taken up [*assumé*] by a human subject, becomes the medium [*le support*] and symbol of this relationship, which we would like to name *transindividual*' (Simondon 2017: 252, emphasis in original). Technical invention creates a special inter-human relation; however, this relationship connects individuals neither by means of their unique individuality, nor by their identity, but by the pre-individual reality which is contained in every individual. Thus, the transindividual relation connects individuals through the mediation of the technical object which, in its turn, always carries something of human nature, if by 'nature' we understand this pre-individual charge containing potentialities and virtualities (Simondon 2017: 253). In this sense, the transindividual relationship encompasses something non-human (the pre-individual charge) within the human and vice versa: 'there is something of human nature in the technical being' (Simondon 2017: 253). Hence, a human being existing in the transindividual mode is always incomplete, unfinished, always negotiating both with its pre-individual potentiality and with other incomplete individuals through the act of technical invention.

## Stiegler's General Organology

Simondon's ideas are elaborated further in Stiegler's *Technics and Time 1: The Fault of Epimetheus*[4] and his other works. Stiegler argues that between the inorganic beings of the physical sciences and the organised beings of biology, there is a third type of being, that of technical objects, which can be described as inorganic organised beings (Stiegler 1998: 17). As far as both organic biological beings and inorganic technical objects are organised in one or another way, the question is to what extent the analogy between biological and technological development can be applicable. Following Leroi-Gourhan, Stiegler analyses technical objects in terms of technological lineage or technological phylum (meaning a major taxonomic division of living organisms). The comparison between technological and biological facts, between technical objects and living beings, is crucial for Stiegler's hypothesis. He argues that a technical object is '*organized inorganic matter*

[4] Bernard Stiegler, *La technique et le temps, 1: La faute d'Epiméthée*, Paris: Galilée, 1994. Translated into English as *Technics and Time, 1: The Fault of Epimetheus*, trans. Richard Beardsworth and George Collins, Stanford, CA: Stanford University Press, 1998.

that transforms itself in time as living matter transforms itself in its interaction with the milieu. In addition, it becomes the interface through which the human qua living matter enters into relation with the milieu' (Stiegler 1998: 49, emphasis in original). In other words, a human (as a living being) interacts with a technical object and through the technical object it interacts with its milieu.

Thus, the technical object is understood as an extension of a living being; in other words, as an exteriorisation of the human body with the help of prosthetic devices. Relying on the investigations of Leroi-Gourhan, Stiegler makes an analogy between an organ as a part of a living organism and an *organon* qua technical instrument. For Stiegler, a human being is always already externalised by means of tools and technologies, but it is precisely this exteriorisation by which interiority is constituted. In a paradoxical and quasi-Derridean manner, Stiegler argues that interiority and exteriority are related in a double bind, because human interiority is created by means of exteriority (by tools as technical objects).

The movement inherent in this process of exteriorization is paradoxical: Leroi-Gourhan in fact says that it is the tool, that is, *tekhnē*, that invents the human, not the human who invents the technical. Or again: the human invents himself in the technical by inventing the tool – by becoming exteriorized techno-logically. (Stiegler 1998: 141, emphasis in original)

In this sense, the origin of technics and the origin of the human coincide in a single moment, that of exteriorisation, which is at the same time the moment of interiorisation. Stiegler compares this moment with Simondon's notion of transductive relation: transduction is an activity which propagates (differentiates) itself in a certain domain and also the materiality of what is differentiated. In a similar vein, exteriorisation for Stiegler is a differential interaction with the milieu and also the result of this interaction.

Another important point is that exteriorisation is a relation that takes place not only in space but also in time, and creates the structure of anticipation. A technical object is not 'passive' or adaptive as a living being is, but implies an anticipation as a projection towards the future: 'Anticipation means the realization of a possibility that is not determined by a biological program' (Stiegler 1998: 151). In his description of time Stiegler relies heavily on Husserl's and Heidegger's phenomenological analyses and, in this sense, he is a docile disciple of a metaphysical tradition. Stiegler believes that a technical object (and also a subject) exists in the temporality of *Dasein*, described by Heidegger, and that a technical object as a specifically human phenomenon cannot be reconciled with biological determinism and genetic programming. The temporality of the technical object is closely related to memory, which can be exteriorised with the help of technical devices. Stiegler asserts that exteriorisation can be thought of as grammatisation, since *grammē*, or writing in general, is the first form of externalised memory, as was demonstrated in Derrida's grammatology.[5] Writing is the first instrument that allows one not only to exteriorise memory, but also to share it with other members of society. In this sense, exteriorisation *qua* grammatisation is a form of transindividuality, as discussed by Simondon, which relates individuals through the invention of technical objects. Grammatisation is seen as a 'general history of life', which allows 'the pursuit of life by means other than life', namely, technics.

Stiegler discusses technicity not only in terms of space (as exteriorisation and interiorisation), but also in terms of temporal structure. For Stiegler, it is temporal structure that defines technicity as an exceptional human phenomenon that allows it to exceed biological determinism and genetic programming. In *Technics and Time, 3: Cinematic Time and the Question of Malaise*,[6] Stiegler develops Husserl's analysis of internal time-consciousness. Husserl examines different modes of consciousness, such as the capacity to remember, which is named as retention, and the capacity to anticipate the future, which is named as protention.[7] Husserl demonstrates these different aspects of time by providing the example of a melody: listening to a melody we perceive the present moment, the now, which in a few seconds passes away but is retained in our memory – it is a retention. At the same time, while listening to the present melodic phrase, we anticipate the next phrase, which is not yet present but forthcoming. This imagination, or anticipation, is a protention. Husserl names these time modes as primary retention and primary protention. However, if we are not listening to the melody in the actual present moment but are trying to recollect it in our memory, we also have to retain those phrases which have already been pronounced and to anticipate those which will come, even if these processes are taking place in our memory. Husserl names these time modes as secondary retention and secondary protention.

In addition to this schema, Stiegler suggests what he names as tertiary retention – a retention that is inscribed not in the actual perception (primary retention), or in our imagination (secondary retention), but in a technological memory of technical objects. It is an artificial, or technological, memory, such as writing or recording, which compresses primary and secondary

---

[5] Jacques Derrida, *De la grammatologie*, Paris: Les Éditions de Minuit, 1967. Translated into English as *Of Grammatology*, trans. Gayatri Chakravorty Spivak, Baltimore, MD: Johns Hopkins University Press, 1974.

[6] Bernard Stiegler, *La Technique et le temps, 3: Le temps du cinéma et la question du mal-être*, Paris: Éditions Galilée, 2001. Translated into English as *Technics and Time, 3: Cinematic Time and the Question of Malaise*, trans. Stephen Barker, Stanford, CA: Stanford: Stanford University Press, 2011.

[7] Edmund Husserl, *Zur Phänomenologie des inneren Zeitbewusstseins 1893–1917*, in *Husserliana*, Bd. 10, The Hague: Martinus Nijhoff, 1969. Translated into English as *The Phenomenology of Internal Time-Consciousness*, ed. Martin Heidegger, trans. James S. Churchill, Bloomington, IN: Indiana University Press, 1964.

retentions in a recording device which can be detached from an actual individual. As Stiegler points out,

> we would then have to say that consciousness is always in some fashion a montage of overlapping primary, secondary, and tertiary memories. Thus, we must mark as tertiary retentions all forms of 'objective' memory: cinematogram, photogram, phonogram, writing, paintings, sculptures – but also monuments and objects in general, since they bear witness, for me, say, of a past that I enforcedly did not myself live. (Stiegler 2011: 27–8)

Technological memory can be externalised and shared by other individuals (it is transindividual in the Simondonian sense) and even by other generations (it is transgenerational). In this sense, tertiary retention avoids the limitations characteristic of other kinds of retentions. As Hui points out,

> The third memory is a compensation to the retentional finitude of the organism, since an organism cannot retain all its experience and cannot transfer this experience to the next generation without having exteriorized them as symbols and tools. Furthermore, the secondary retention, which we call *memory*, can be effectively activated only through the tertiary retention, since it is the tertiary retention (for example, writings or images) that provides the force of synchronization and the diachronization of memory. (Hui 2019: 202, emphasis in original)

In this sense, tertiary retention exceeds both the biological limitations of the organism and the existential finitude of the individual.

Thus, exteriorisation creates temporality, which, according to Stiegler, is exceptionally human, distinguishing human beings from other species. 'The temporality of the human, which marks it off among other living beings, presupposes exteriorization and prostheticity: there is time only because memory is "artificial," becoming constituted as already-there *since* [. . .] its "having been placed outside of the species"' (Stiegler 1998: 172, emphasis in original). Stiegler believes that at the moment of exteriorisation (*qua* temporalisation and grammatisation) the human being is released from biological determinism and genetic programming, and is 'born' as an individual with its unique experience (which is defined as epigenesis). However, with the help of the third memory, or tertiary retention, this individual enters into the field of transindividual memory, which is always-there, collecting the experience of past generations. In this sense, Stiegler differentiates between three types of memory: the genetic memory of the biological individual, the epigenetic memory of the existential individual, and the epiphylogenetic (techno-logical) memory, which is transindividual and which designates technicity in general (Stiegler 1998: 177). For Stiegler, genesis is a 'program' in a quasi-deterministic biological sense, whereas epigenesis is the development of a unique individual which, unfortunately, is finite and disappears when its life ends. It is only with epiphylogenesis, that is, with technological artificial memory, that epigenesis can be retained and memorised: 'this epigenetic sedimentation, a memorization of what has come to pass, is what is called the past, what we shall name the *epiphylogenesis* of man, meaning the conservation, accumulation, and sedimentation of successive epigeneses, mutually articulated. Epiphylogenesis is a break with pure life' (Stiegler 1998: 140, emphasis in original). Epiphylogenesis, or tertiary retention, allows one to access a past that one never lived in and share it with other individuals and other generations.

As far as epiphylogenesis is a memory shared with other individuals and other generations, it is transindividual in the Simondonian sense. Technological memory, or tertiary retention, is the necessary condition for organising society. Thus, on the one hand, Stiegler differentiates between different kinds of memory (biological, existential and technological); on the other hand, he relates these diverse modes of being into a unified theory of 'general organology', which includes biological organs, technical objects (*organon*) and the organisation of society.[8] The concept of general organology is synonymous with the term epiphylogenesis, which encompasses biological memory, individual memory and the transindividual technological memory. In his book *For a New Critique of Political Economy*,[9] Stiegler asserts that general organology is

> a theory of the articulation of bodily organs (brain, hand, eyes, touch, tongue, genital organs, viscera, neuro-vegetative system, etc.), artificial organs (tools, instruments and technical supports of grammatization) and social organs (human groupings [. . .] political institutions and societies, businesses and economic organizations [. . .], and social systems in general). (Stiegler 2010: 34)

Similarly to Simondon, Stiegler establishes a kind of analogical paradigmatism between biological, psychosocial and technical individuation. However, Stiegler thinks that 'general organology' is a better term than Simondon's 'mechanology'. Stiegler argues that 'General organology is a method of thinking, at one and the same time technical, social, and psychic becoming, where technical becoming must be thought via the concept of the technical system, as it adjusts and is adjusted to social systems, themselves constituted by psychic apparatuses' (Stiegler 2017: 130). In other words, Stiegler uses the

---

[8] As Yuk Hui points out, Stiegler developed the term 'organology' in 2003, when he was the director of IRCAM at the Centre Georges Pompidou; however, for him the term is derived less from Bergson's and Canguilhem's philosophy of life and more from musicology (Lovink 2019; Hui 2019: 200).

[9] Bernard Stiegler, *Pour une nouvelle critique de l'économie politique*, Paris: Éditions Galilée, 2009. Translated into English as *For a New Critique of Political Economy*, trans. Daniel Ross, Cambridge: Polity, 2010.

notion of general organology as a kind of pharmacology which helps to diagnose the divergence between technological individuation and psychosocial individuation observed in contemporary society.[10] Although admitting that technology has a crucial role in constituting the individual and the society, Stiegler assumes that technologies might be poisonous (*pharmakon*) in the sense that they create prostheses for memory and thus increase the proletarianisation of knowledge. However, these pharmacological ambitions, being at the same time diagnostic and therapeutic, compromise Stiegler's project as far as they rest on a humanistic presumption that there is an 'authentic' experience and knowledge.

To conclude, we can argue that Stiegler elaborates Simondon's ideas and asserts that human development and technical epiphylogenesis are inseparable. At the same time, he moves away from the originality of Simondon's project by taking a diagnostic and therapeutic stance. As Mills observes,

> A key difference between the two thinkers is that Simondon doesn't describe technics as being originary for humanity ... This also means that technics doesn't constitute the pre-individual for Simondon, as it does for Stiegler, for whom the history of the human is also the history of technology and vice versa. (Mills 2016: 162)

For Simondon, the technical object is part of a general ontogenesis; therefore it is determined by pre-individual potential and by the associated milieu, whereas a human being, an inventor, is only a part or a side-effect of this development. By contrast, for Stiegler, a human being and a technical object are co-constituted: a human being originates at the moment when it is externalised in technical tools and prostheses. In this respect, human development is co-constitutive with technological development. This approach is radically different from Simondon's belief that a technical object has its own 'mode of existence' and that it is quasi-autonomous from the human being. As Mills points out, 'Stiegler's organology shares some aspects of Simondon's mechanology but ultimately betrays Simondon's core insight that the technological mode of individuation is in a very real way independent' (Mills 2016: 170). For Simondon, the technical object is defined in relation to the pre-individual potential of the inventor, and also through its interaction with an associated milieu. In other words, for Simondon, technics is always associated with nature (a good example of this

---

[10] As Stiegler points out, 'general organology defines the rules for analyzing, thinking, and prescribing human facts at three parallel but indissociable levels: the psychosomatic, which is the endosomatic level, the artifactual, which is the exosomatic level, and the social, which is the organizational level. It is an analysis of the relations between organic organs, technical organs, and social organizations. As it is always possible for the arrangements between these psychosomatic and artifactual organs to become toxic and destructive for the organic organs, general organology is a pharmacology' (Stiegler 2017: 130).

is the interaction between a river and a machine in the Guimbal turbine), whereas for Stiegler, the dimension of nature is seen as a certain kind of limitation.

At this point we have to say that the initial hypothesis about the analogy between the development of organised biological beings and organised inorganic beings (technical objects) is compromised, since Stiegler presents technicity in exceptional humanistic terms. However, if we take into account the recent discoveries in developmental biology, we can argue that biological individuals also have the capacity to anticipate and memorise, and are capable of using tools as the exteriorisations of their bodies. Thus, the invention of tools is not something exceptionally human and can be found in the realm of animals. If we consider Uexküll's works, we can see that, for example, a spider uses its web as a certain kind of prosthetic device that allows it to interact with the milieu. The spider's web is configured in a 'fly-like' mode; in other words, it already anticipates a fly and this anticipation is crucial in constructing web technology. In a similar way, Ruyer argued that technological inventiveness is a continuation of organic inventiveness: first tools appear as internal organs; then internal organs are externalised into the world (a spider's web as the extension of silk glands); and finally they become detachable artefacts. Biological inventiveness is prolonged in technological inventiveness. Therefore we can argue, contra Stiegler, that technological invention is not an exceptional human capacity; animals are also capable of exteriorisation, temporality (memory and anticipation) and tool invention.

## Hui's Cosmotechnics

Simondon's and Stiegler's ideas are significantly elaborated in Hui's *Recursivity and Contingency*, which can be described as a new theory of organology. Hui asserts that organology can be interpreted as a continuation and elaboration both of organicism[11] and cybernetics (or mechano-organicism). Cybernetics, as it is defined by Norbert Wiener, asserts that the physical functioning of the living individual and the operation of some of the newer communication machines are parallel in their analogous attempts to control entropy through feedback (Wiener 1989: 26). This analogy allows Wiener to define both an organism and a machine with the help of the concept of feedback, which means the circularity between a being (living

---

[11] As Hui points out, 'in between vitalism and mechanism there is also the "third way" known as *organicism*, associated with authors such as Ludwig von Bertalanffy, Joseph Needham, Joseph Woodger, and Conrad Waddington [...] and many others. The organicists wanted to overcome the opposition between vitalism and mechanism, and show that, for example, a cell can neither be reduced to physico-chemical explanations nor be understood as a mysterious vital force, but rather comprises different forms and levels of organization' (Hui 2019: 70).

or mechanical) and its environment. Having in mind this circularity, Hui makes an interesting comparison between the reflective judgement found in German idealist philosophy (from Kant to Fichte and Hegel), when the mind comes back to itself to determine itself, and the recursive movement operating in cybernetic machines. According to Hui, cybernetics is a continuation of metaphysics rather than its end, as suggested by Martin Heidegger (1976). In other words, like the reflective judgement in transcendental philosophy which constantly comes back to itself to determine itself, feedback in cybernetics refers to a self-regulatory process, during which a machine adapts itself to a spontaneous finality. In this sense, the concept of recursivity (and feedback) questioned linear causality and introduced a new temporal structure, 'one that was no longer based on a linear form but was rather more like that of a spiral' (Hui 2019: 238). This means that recursivity is closely related to contingency: in the mechanical mode of operation, based on linear causality, a contingent event may lead to a collapse, whereas in a recursive mode of operation contingency is integrated in such a way that it enriches the system and allows it to progress and develop. As Hui asserts, cybernetic machines are becoming-organic in the sense that they integrate contingency and recursivity – the features that characterise living organisms.

However, cybernetics (or mechano-organicism) is criticised by many authors, including Simondon, for reducing the functioning of both living beings and machines. As I pointed out earlier, Simondon argues that it is a mistake to postulate an identity between a living being and a self-regulating technical object, because it is only a tendency and not an entirely concrete existence: 'one mustn't go right to the limit and speak of technical objects as if they were natural objects' (Simondon 2017: 51). Machines cannot create other machines, and behind every machine there is always a human living being – it is precisely this human–machine relation that is missing in the discourse of cybernetics. For this reason, Hui suggests moving from cybernetics to organology – as a philosophy of life.

> As the first principle of organology, it is important to avoid drawing an *equivalence* between machine and organism – a common mistake of reductionism – and measuring the progress of technology according to its closeness to 'human intelligence' [. . .] Conventional Cartesian mechanism is based on the belief in a linear logic immanent in the living form, thus leading to the mechanization of the organism, and by doing so the *analogy* between mechanism and organism is taken as an *equivalence*. (Hui 2019: 146, emphasis in original)

In contrast to cybernetics, organology examines not the equivalence between machine and organism but the possibility of their coexistence. At the same time, organology has to be differentiated not only from cybernetics (organo-mechanism) but also from organicism. Organicism examines only organic entities and the forms of their organisation in terms of an organic whole, whereas organology examines the relations between the organic and the inorganic and their forms of hybridisation. 'This could be seen as a fundamental difference between organicism and organology; that is, whereas organicism studies the relations between different parts in the system – for example, an organism – organology extends beyond organic form to reintegrate the inorganic into an organized whole' (Hui 2019: 174). The organic life (including human life) can be maintained only through the organisation of the inorganic, through the invention of machines and tools. To put it in Stiegler's words, organology examines the inorganic as the pursuit of life by other means than life.

Stiegler's organology examines technical objects in terms of the organised inorganic, whereas Hui suggests that organology should rethink technical objects in their organising capacity. 'What we are witnessing today is a shift from the *organized inorganic* to the *organizing inorganic*, meaning that machines are no longer simply tools or instruments but rather gigantic organisms in which we live' (Hui 2019: 28, emphasis in original). In this respect, Hui incorporates Stiegler's project into his own organology, and yet the ontological weight is balanced differently: for Stiegler, a human being creates technology to extend and expand its own subjectivity; for Hui, both human beings and technologies coexist inside a general cybernetic organism which can be imagined as a smart home, smart city or the Anthropocene as a technological project. A good example of such a gigantic cybernetic organism is James Lovelock's Gaia theory, which defines the Earth as a self-regulating system incorporating both organic and inorganic sub-systems into an organised whole. 'The inorganic is no longer organized by the human body as was the case with simple tools, but rather constitutes an enormous technical system we can only live inside of, while submitting to its rules' (Hui 2021: 224). Thus, the 'new organology' has two important consequences: first, the new cybernetic machines are becoming organic in the sense that they incorporate organic features – recursivity and contingency; second, these machines are no longer individual machines but gigantic technological systems which are exponentially growing with the help of recursive operations (Hui 2021: 52). In this respect, the opposition between machine and organism becomes irrelevant and obsolete.

This evolution of technological systems and their capacity to expand with the help of recursive operations and algorithms forces us to invent a new computational hermeneutics and reconsider our conceptual apparatus. These new forms of technology imply a new mode of determination, which is associated not with what is most possible but with what is most probable. Critically revisioning Stiegler's project, Hui points out that Stiegler's schema of temporality can be described in terms of recursivity because primary retention and protention are becoming more complex in secondary retention and protention, which, in their turn, can be enriched and extended in tertiary retention.

> Primary, secondary, and tertiary retention together with primary and secondary protention thus form a circuit in which the soul is no longer simply a movement that returns to itself to determine itself, but rather the soul, whose activity is the *noesis*, is also a *tekhnesis*, whose organization depends on the third memory. (Hui 2019: 201, emphasis in original)

Our capacity to anticipate rests on the organisation of our memory (secondary retention), which can be effectively activated only through artificial technological memory (tertiary retention). However, what is missing in this scheme of recursive circularity is the element of tertiary protention (Hui 2016: 221–52). Tertiary protention would refer to a certain temporal structure of anticipation created not by humans but by digital technology. Tertiary protention also presents a new form of determination which is 'always preemptive, in the sense that the machine has already anticipated what the options will be: in this case, freedom means choice. This precisely means that it is a reduction of the contingent to the *most probable*' (Hui 2019: 211, emphasis in original). Tertiary retention conceptualises artificial memory retained in machines, whereas tertiary protention conceptualises anticipations generated artificially by machines.

> The preemption of the tertiary protention is possible only because of the computational hermeneutics, which is essentially recursive: it constantly evaluates the past in order to anticipate the future, which in turn determines the present. Human beings are reintegrated into the temporality of machines, not only as individuals but also as collectives and communities. (Hui 2019: 243)

This new structure of temporality forces us to imagine different forms of knowledge where human anticipation and technological pre-emption become indistinguishable.

This indistinguishability between human intelligence and artificial intelligence is also discussed in Malabou's latest book, *Morphing Intelligence: From IQ Measurement to Artificial Brains*.[12] Malabou argues that the latest advances in artificial intelligence, such as the creation of IBM's SyNAPSE chip, or the Blue Brain project, forced her to rethink her earlier assumptions, elaborated in *What Should We Do with Our Brain?* Malabou's notion of brain plasticity was built on the presumption that biological organisms, in contrast to machines, are capable of reorganising themselves in their form-taking activity. The plasticity of the biological brain cannot be measured or calculated in quantitative terms because it is capable of qualitative change.

---

[12] Catherine Malabou, *Metamorphoses de l'intelligence: Que faire de leur cerveau bleu?*, Paris: PUF, 2017; translated into English as *Morphing Intelligence: From IQ Measurement to Artificial Brains*, trans. Carolyn Shread, New York: Columbia University Press, 2019.

However, recent developments in artificial intelligence, namely the creation of a new type of chip, a 'neuro-synaptic processor', prove that artificial intelligence is also capable of a certain form of plasticity, or epigenesis. 'The subtlety of algorithmic calculation today derives precisely from the fact that it is capable of simulating noncalculation, that is, spontaneity, creative freedom, and the directness of emotion' (Malabou 2019: 150). Machines appear to be more and more natural and can even simulate spontaneous behaviour. To the common-sense conclusion that AI simply 'mimics' the biological brain, Malabou opposes a much more interesting idea: that AI is not only imitating the biological brain but, through this imitation, relates to its own 'technological self' (Malabou 2023). Thus we can follow not only an epigenesis of organisms but also an 'epigenesis of technology', which means that technology develops by relating to nature and also to its 'technological self'. Technology mimics itself and comes back to itself through nature, and this is exactly the same phenomenon that Hui describes as recursivity. It is a new kind of intelligence, or cognition, which no longer draws on the human imagination but develops in a quasi-autonomous way.

In this sense, both Malabou and Hui oppose Stiegler's conviction that human intelligence is non-calculable and qualitative, and in this respect can be opposed to calculable machines. Hui asserts that instead of creating a false opposition between the organic and the machinic, we have to reconceptualise the becoming-organic of machines. 'The inorganic is no longer organized by the human body as was the case with simple tools, but rather constitutes an enormous technical system we can only live inside of, while submitting to its rules' (Hui 2021: 224). It is obvious that these gigantic technological systems – cybernetic organisms – go beyond humans and machines. However, this new scale should be reconsidered not as a deprivation or a degradation of human rationality, but as an opportunity to think about another dimension – that of nature or cosmos. In this respect, Hui is closer to Simondon's project than Stiegler's. Simondon not only attempted to reconcile technics and culture, but also examined the relation between technics and nature. What is left out in Stiegler's project is the relationship between technics and nature, because technics is described in purely humanistic terms. For Simondon, a technical object is defined through its relation to a geographical world with which it creates an associated milieu (Simondon 2017: 59). Hui elaborates this insight further by suggesting that nature and technics not only define each other in some specific phases of technical invention, but create a priori conditions for each other:

> I suggest, firstly, to consider the *technical* a priori in the concept of nature, which allows us to abandon a pure and innocent image of nature and gives us a 'second nature'; and, secondly, the *cosmic* a priori in technological development, meaning that technics are always already cosmotechnics from the beginning. (Hui 2017: 11, emphasis in original)

Hui returns to Simondon's example of the Guimbal turbine: the turbine produces so much heat that it would destroy itself, therefore it needs a natural element, namely, a river, to be integrated. The current of the river forces the turbine to move and, at the same time, it cools it down and prevents it from overheating. In this sense, the technical and the geographical milieus are connected by recurrent causality: the stronger the current, the more heat the turbine produces, and because the water flows faster, the cooling process is more efficient (Hui 2019: 191). In this sense, we can argue that the technical object adapts to the environment and also adopts it as a necessary part of its functioning. Hui defines this process of adaptation–adoption in terms of cosmotechnics: 'it means the unification of the cosmic order and moral order through technical activities. Human activities, which are always accompanied by technical objects such as tools, are in this sense always cosmotechnical' (Hui 2017: 4).

In other words, cosmotechnics refers to a new notion of organology which makes connections not only between living beings and technical objects, but also between technical objects and 'natural' cosmic forces, which are understood as technical a priori. This new notion of organology understood as cosmotechnics allows us to reconceptualise the relation between 'nature' and technology and can be seen as a critical response to the Anthropocene. If the Anthropocene reduces all natural potentials to 'resources' which can be exploited without limitations, then cosmotechnics implies an ethical balance between cosmic order and technological order. Relying on the Oriental tradition, Hui argues that both cosmic forces and technical objects can coexist in cosmotechnics and maintain their quasi-autonomous status. In this context cosmotechnics can be seen as a new organology that makes connections between natural objects, organising organic beings (humans) and organised/organising inorganic beings (technical objects and cybernetic machines which are becoming organic).

However, what is missing in this new organology is the concern with real organisms – organised organic beings. While discussing the integration of the natural world in the functioning of the Guimbal turbine, Hui asks: 'how about those other living beings, for example fishes swimming in the river?' (Hui 2017: 16). As Hui admits himself, this question remains outside the scope of the Simondonian opposition between nature and technics. The same criticism can be directed to Hui's new organology: on the one hand, it is a timely attempt to rethink the becoming-organic of the machines; on the other hand, his new organology is reluctant to discuss real organisms.

## Conclusion

To summarise, we can argue that the theory of organology, extending from Simondon to Stiegler and Hui, is a thinking about technology through other means than technology. For Simondon, mechanology is understood as a connection between technical objects, natural forces and the potentiality of an inventor. For Stiegler, general organology designates a connection between technical objects, the human psyche and social systems. Hui defines new organology as cosmotechnics, which brings together the cosmic, the moral and the technological order. In this respect, organology allows one to resolve the dispute between mechanism and vitalism by demonstrating that living beings and technical objects are interrelated in many different but at the same time systemic ways. Organology examines living beings and technical objects as being integrated into an associated milieu through which they adapt and attune to each other. This approach to technology clearly differs from that of cybernetics because it examines technical objects according to those features that they share with organic beings, such as development (genesis, epigenesis, epiphylogenesis), recursivity and contingency, multiplicity, and the potentiality for change. These features, already discernible in Simondon's philosophy, are what differentiates organology from cybernetics and information theory: they explain technical objects not in quantitative but in qualitative terms (Massumi 2012: 32).

These qualitative features allow one to inscribe technical objects into the evolution of living beings. Stiegler elaborates this qualitative turn by asserting that epiphylogenesis of technological objects is a transindividual and transgenerational process which overcomes the genesis of organisms and the epigenesis of human individuals. Hui extends this qualitative dimension even further by asserting that new cybernetic machines are becoming-organic in the sense that they incorporate recursivity and contingency. In this respect, organology can be seen as the potentialisation of technologies, and, at the same time, the potentialisation of life. As Stiegler points out, organology is a negentropy – a fight against entropy and the disintegration of life – and a pursuit of life by other means than life.[13] Thus, organology can be seen as an alternative to the Anthropocene, which is a purely technological project in the sense that it covers a belief that the ecological crisis (the exhaustion of natural forces) can be solved with the help of technological means, such as geoengineering. In contrast to this, organology proposes to rethink the organic condition of philosophising and in this way suggests the possibility of qualitative change.

---

[13] Stiegler challenges the Anthropocene with his notion of the 'Neganthropocene': the Anthropocene is the time of entropy, whereas the Neganthropocene should explore the organological reorganisation of matter giving rise to a new form of life, namely, negentropy (Stiegler 2018: 42).

# 6
# Planetary Organism

The theory of organology, relating biological (organised organic), technical (organised inorganic) and cybernetic (organising inorganic) beings, leads to a more general methodological question: how can these different levels of organisation be combined with each other? How can we imagine and explain their interactions on a planetary scale? Gaia theory is one of the attempts to reconcile different kinds of organological development into a consistent whole. However, the Gaia theory itself was developing and changing in trying to explain these planetary interactions either in terms of a superorganism, or as a cybernetic machine. In this chapter I will discuss the development of the Gaia hypothesis as it was defined by James Lovelock in the 1970s and later elaborated in his collaboration with biologist Lynn Margulis. Margulis's research in symbiogenesis and her interest in Maturana and Varela's theory of autopoiesis helped to reshape Gaia theory from first-order systems theory to second-order systems theory. In contrast to a first-order systems theory which is concerned with the processes of homeostasis, second-order systems incorporate emergence, complexity and contingency.

The recent discontent with the conceptualisation of the Anthropocene has forced many contemporary philosophers and theorists to return to the notion of Gaia. In recent years many thinkers, such as Bruno Latour, Isabelle Stengers and Donna J. Haraway, have addressed Gaia theory in one or another respect. In this chapter I want to compare the original Gaia theory with these new interpretations, which come from different backgrounds and employ different methodologies. Gaia is interpreted either as an autopoietic or sympoietic system, or, by contrast, as an 'outlaw', an anti-system. Despite these different interpretations, the recent theoretical interventions can be read as various versions of second-order systems theory. In this respect, even Latour's and Stengers's takes on Gaia, defining it as an 'outlaw' or an anti-system, can be interpreted as a specific kind of systems thinking.

## The Gaia Hypothesis

The Gaia hypothesis was formulated by the chemist James Lovelock in the 1970s and was later significantly remodelled through Lovelock's collaboration with biologist Lynn Margulis. The first insights of the Gaia hypothesis emerged during the 1960s in a NASA laboratory, where Lovelock was assigned to examine the physical and chemical properties of Mars and determine the planet's suitability for life. It was noticed that Mars is in a chemical–physical balance, which leads to a perfect equilibrium. Lovelock turned the question about life on Mars upside down: he started from the obvious fact that there is life on Earth and that Earth expresses a disequilibrium of atmospheric phenomena. Thus, if the disequilibrium of atmospheric phenomena is related to the existence of life on Earth, then a perfect equilibrium of atmospheric processes on Mars leads to the conclusion that there is no life there. Later this assertion was confirmed by the *Viking* mission in 1976. But what is important in formulating the Gaia hypothesis is not the possibility of life on Mars but the first part of this equation – the relationship between life and the disequilibrium of atmospheric processes on Earth. Lovelock formulated a hypothesis that living organisms (the biota) are able to regulate temperature and other planetary conditions in the same way that they are able to regulate their own body temperature. He asserted that chemical, physical and biological processes taking place on Earth seek for a homeostasis, or the optimal conditions for life, that is achieved through feedback loops operated automatically by the biota. In other words, he formulated the hypothesis that the Earth as a whole is a living and self-organising system.

To test this hypothesis, Lovelock and his former student Andrew Watson developed a model called Daisyworld – a computer model of a planet, warmed by increasing heat from the sun. The Daisyworld is a simplified model, where the environment is reduced to a single property – temperature – and the biota is reduced to two species, namely, black daisies and white daisies. The crucial question Lovelock asked himself was would the evolution of the Daisyworld ecosystem lead to the self-regulation of the climate (Harding 2014: 166)? Thus, as the climate on this simulated planet warms up and becomes suitable for life, black daisies appear first, because they can absorb solar energy better than white daisies. As the temperature on the planet increases, the black daisies disappear and white ones appear. The white daisies reflect the solar energy and hence cool down the planet. Thus, throughout the evolution of Daisyworld the temperature was kept constant:

> When the sun is relatively cold, Daisyworld increases its own temperature through solar energy absorption by the black daisies; as the sun gets hotter, the temperature is gradually lowered because of the progressive predominance of energy-reflecting white daisies. Thus Daisyworld, with-

out any foresight or planning, regulates its own temperature over a vast time range by the dance of the daisies. (Harding 2014: 167)

The purpose of this model was to demonstrate that feedback loops interlinking non-living and living systems (temperature and plants) can regulate the climate and achieve the most favourable conditions for living organisms.

These experiments asserted the idea that all life and its environment are coupled in such a way as to form a self-regulating system. Lovelock formulated this idea and presented it publicly for the first time in 1969 in Princeton. His friend, the novelist William Golding, author of *Lord of the Flies*, suggested the name Gaia (the Greek word for mother Earth) as a suitable title for his theory. In 1972 Lovelock published a first paper on his theory titled 'Gaia as Seen Through the Atmosphere' (Lovelock 1972). At the same time a microbiologist, Lynn Margulis, was working on similar questions and investigating the smallest micro-organisms. Margulis argued that the Earth's atmosphere is transformed by biological organisms and that bacteria play a crucial role. All life is dependent on the metabolism of microbes which modulate the biosphere in which we live.

> During the first billion years of evolution, bacteria – the most basic forms of life – covered the planet with an intricate web of metabolic processes and began to regulate the temperature and chemical composition of the atmosphere so that it became conducive to the evolution of higher forms of life. (Capra and Luisi 2014: 351)

Thus, Margulis helped Lovelock to revise his theory and propose that Gaia is not a single superorganism but a symbiogenesis of a variety of organisms. In *Symbiotic Planet: A New Look at Evolution*, Margulis points out that

> Gaia, the living Earth, far transcends any single organism or even any population [...] The sum of planetary life, Gaia, displays a physiology that we recognize as environmental regulation. Gaia itself is not an organism directly selected among many. It is an emergent property of interaction among organisms, the spherical planet on which they reside, and an energy source, the sun. (Margulis 1998: 119)

Gaia can be seen as a self-regulating system, which connects the metabolic processes of micro-organisms and the atmospheric processes of the Earth in feedback loops. As Greg Hinkle, a former student of Margulis, pointed out, 'Gaia is just symbiosis as seen from space' (Margulis 1998: 2); in other words, it is a symbiosis extended to a planetary scale.

Both Lovelock and Margulis describe Gaia as a metastable system, stable in its instability. Gaia is an emerging property, incessantly creating new environments and new organisms. For example, Margulis argues that bacteria can regulate the atmosphere by taking chemical elements they need for their bodies from the air and volcanoes. 'Eventually, blue-green bacteria wrenched hydrogen atoms from water ($H_2O$). Oxygen was expelled as a metabolic waste product. This waste, at first disastrous, eventually powered life's continued growth [. . .] The oxygen we need to breathe began as a toxin; it still is' (Margulis 1998: 121). Thus, Gaia is seen as 'a genius of recycling', because the waste produced by one species becomes the food for another. Oxygen makes up one-fifth of the Earth's atmosphere and, combined with other gases, is highly explosive. However, the ecosystem reduces these gases faster than they can react, thus maintaining an optimal equilibrium. As Margulis observes, 'The entire planetary surface, not just the living bodies but the atmosphere that we think of as an inert background, is so far from chemical equilibrium that the entire planetary surface is best regarded as alive' (Margulis 1998: 122–3). In this respect, there is no clear separation between the organic and the inorganic, because the Earth's atmosphere is not simply chemical or geological, but rather geophysiological: it expresses the features of a living organism which can manipulate and change its environment.

The Gaia hypothesis was strongly criticised by scientists. Many critics claimed that Gaia theory was unscientific because it was implying a certain teleology. As Capra and Luisi point out, 'The scientific establishment attacked the theory as teleological, because they could not imagine how life on Earth could create and regulate the conditions for its own existence without being conscious and purposeful' (Capra and Luisi 2014: 165). The most important issue here is the question, in what sense is Gaia considered to be alive? As Capra and Luisi point out, there are several criteria that define a system of life: the first is self-organisation, the capacity to assume an organised structure thanks to the inner rules of the system; the second is autopoiesis, when the self-organising structure can regenerate from within all its own components; and there is the level of the living organism, when autopoiesis becomes associated with cognition (Capra and Luisi 2014: 165). The first and second criteria are met by both living and non-living systems. Thus, only the third criterion would characterise Gaia as alive – the assumption that Gaia is driven by purposeful, directed and cognitive behaviour. Margulis affirms this possibility without any hesitation:

> Life produces fascinating 'designs' in a similar way by repeating the chemical cycles of its cellular growth and reproduction. Order is generated by nonconscious repetitious activities. Gaia, as the interweaving network of all life, is alive, aware, and conscious to various degrees in all its cells, bodies, and societies. (Margulis 1998: 126)

In fact, synthetic biology confirms that life is built on these repetitive patterns and can be reproduced artificially.

Another answer to this criticism is Margulis's notion of proprioception or the self-awareness characteristic of living beings. Similarly to Ruyer, who argued that every organism has a primary consciousness, Margulis introduces the notion of proprioception, the sensing of self. 'Proprioception, as self-awareness, evolved long before animals evolved, and long before their brains did. Sensitivity, awareness, and responses of plants, protocists, fungi, bacteria, and animals, each in its local environment, constitute the repeating pattern that ultimately underlies global sensitivity and the response of Gaia "herself"' (Margulis 1998: 126). Like simple organisms, plants and animals, which are aware of themselves without any reflective consciousness, Gaia also has this primary sensitivity or proprioception, which occurs in the absence of any central 'head' or 'brain'. In this respect, Margulis indicates that Gaia exerts a certain 'planetary cognition' which makes it similar to an autopoietic system.

## Gaia and the Theory of Autopoiesis

At the same time as Lovelock and Margulis were trying to conceptualise the Gaia theory, the Chilean biologists Humberto Maturana and Francisco Varela were working on the theory of autopoiesis. The concept of autopoiesis was coined in the 1970s and it refers to the minimal organisation of life, such as a cell (*auto* means 'self' and refers to self-organising systems, and *poiesis* means 'making or creating'). The first publication on the theory of autopoiesis, entitled 'Autopoiesis: The Organization of Living Systems', appeared in English in 1974 (Varela et al. 1974) with the help of Heinz von Foerster, a founder of cybernetics. Autopoiesis refers to the minimal organisation of a living system, which is capable of maintaining itself in a closed circular process of self-production, and is also capable of interacting with an environment in order to get nutrients and energy. In this respect, an autopoietic organisation is defined by several features. The first is self-maintenance, which means that the cell's main function is to maintain its individuality despite the many chemical reactions taking place in it (Maturana and Varela 1980). This also means that an autopoietic entity is autonomous, capable of reproducing itself from within. In this sense, an autopoietic organisation is operationally closed. Second, an autopoietic unity interacts with the environment and gets information or energy from it. What distinguishes living systems from non-living systems is that the interaction between a living system and its environment creates a 'structural coupling': 'a living system relates to its environment *structurally* – that is, through recurrent interactions, each of which triggers structural changes in the system. For example, a cell membrane continually incorporates substances from its environment; an organism's nervous system changes its connectivity with every sensory perception' (Capra and Luisi 2014: 135, emphasis in original). In other words, every encounter with the environment produces a structural change in the system, which then again becomes autonomous. In this sense, autopoietic entities are 'structurally determined', that is, they are determined not by external forces (as in the case of non-living systems) but by their own internal structure. This leads to the third characteristic of living entities – life is an emergent property that cannot be reduced to the properties of the components (Capra and Luisi 2014: 133). Emergence can be seen as the necessary condition of self-organisation.

Thus, an autopoietic entity is self-maintaining and autonomous, it is structurally coupled with its environment and is constantly creating emergent properties that change its internal structure. Such a definition might seem contradictory, because autonomy and coupling with the environment seem to go in different directions. However, what it is important to understand is that this self-transcending movement is the necessary condition of life. As Evan Thompson observes,

> The self-transcending movement of life is none other than metabolism, and metabolism is none other than the biochemical instantiation of the autopoietic organization. That organization must remain invariant – otherwise the organism dies – but the only way autopoiesis can stay in place is through the incessant material flux of metabolism. In other words, the operational *closure* of autopoiesis demands that the organism be an *open system*. (Thompson 2009: 85, emphasis in original)

Thus, the main feature of autopoietic systems is that they have to change in order to be alive – a total closure or homeostasis would lead to death. This feature is also something that is shared by second-order systems. As Cary Wolfe points out, 'all autopoietic entities are *closed* [...] on the level of *organization*, but *open* to environmental perturbations on the level of *structure*' (Wolfe 1995: 53, emphasis in original). In this sense, autopoietic systems are structurally open and organisationally closed at the same time.

The notion of structural coupling allows one to distinguish between living and non-living systems. If a non-living entity is disturbed by the environment, it will react according to a linear line of cause and effect, which is more or less predictable; if a living being is disturbed, it will respond with structural changes that are unpredictable (Capra and Luisi 2014: 136). In this sense, Maturana and Varela argue that the interactions between a living system and its environment are cognitive interactions, and the structural changes that a living being is undergoing are acts of cognition. In *Autopoiesis and Cognition* (1980), Maturana and Varela assert that the process of cognition, or the process of knowing and learning, is coextensive with the process of life. '*Living systems are cognitive systems, and living as a process is a process of cognition.* This statement is valid for all organisms, with and without a nervous system' (Maturana and Varela 1980: 13, emphasis in original). In other words, the capacity of interaction is seen as a cognitive activity which can be discerned at all levels of life, from cells to human and non-human animals. 'The interactions of a living organism – plant, animal, or human – with its environment are cognitive interactions. Thus life and cognition are inseparably connected. Mind – or, more accurately, mental activity – is immanent in matter at all levels of life' (Capra and Luisi 2014: 254). In this sense, cognition is a characteristic not only of animals with reflective consciousness, such as humans, but also other living beings with or without a nervous system and brain.

Extending the notion of cognition to all processes of life, Maturana and Varela assert the continuity of life and mind. This reminds us of Ruyer's notion of primary consciousness, discussed in Chapter 2. Primary consciousness is characteristic of simple organisms without brains and it conveys the capacity of self-survey and self-enjoyment (Ruyer), or 'the feeling of what happens' (Damasio). Similarly, Margulis argued in her text 'The Conscious Cell' (2001) that micro-organisms possess a certain 'microbial consciousness', which later evolves and transforms itself into the nervous system of higher vertebrates. However, in this context 'consciousness' refers not to a self-reflective consciousness of complex animals and humans, but to consciousness as sentience. As Thompson points out, 'One might summarize these threads by saying that consciousness as sentience is a kind of *primitively self-aware liveliness or animation of the body*' (Thompson 2009: 84, emphasis in original). N. Katherine Hayles (2017) also adds a significant elaboration to this problem by proposing a tripartite framework of cognition: this is awareness, or consciousness in a conventional sense, the nonconscious cognition (associated with Damasio's notion of 'proto-self' and Maturana and Varela's notion of cognition), and the material processes taking place within the body. What makes the notion of non-conscious cognition so interesting is that it includes not only cognitive capacities of living organisms, but also cognitive processes of computational media. In this respect, Maturana's and Varela's positions differ: Maturana reserved the term exceptionally for living beings, whereas Varela extended it to technological systems and compared cellular automata and the emergence of cognition in biological cells (Varela et al. 1991).

In this respect, Maturana and Varela's theory of autopoiesis and cognition could be seen as a universal methodology applicable to different fields of organisation, such as an ecosystem or a social domain. Although theorists were reluctant to extend the concept of autopoiesis to other fields, some applications were very successful. For example, sociologist and system theorist Niklas Luhmann interpreted autopoiesis as a general form of system building by using a self-referential closure, and argued that general principles of autopoietic organisation can be applied to social systems (Luhmann 1990: 2). In a similar way, autopoietic organisation was applied to Gaia theory. In 1988 Lovelock, Margulis and Varela met at a Gaia theory symposium in Italy, where Varela made an explicit connection between the self-referential system and Gaia theory.

> The quality we see in Gaia as being living-like, to me is the fact that this is a fully autonomous system [. . .] it is a system whose fundamental

organization corresponds to operational closure [...] It is this quality of self-identity that I see in Gaia [...] So it seems to me that autonomy, in the sense of full operational closure, is the best way of describing that living-like quality of Gaia, and that the use of the concept of autonomy might liberate the theory from some of the more animistic notions that have parasitized it. (cited in Thompson 1991: 211)

Varela made an important observation that Gaia is not alive but living-like; thus it can be credited as a scientific theory and not as a New Age animistic interpretation. The next important point is that Varela acknowledged that Gaia can be described in terms of autopoiesis. In this sense, autopoiesis is understood as a general mode of systemic self-reference, which can be applied both to living and living-like systems. Margulis seems to take Varela's point into account when she writes that

The simplest, smallest known autopoietic entity is a single bacterial cell. The largest is probably Gaia – life and its environment-regulating behavior at the Earth's surface. Cells and Gaia display a general property of autopoietic entities: as their surroundings change unpredictably, they maintain their structural integrity and internal organization, at the expense of solar energy, by remaking and interchanging their parts. (Margulis 1997: 267)

In this sense, Margulis adopted the theory of autopoiesis and reframed Gaia theory in terms of an autopoietic system.

As Bruce Clarke observed, Varela's critique of Gaia theory at the 1988 symposium engendered a conceptual shift from first-order cybernetics to second-order cybernetics, from homeostatic regulation to autopoietic recursivity (Clarke 2012: 71). Similarly, Onori and Visconti agreed that, influenced by Margulis's investigations into autopoietic systems, Gaia theory moved to second-order cybernetics (Onori and Visconti 2012: 381). First-order cybernetics refers to operational circularity in natural and technological systems, whereas second-order cybernetics turns the logic of operational circularity upon itself. As Clarke asserts, 'First-order cybernetics is hetero-referential, it concerns "objects" such as natural and technological systems. Second-order cybernetics observes the self-reference of "subjects", that is, the necessary recursivity of cognitive systems capable of producing observations in the first place' (Clarke 2012: 59). In this respect, second-order systems, from cells to Gaia, are not only observed but also observing; in other words, they have the capacity of learning and cognition. Thus, according to Clarke, 'The Gaia hypothesis began as a thought experiment drawing on homeostasis, a basic first-order cybernetic model of self-regulation using negative feedback to correct deviations from a desired state of operation' (Clarke 2017: 15). However, after adopting the theory of autopoiesis, Gaia discourse was remodelled according to second-order systems theory, which turned the logic of operational circularity upon itself and thus implied the notion of cognition.

Thus, with Margulis's take on Gaia, the notion of autopoiesis becomes a universal blueprint encompassing both living and non-living processes. As Clarke points out, defined in this way, the Gaian system incorporates both biotic and abiotic, or living and non-living elements. In this sense, 'Gaia is fundamentally *metabiotic*' (Clarke 2017: 18, emphasis in original) because it allows the extension of the theory of autopoiesis from biological autopoietic systems to non-living autopoietic systems, and, in addition, explains the structural couplings between living autopoietic systems and non-living non-autopoietic milieus. Thus, Gaia theory overcomes the traditional scientific distinction between living and non-living matter. Gaia is neither a living superorganism, nor a mathematical model of self-referentiality. Rather,

> Gaia is a self-referential system of planetary cognition operating to produce globally regulative processes binding geological and biological processes and developments together into a superordinate system rendering its subsystem's evolutions interdependent, that is, mutually contingent in the final but not necessarily in the individual instance. (Clarke 2017: 19–20)

Gaia can be defined as a system–environment hybrid (to use Hansen's term), which couples biotic autopoietic systems with abiotic non-autopoietic milieus but doesn't subsume them in a higher order super-system and doesn't reduce their differences. The different kinds of biological, technological or geological systems are seen as '*operationally* incommensurable' (Clarke 2017: 20, emphasis in original); therefore Gaia refers not to planetary aliveness but to planetary interconnectedness between different systems.

## Gaia and Actor-Network Theory

Another important reconceptualisation of Gaia theory is presented in Bruno Latour's *Facing Gaia: Eight Lectures on the New Climatic Regime*. Latour distances himself from cybernetic discourse and prefers to investigate Gaia in terms of his own Actor-Network Theory (Latour 2005). First, Latour argues that Gaia is not a totality, a whole that is made of parts. The part–whole distinction is applicable only to technological systems, whereas Gaia is not a technology or a machine. Latour asserts that 'as Gaia cannot be compared to a machine, it cannot be subjected to any sort of *re-engineering*' (Latour 2017a: 96–7, emphasis in original). The whole–part distinction can be made only on a dead planet; and yet the Earth is alive, therefore such a distinction is not possible. Second, Gaia is not a totality in terms of a superorganism. What Latour finds problematic here is not the concept of an organism, but an organism understood as a whole, or a totality determining its parts. Thus, instead of conceptualising Gaia in terms of a totality, understood either as a machine or an organism, Latour prefers to define it in terms of agency that is involved in different interactions. Margulis's investigations into the kingdom of micro-organisms, similar to those conducted by Louis Pasteur, reveal that the Earth is composed of invisible agents which can manipulate mountain formations, cloud layers and even the movement of tectonic plates. As Latour points out,

> The Earth's behavior is inexplicable without the addition of the work accomplished by living organisms, just as fermentation, for Pasteur, cannot be started without yeast. Just as the action of micro-organisms, in the nineteenth century, agitated beer, wine, vinegar, milk, and epidemics, from now on the incessant action of organisms succeeds in setting in motion air, water, soil, and, proceeding from one thing to another, the entire climate. (Latour 2017a: 93)

Latour interprets Gaia as a network of agents where each agent is trying to manipulate the environment for its own interest.

> Beavers, birds, ants, and termites are not the only ones who bend the environment around them to make it more favorable; so too do trees, mushrooms, algae, bacteria and viruses. Is there a risk of anthropomorphism here? Of course . . . the capacity of humans to rearrange everything around themselves is a *general property of living things*. (Latour 2017a: 99, emphasis in original)

In other words, both human and non-human agents express a certain intentionality and create an entire network of effects and connections. What is important for Latour is to discuss Gaia as a 'connectivity without holism' (Latour 2017b: 75), and to explain the connections among agencies without relying on the conception of the whole (Latour 2017a: 95, 97).

However, Latour's critique of totalities seems far-fetched and should be carefully examined. First, Latour interprets Lovelock's cybernetic discourse as necessarily leading to holistic constructions. As Clarke observes,

> Latour's text constrains cybernetic discourse to one or another dialect of the holistic juggling of parts and wholes. It reads systemic unity as false totality. But there is no conceptual inevitability to these outcomes. On the contrary, the strongest cybernetic formulations in both first- and second-order systems theories place multiplicities, differences, and distinctions before or at least alongside oneness, wholeness, and totality. (Clarke 2020: 68)

In other words, the system doesn't mean wholeness. Second, Latour's other target – the notion of an organism – is also misrepresented. Latour reminds us that there is a general tendency to transpose organismic metaphors from biology to social sciences: 'All the sciences, natural or social, are haunted by the specter of the "organism," which always becomes, more or less surreptitiously, a *"superorganism"* – that is, a dispatcher to whom the task – or rather the holy mystery – of successfully coordinating the various parts is attributed' (Latour 2017a: 95, emphasis in original). Here again Latour is misinterpreting the notion of an organism and doesn't take into account the fact that an organism can be interpreted not as a whole but as an autopoietic organisation. Latour refuses to admit that autopoietic systems (from cells to ecosystems) are capable of incorporating within themselves differences and multiplicities. Thus, going against the grain of Lovelock and Margulis's orientation towards systems theory, Latour argues that Gaia is anti-systemic: 'Gaia, the outlaw, is the anti-system' (Latour 2017a: 87). However, as Clarke points out, it is important not to conflate the notion of the whole with that of the system (Clarke 2017: 14). If Gaia is not a whole, it doesn't mean that it cannot be a system.

Latour associates this anti-systemic character of Gaia with Isabelle Stengers's interpretations. As Stengers points out, Gaia exists on its own terms:

> It is not a living being, and not a cybernetic one either; rather it is a being demanding that we complicate the divide between life and non-life, for Gaia is gifted with its own particular way of holding together and of answering to changes forced on it [. . .] thus breaking the general linear relation between causes and effects. (Stengers 2015b: 137)

In her book *In Catastrophic Times: Resisting the Coming Barbarism*, Stengers describes Gaia as an intruder that is incompatible with our expectations and conceptualisations. Gaia is 'a ticklish assemblage of forces' that is absolutely transcendent in relation to our reasons and projects.

> The intrusion of this type of transcendence, which I am calling Gaia, makes a major unknown, *which is here to stay*, exist at the heart of our lives. This is perhaps what is most difficult to conceptualize: no future can be foreseen in which she will give back to us the liberty of ignoring her. (Stengers 2015a: 47, emphasis in original)

Defined in this way, Gaia is intrusive, ticklish and unforeseen, ready to destroy our human order. This radically unknown and unforeseen character of Gaia can be traced to Stengers's theoretical background in far from equilibrium systems theory, which she elaborated together with Ilya Prigogine (Prigogine and Stengers 1984). Interpreting Gaia from this point of view, we can recognise some contours of dissipative structures. Dissipative structures not only maintain themselves in a state far from equilibrium but may evolve into more complex structures (Capra and Luisi 2014: 159). In this regard Gaia the intruder, even being chaotic and unforeseen, may evolve into a new complex order, and, in this sense, is perfectly compatible with systems theory. Clarke comes to a similar conclusion when he asserts that, regardless of both Latour's and Stengers's attempts to extract the concept of Gaia from its cybernetic origin, it still retains its systemic character: 'the Gaia discourses of Stengers and Latour may be positively aligned with the systems theory that supports Lynn Margulis's autopoietic Gaia concept' (Clarke 2017: 7).

Cary Wolfe provides a less sympathetic reading of Latour's *Facing Gaia* and of his attempts to shape Gaia in terms of Actor-Network Theory. According to Wolfe, the main problem in Latour's theory is the insufficient understanding of the difference between first-order and second-order systems theory. 'A crucial underlying problem [. . .] is that Latour continues to understand the terms "system" and "autopoiesis" as if they were simply synonyms for homeostasis and command-and-control, and the fingerprints of this misunderstanding in *Facing Gaia* are all over his use of the term "cybernetics"' (Wolfe 2020: 140). It seems that Latour understands cybernetics as based on 'mereological' relations between parts and wholes. As Wolfe points out, 'it should come as no surprise that Latour cannot understand that, in second-order systems theory, the account of the relationship between the "part" and the "whole" [. . .] is actually the *opposite* of the caricature he offers here' (Wolfe 2020: 140, emphasis in original). Latour's critique of cybernetics and systems theory misses the target because second-order cybernetics reconceptualises the notion of the system in such a way that it incorporates recursivity and contingency (Hui 2019).

Another problem appears when Latour is trying to explain the nature of the relationships between an organism and its environment. As was said before, Latour is describing every agent as trying to manipulate its environment and to rearrange everything around itself. In this sense, Latour argues that

> there is *no longer any environment* to which one might adapt. Since all living agents follow their own intentions all along, modifying their neighbors as much as possible, there is no way to distinguish between the environment to which the organism is adapting and the point at which its own action begins. (Latour 2017a: 100, emphasis in original)

Latour is trying to explain this intentionality of agents by referring to Richard Dawkins' theory of the 'selfish gene'; however, he himself admits that the notion of 'self' in biology is very problematic. Thus, all agents are interacting quite chaotically in 'waves of action', which subvert all borders in such a way that it becomes impossible to distinguish between an individual and an environment to which it would adapt. In this respect, it becomes even more difficult to explain how these agents can interact if the distinction between an organism and its environment, the inside and the outside, is subverted. According to Wolfe,

What Latour is unable to theorize here is the relationship [...] between 'inside' and 'outside', 'neighbor' and 'environment,' because he doesn't grasp the key insight of second-order systems theory and the theory of autopoiesis: that the *contingency* of the self-reference of autopoietic organisms *is* the 'wild card,' the 'outlaw,' at the core of everything Latour wants from the unpredictable 'agency' and 'intentions' ... (Wolfe 2020: 141, emphasis in original)

What Latour describes as sporadic actions and intentions of agents is nothing other than the self-referential character of autopoietic systems, which include contingency and recursivity. Organisms not only manipulate and change their environments, but also change themselves in recursive operations. In other words, they are closed and bounded individuals at an organisational level and open at an environmental level. As Luhmann points out,

The concept of a self-referentially closed system does not contradict the system's *openness to the environment*. Instead, in the self-referential mode of operation, closure is a form of broadening possible environmental contacts; closure increases, by constituting elements more capable of being determined, the complexity of the environment that is possible for the system. (Luhmann 1995: 37, emphasis in original)

In second-order systems, recursivity works in such a way that, by incorporating contingency, it makes the system more complex. This contingency explains the 'anti-systemic' and 'outlaw' character of Gaia which Latour's theory fails to address.

Another important point of critique is that the notion of 'agent', or 'actor', fails to maintain the difference between living and non-living (physical) systems. As Wolfe points out,

Flat Ontologies (and finally Latour's own Actor-Network Theory) evacuate the radical discontinuity between qualitatively different orders of causation that obtain in living vs. physical systems – different orders that impact in fundamentally different ways the evolution of the biosphere, climate change, and, ultimately, the entire concept of Gaia. (Wolfe 2020: 132)

Living systems imply relations that are much more unpredictable and act as an 'outlaw'. In this respect, Latour's Actor-Network Theory flattens the distinction between living and non-living systems, and the different orders of causality that these systems imply. Living organisms imply a different order of causality, which incorporates recursivity and contingency and which allows them to change themselves and their environment. In second-order systems, recursivity is the source of internal transformation, which, in its turn, is the main characteristic of living organisms. The difference between living and non-living systems is crucial if we want to understand the functioning of Gaia and the interface between physical, biological and technological systems.

## Gaia and the Theory of Sympoiesis

Gaia theory takes an important place in Donna J. Haraway's works, from her early writings dedicated to cyborgs to the latest theory of sympoiesis described in *Staying with the Trouble: Making Kin in the Chthulucene*. In her short text 'Cyborgs and Symbionts' (1995), Haraway asks what is the nature of Gaia: is it a cybernetic entity, as Lovelock suggested, or is it a symbiotic monster, as described by Margulis? For Lovelock, 'the whole earth was a dynamic, self-regulating, homeostatic system; the earth, with all its interwoven layers and articulated parts, from the planet's pulsating skin through its fulminating gaseous envelopes, was itself alive' (Haraway 1995: xiii). However, it is alive not in the sense that it is a living organism, but because it brings into a complex system different layers of the earth. 'Lovelock's earth – itself a cyborg, a complex auto-poietic system that terminally blurred the boundaries among the geological, the organic, and the technological – was the natural habitat, and the launching pad, of other cyborgs' (Haraway 1995: xiii). Thus, there are two versions of Gaia: the cyborg-like Gaia which can be seen as a self-regulating man–machine system; and a symbiotic Gaia, a hybrid born from non-innocent couplings of creatures with different genomes, such as in the case of *Mixotricha paradoxa*. It is interesting to see that this early text already marks both the machinic and organismic pedigree of Gaia and also introduces the term autopoiesis in quite an unproblematic way.

A different take on Gaia appears in Haraway's *Staying with the Trouble: Making Kin in the Chthulucene*.[1] Haraway seems sympathetic to Latour's and Stengers's theories of Gaia (although omitting their different backgrounds) and reads them as a continuation of Lovelock and Margulis's hypothesis:

> In this hypothesis, Gaia is autopoietic – self-forming, boundary maintaining, contingent, dynamic and stable under some conditions but not others. Gaia is not reducible to the sum of its parts, but achieves finite systemic coherence in the face of perturbations within parameters that

---

[1] In *Staying with the Trouble: Making Kin in the Chthulucene* (2016), Haraway constructs her theory of Gaia in opposition to the theories of the Anthropocene. The Anthropocene is a term suggested by Paul Crutzen and Eugene Stoermer (Crutzen and Stoermer 2000; Crutzen 2002) to name a new geological epoch, which marks the irreversible effects on the planet produced by human activity. The term was criticised by many authors for reintroducing the notion of the Anthropos back into the scene (Demos 2017). Some other authors suggested such terms as 'Capitalocene' (Moore 2016) or 'Plantationocene' (Haraway 2015). Haraway suggests the new term 'Chthulucene', which will be discussed in the next chapter.

are themselves responsive to dynamic systemic processes. (Haraway 2016: 43–4)

Thus, Gaia exposes a certain systemic coherence, but the nature of this systematicity is not discussed. Haraway seems more sympathetic to Margulis's idea that life emerges through symbiosis and symbiogenesis, which leads to the increasing complexity of life forms. This is why Haraway questions the underlying assumption that these emerging life forms are autopoietic and argues that Margulis perhaps 'would have chosen the term *sympoietic*, but the word and concept had not yet surfaced' (Haraway 2016: 61). Haraway asserts that nothing can really create itself,[2] therefore, nothing is really autopoietic but needs other organisms and environments to become what it is. In this regard the theory of autopoiesis should be coupled with the theory of sympoiesis, which refers not to autonomous but to collectively produced systems.

Haraway takes the term sympoiesis from M. Beth Dempster's (2000) work, where she distinguishes between autopoietic and sympoietic systems. Autopoietic systems, as defined by Maturana and Varela, are characterised by two basic features: first, they produce relations between their components that allow them to reproduce the same pattern of relations (they are self-referential); second, they have the ability to reproduce their own boundaries (they are self-defining). Autopoietic systems are organisationally closed, but structurally open: this means that they are not absolutely autonomous but that they internally define their boundaries and relationships with the environment. Sympoietic systems are defined as organisationally ajar, with loosely defined boundaries. 'Lacking self-defined boundaries, sympoietic systems consequently lack the same degree of control and are open to a continual flux of organizationally relevant information [. . .] This dynamic, though restricted, flux of information allows sympoietic systems to evolve continuously by adapting to changing conditions and by generating new ones' (Dempster 2000: 9). Autopoietic and sympoietic systems manage information in different ways: autopoietic systems carry a kind of 'packaged' information, whereas sympoietic systems carry different bits of information in their components (which are autopoietic in themselves) and lack a central control. This makes sympoietic systems more flexible and adaptive, therefore they can easily adapt to changing environments, and also produce new forms of organisation (in this regard they are allopoietic):

[2] In *When Species Meet* (2008), Haraway attributes this thought to Scott F. Gilbert: 'I am instructed by developmental biologist Scott Gilbert's critique of autopoiesis for its emphasis on self-building and self-maintaining systems, closed except for nourishing flows of matter and energy. Gilbert stresses that nothing makes itself in the biological world, but rather reciprocal induction within and between always-in-process critters ramifies through space and time on both large and small scales in cascades of inter- and intra-action' (Haraway 2008: 32).

'autopoietic systems follow some sort of path from a less to a more developed stage, whereas sympoietic systems are continually, although not necessarily consistently, changing' (Dempster 2000: 10–11). This explains why sympoietic systems have greater potential for change: if autopoietic systems are homeostatic, predictable and development-oriented, then sympoietic systems are allopoietic (producing otherness), unpredictable and evolution-oriented. In this sense, sympoietic systems, which also include autopoietic systems as their components, have the ability to maintain their identity and the status quo, and, at the same time, have the potential to change and to adapt to changes coming from the environment.

Thus, Haraway promotes the theory of sympoiesis and suggests that 'Gaia is a system mistaken for autopoietic that is really sympoietic' (Haraway 2016: 180, n. 38). According to Haraway, autopoiesis can explain the functioning of bounded units or individuals, whereas sympoiesis is a better term to explain the collaborative assemblages that acquire their identity in the process of interaction and becoming. By fusing different components, sympoiesis creates more complex life forms and gives rise to new emergent properties. Haraway refers to Margulis's notion of the holobiont, which indicates an organism plus persisting symbionts, such as the poster critter *Mixotricha paradoxa*. For Haraway, the notion of the holobiont questions the idea of a self-organised individual and indicates that all living beings appear as a result of dynamic organising processes:

> Like Margulis, I use *holobiont* to mean symbiotic assemblages, at whatever scale of space or time, which are more like knots of diverse intra-active relatings in dynamic complex systems, than like the entities of a biology made up of preexisting bounded units (genes, cells, organisms, etc.) in interactions that can only be conceived as competitive or cooperative. (Haraway 2016: 60, emphasis in original)

In this respect, Haraway thinks that sympoiesis 'is a word proper to complex, dynamic, responsive, situated, historical systems [. . .] Sympoiesis enfolds autopoiesis and generatively unfurls and extends it' (Haraway 2016: 58). That means that sympoiesis and autopoiesis are not in opposition to each other, but, rather, they designate different aspects of systemic complexity.

Haraway takes the notion of the holobiont even further by trying to decentralise the relationships between a host and its symbionts: 'my use of *holobiont* does not designate host + symbionts because all of the players are symbionts to each other, in diverse kinds of relationalities and with varying degrees of openness to attachments and assemblages with other holobionts' (Haraway 2016: 60, emphasis in original). The idea that 'all of the players are symbionts to each other' echoes Latour's formulation that every agent is trying to manipulate another in such a way that all borders between an organism and its environment, between the inside and the outside, are subverted. But this subversion poses another methodological question: if the borders are subverted, how can we distinguish between organisms and environments, or symbionts and hosts? Is it still possible to talk about any systemic approach, if all symbionts dissolve in their environment? As Wolfe critically formulates it, if all boundaries between an organism and its environment collapse, to what is this system still open? Wolfe asserts that to theorise this mode of interaction, first we have to define the entity which is interacting, and only then can we define the nature of this interaction. In other words, first we have to explain the organisation of an autopoietic entity, and only then can we define their sympoietic interactions. In Wolfe's view, 'approaching complex system/environment interactions from the theoretical framework of autopoiesis is coherent and rigorous, while the theory of "sympoiesis" is not' (Wolfe 2023: 216).

To answer this critique, we can argue that a systems theory approach, even being coherent and rigorous, might also have its limitations. Here we can quote Haraway's interview where she says that she is sympathetic to certain efforts to rethink Gaia through autopoiesis, but in general she is resistant to systems theory: 'I am nonetheless deeply resistant to systems theories of all kinds, including so-called third-order cybernetics and the autopoiesis and structural coupling approaches' (Gane 2006: 139). This assertion should be taken into account – what if systems theory is insufficient to account for the relational and processual nature of sympoietic intra-actions? Maybe first we have to understand the nature of this interaction, and only then analyse the agents or actors, having in mind that they are just temporal effects of this interaction.

Another point of Wolfe's critique is related to the paradoxical position of the observer: if we agree with the statement that 'everything is connected', then we imply an observer's position from which this connectedness can be seen or observed. However, this is the impossible position of the 'God's-eye view' which Haraway criticises herself. The observer's position always implies a particular place and has unavoidable limitations. Having this in mind, Wolfe argues that the second-order systems theory approach, which maintains the self-referential closure and the boundaries between the system and its environment, is a better theoretical model. In other words, to increase the connections with the environment and to reach a higher complexity, an entity first has to be a closed autopoietic system. Wolfe formulates his 'openness from closure' principle (Wolfe 2010: 117), meaning that self-reference in autopoietic systems refers not to closure or the homeostatic 'repetition of the same', but to recursive operations which can incorporate contingency (Wolfe 2020: 141). Without this autopoietic self-referential closure there would be no recursivity, and without recursivity there would be no actual connectivity between an organism and its environment. As Wolfe points out, 'when it comes to the biosphere and its role in the larger system of Gaia, second-order closure and the recursivity it enables between organism and environment *is* the joker in the deck, both ontogenetically and phylogenetically, the most unpredictable source of the "outlaw" characteristics of alterity and contingency' (Wolfe 2020: 142, emphasis in original). And yet, even though this second-order systems approach seems justifiable in discussing the theory of Gaia, the question still remains whether it is appropriate to accept the theory of sympoiesis. If we think about Gaia as a thin layer of the atmosphere, we have to admit that it is not just an autopoietic system having a boundary or a membrane; *it is* a boundary or a membrane itself (Clarke 2017: 222). If Gaia is a bounded entity and a boundary itself, then the notion of autopoiesis perfectly fits this description. However, if we think about the holobiont and the processes of sympoiesis, the notion of boundary becomes irrelevant. The ontological weight here is laid not on entities and their boundaries, but on the relations between different centres of cognition. Thus, the notion of sympoiesis requires not systems theory, but a cognitivist approach, which will be discussed in the next chapter.

## Conclusion

As we have seen, the original Gaia hypothesis had two 'parents': it is Lovelock's cybernetic model and Margulis's notion of symbiosis and symbiogenesis. After meeting Varela, Lovelock and Margulis were persuaded to describe Gaia in terms of self-referential and self-maintaining autopoietic system, connecting living and non-living components. However, other authors, such as Latour and Haraway, invite us to rethink Gaia not as an autopoietic unity, closed unto itself in repetitive patterns, but as a complex and dynamic network, which is open to contingency and otherness. In this respect, Gaia is not quite an organism or a living being, but a living-like agent, driven by its formative activity. As Latour points out,

> The simplification introduced by Lovelock in the comprehension of terrestrial phenomena is not at all that he added 'life' to the Earth, or that he made the Earth a 'living organism', but, quite to the contrary, that he *stopped denying* that living beings were active participants in biochemical and geochemical phenomena. (Latour 2018: 76, emphasis in original)

Lovelock refused to de-animate the Earth and to deny that there are many actors or agents that produce and engender qualitative changes.

In this respect, the theory of living-like Gaia is a better theoretical tool to reflect our climatic condition than the discourse on the Anthropocene. The Anthropocene (and Capitalocene or Plantationocene) deals with measurable or quantitative effects which are mostly irreversible. By contrast, Gaia theory reflects qualitative connections between living and non-living systems. Gaia theory implies the planetary cognition that organises different living and non-living (geological or technological) systems in such a way that they can reach the most favourable conditions. In this respect, Gaia theory is nothing other than organology, the extension of life by other means than life: living beings are exteriorised into non-living environments or technologies, and vice versa: non-living substances are interiorised by living beings and transformed into vital energy. Gaia is this planetary organism that collects different organic and inorganic components and produces new forms of life.

# 7
# Hybrid Organism

In this chapter I will discuss Haraway's notion of sympoiesis and will examine different modes of cohabitation or hybridisation with non-human others. Such concepts as sympoiesis, or the holobiont, question the notion of the biological individual and also change our understanding of what it means to be human. As Richard Grusin pointed out, 'we have never been human', for the reason that 'the human has always coevolved, coexisted, or collaborated with the nonhuman – and that the human is characterized precisely by this indistinction from the nonhuman' (Grusin 2015: ix–x). We have never been human, because we have always been dependent on other species living within or beyond our bodies. However, the question that still needs to be answered is whether all forms of coexistence are profitable and welcomed. How does one define the limit at which this coexistence is collaborative and productive ('posthuman'), and beyond which it becomes damaging and lethal, in other words, 'posthumous', e.g. coming after life? (Weinstein and Colebrook 2017). For this reason, the interrelations between different life forms should be discussed together with the concepts of immunity and contagion. The notion of immunity expresses an ambivalent character of life: on the one hand, it protects an organism against everything that is beyond its boundary; on the other hand, it helps to collaborate with other organisms and to create a new community, or an ecosystem. In this sense, immunity can be thought as a possibility for a new community connecting human and non-human beings. At the end of this chapter, I will examine different modes of interspecies communication in contemporary art practices.

## Sympoiesis as 'Making-With'

Haraway's discursive interventions, from cyborgs to symbiotic creatures, deconstruct the myth of the organism as a natural wholeness. Instead, she persuasively demonstrates that every living being is a multiplicity, an assemblage, which might be arranged and rearranged in many different ways. In this respect, Haraway, without acknowledging it,[1] elaborates further Deleuze and Guattari's attempts to disarticulate the idea of an organism and open it to becoming and 'unnatural participations', which was discussed in Chapter 3. For Deleuze and Guattari, an organism is an assemblage-like construction, the body without organs, which demonstrates the disorganisation of the organism and the denaturalisation of nature. Deleuze and Guattari are interested in different modes of becoming, defined as expansion, propagation, occupation, contagion, peopling. It is a multiplicity, which is organised not by filiation or heredity, but through epidemic or contagion. Haraway also insists on the contingent and undetermined mode of every multiplicity; however, she stresses symbiotic cooperation and sympoietic entanglements.

In this chapter I will discuss Haraway's notion of sympoiesis not in relation to the Gaian system but as a mundane practice of 'making-with' or 'becoming-with' (Haraway 2016; 2017). Haraway is sympathetic to Lynn Margulis's idea that life emerges through symbiosis and symbiogenesis, which leads to the increasing complexity of life forms. In *Symbiotic Planet* (1998), Margulis proved that life originated from the interaction between different life forms, such as bacteria and archaea. By fusing with each other, bacteria and archaea invented a complex cell made of a nucleus and extranuclear organelles. As Haraway suggests, symbiosis is the basic law of life: 'The core of Margulis's view of life was that new *kinds* of cells, tissues, organs, and species evolve primarily through the long-lasting intimacy of strangers' (Haraway 2016: 60, emphasis in original). Haraway asserts that the notion of autopoiesis should be coupled with the notion of sympoiesis because, as she says, nothing creates itself; thus nothing is really autopoietic, or self-organising. Everything needs others to create itself. Haraway asserts that organisms are never quite autonomous: 'neither biology nor philosophy any longer supports the notion of independent organisms in environments ... Bounded (or neoliberal) individualism amended by autopoiesis is not good enough figurally or scientifically; it misleads us down deadly paths' (Haraway 2016: 33). Instead, she says, we have to adopt Karen Barad's (2007) agential realism and intra-active complex systems of relations, where the elements of the system do not pre-exist the relations but are created precisely by them. Such a model of intra-active relationships is better than the model of autopoietic systems.

> Autopoietic systems [...] are not good models for living and dying worlds and their critters. Autopoietic systems are not closed, spherical, deterministic, or teleological, but they are not quite good enough models for the mortal SF world. Poiesis is symchthonic, sympoietic, always partnered

---

[1] We find a harsh critique of Deleuze and Guattari's notion of becoming in the first chapter of Haraway's *When Species Meet* (2008: 3–44). However, a more positive and careful approach is lacking.

all the way down, with no starting and subsequently interacting 'units'. (Haraway 2016: 33)[2]

Haraway suggests that a living being (she prefers a tentacular one) is never closed unto itself, but is always entangled and attached to other living beings and forms interspecies assemblages.

In other words, Haraway does not completely reject the theory of autopoiesis but insists that autopoiesis and sympoiesis are different aspects of systemic complexity, and that they rather enfold than oppose each other. At this point it is important to stress that Maturana and Varela do not assert that autopoietic systems are closed and devoid of interaction with other systems. For example, they argue that 'Autopoietic systems may interact with each other under conditions that result in behavioral coupling' (Maturana and Varela 1980: 119–20). The interacting organisms as dynamic systems trigger each other and thus become continuously changing structures, but never lose their autopoietic character. In this respect, autopoietic systems are not neglected but rather complicated, and they become the source of each other's change and development. Haraway is saying the same thing when she adopts Margulis's notion of the holobiont and reinvents it in the sense that the holobiont does not merely designate the host plus the symbionts, but means that 'all of the players are symbionts to each other, in diverse kinds of relationalities and with varying degrees of openness to attachments and assemblages with other holobionts' (Haraway 2016: 60). In this sense, sympoiesis is always an allopoiesis, or heteropoiesis, an attempt to deal with otherness and cope with differences.

To assert her theory of sympoiesis as a 'making-with', Haraway refers to the works of biologists which give clear evidence that symbiosis has always been a dominant mode of existence. For example, in a famous article 'A Symbiotic View of Life: We Have Never Been Individuals' (2012), Scott F. Gilbert, Jan Sapp and Alfred Tauber argue that biological individuals are always inhabited by other forms of life, such as viruses or bacteria. After examining biological individuals according to anatomical, developmental, physiological, genetic and immunological criteria, the authors come to the conclusion that all organisms are related to each other in an all-pervading symbiosis. Before Margulis's work, symbiosis was seen as rare or exceptional; now symbiosis 'is becoming a core principle of contemporary biology, and it is replacing an essentialist conception of "individuality" with a conception congruent with the larger systems approach now pushing the life sciences in diverse directions' (Gilbert et al. 2012: 326).

There are many criteria for defining biological individuality. According to anatomical criteria, a biological individual is regarded as a structured whole. However, our favourite critter *Mixotricha paradoxa* is a chimeric individual,

---

[2] SF here refers to science fiction, speculative feminism, speculative fabulation, string figures, etc.

'a beast with five genomes' (Margulis and Sagan 2001: 38–41), which is composed of a host and persistent populations of symbionts. Now, if we examine a biological individual according to developmental criteria, we can see that development is closely related to interspecies communication. For example, the newborn of the Hawaiian bobtailed squid *Euprymna scolopes* lacks a light organ, which is developed in cooperation between the squid and the luminescent bacteria called *Vibrio fischeri* (Gilbert et al. 2012: 328). Thus, the vibrio bacteria are essential for inventing a new organ and also bringing the squid into being. The vibrio bacteria also initiate changes in the squid's gene expression, thus altering the development of its body and immune system. As Margaret McFall-Ngai points out, 'These observations challenged what we thought we knew about organismal development, namely, that it was driven primarily by inherited genetic codes. In contrast, our research showed us that squid develop, in part, through relations with microbes, not exclusively through inherited genetic scripts' (McFall-Ngai 2017: 61). These and many other examples provide evidence that animals cannot be considered individuals by anatomical, developmental, physiological, immunological, genetic or evolutionary criteria. Their bodies must be understood as holobionts that developed through interspecies communication.

However, the notion of the holobiont changes not only our understanding of the animal world but also the idea of what it means to be human. In a more recent article Gilbert observes that 'The holobiont is powerful, in part, because it is not limited to nonhuman organisms. It also changes what it means to be a person' (Gilbert 2017: 75). Seen from this perspective, the human body is not a bounded individual but a complex ecosystem, which is related to other organisms through the reciprocal process of symbiosis. For example, in defining anatomical individuality, Gilbert suggests that only about half the cells in our bodies contain a 'human genome', and the other cells include about 160 different bacterial genomes (Gilbert 2017: 75). Thus, from the anatomical point of view, human bodies contain a plurality of bacterial ecosystems. From the genetic point of view, we are not individuals either because, while humans have about 22,000 different genes, the bacteria in us provide eight million more. The co-metabolism between humans and their bacterial symbionts proves that we are not individuals from the physiological point of view. Gilbert gives an interesting example of such a physiological symbiosis: a mother has two different kinds of nutrients in her milk – one is for the newborn baby, and the other for the bacteria that will help to build its gut and immune system. 'A human mother's milk contains several oligosaccharides, complex sugars, that cannot be digested by the baby. These are not sugars for the baby; these are sugars for bacteria such as *Bifidobacteria*, which has genes that encode enzymes capable of digesting those special milk sugars' (Gilbert 2017: 81). Thus, the maternal body creates conditions for a new symbiotic community. According to immunological criteria, humans are also far from individuals because our immune system allows countless microbes to become parts of our bodies. As Gilbert points out, 'Without the proper microbial symbionts, important subsets of immune cells fail to form [. . .] We are thus not individuals by immune criteria' (Gilbert 2017: 82). Recent research in immunology reveals that there is no such thing as an individual 'self' because our bodies couldn't survive without hosting microbial organisms.

Thus, after discussing anatomical, genetic, developmental, physiological, immunological and evolutionary criteria, Gilbert comes to the conclusion that we are not individuals but holobionts – organisms persistently cooperating with communities of symbionts. This means that symbiosis is not an exceptional or marginal case but an all-encompassing principle of life. 'These major symbiotic webs rule the planet, and within these big symbioses are the smaller symbiotic webs of things we call organisms [. . .] Symbiosis is the way of life on earth; we are all holobionts by birth' (Gilbert 2017: 84). But if we are all holobionts by birth, what do these modes of symbiosis and cohabitation mean for us and for other species?

This forces us to think about how we can harmonise these biological insights and our philosophical predispositions. Are we ready to give up the notion of the human individual? Inspired by recent biological research, Haraway enthusiastically invites us to engage in interspecies communication, which is understood as sympoiesis. In contrast to biological symbiosis and symbiogenesis which is simply found in the natural world, sympoiesis means an active 'making-with' with other species, which is understood as a way to counter both anthropocentrism and the Anthropocene. Taking as a metaphor the spider *Pimoa cthulhu*, and making a small change in spelling from cthulhu to chthulu, Haraway invents a new term – the Chthulucene[3] – that should replace the Anthropocene.

> [T]he Chthulucene is made up of ongoing multispecies stories and practices of becoming-with . . . Unlike the dominant dramas of Anthropocene and Capitalocene discourse, human beings are not the only important actors in the Chthulucene, with all other beings able simply to react. The order is reknitted: human beings are with and of the earth, and the biotic and abiotic powers of this earth are the main story. (Haraway 2016: 55)

Haraway invites us to create tentacular webs and assemblages with other species. However, what I find problematic in this project is that these connections work only on the imaginary and speculative level, avoiding the real interaction with other species. The relationship with animal partners remains vaguely defined, and in some cases – such as poetically described interactions with companion species (Haraway 2008) – looks very problematic because it is still embedded in the logic of anthropocentrism and asserts the supremacy of the human species.

---

[3] Haraway refers to a spider, *Pimoa cthulhu*, that lives in the redwood forests of Sonoma and Mendocino counties, near where she lives in north central California.

How can we imagine interspecies communication beyond these beautiful poetic SF speculations? Even if the notion of symbiosis is now widely accepted in biology, sympoiesis, or 'making-with', between human and non-human species still needs to be accounted for and explained. What is problematic here is that the entire history of philosophy rests on the idea of the bounded individual. To renounce the boundaries would mean to destroy the individual, the human subject, and thus to deprive the world of the source of thinking and reasoning. When Gilbert, Sapp and Tauber announce that 'we are all lichens', or, as Haraway asserts, 'we are humus, not humans', to what extent can we accept these statements? Can we renounce our human individuality and dissolve into the mud of compost? At this point, some other terms and concepts should be found or invented. I think that the notion of sympoiesis should be discussed in relation to the question of immunity and contagion. Are all connections and relations profitable to the host and its symbionts, or not? If they are, then everyone can enjoy interspecies collaboration; but if they are not, then these connections might be fatally contagious and lead to destruction. In other words, to explain the interaction with otherness, we have to explain the functioning of the immune system.

## Immunity and Contagion

Haraway discusses the notion of immunity in one of her earlier texts, 'The Biopolitics of Postmodern Bodies: Constitutions of Self in Immune System Discourse'.[4] What is important for Haraway is that the individual body is not something given but is permanently constructed: paraphrasing Simone de Beauvoir, she asserts that 'one is not born an organism. Organisms are made; they are constructs of a world-changing kind' (Haraway 2013: 279). The immune system is a good example of organisms being assemblages, which are constantly shaped by the environment. As Haraway points out, '"Organism" and "individual" have not disappeared; rather, they have been fully denaturalized. That is, they are ontologically contingent constructs from the point of view of the biologist, not just in the loose ravings of a cultural critic or feminist historian of science' (Haraway 2013: 292–3). The immune system, as it was defined in the twentieth century, draws the boundary between the 'self' and the 'non-self', and in this respect immunological discourse imitates the discourse of biopolitics. The immune system creates a defensive mechanism to fight against the 'non-self' in the same way as biopolitical power discriminates against the 'other'.

However, the distinction between the 'self' and the 'non-self' is not so clear if we want to explain it biologically. What remains to be explained is what defines this 'self' and why the immune system is silent in relation to its own cells and tissues. What happens when a part of the so-called 'self'

---

[4] First published in *differences: A Journal of Feminist Cultural Studies*, 1, 1989, pp. 3–43.

changes and becomes a stranger to itself? Is the biological 'self' identical with philosophical and psychological notions of individuality? As Alfred I. Tauber explains, the notion of selfhood was not only imported from philosophical discourse but quickly became an idiom that was explained as if it grew within the science of immunology (Tauber 2017: 42). The notion of 'self', which comprises both the organismal self and the immunological self, was a very convenient and recognisable model with which to think about our immunological identity. However, as immunology developed, some important questions had to be answered. First, the immunological 'self' is never given all at once, but develops throughout the organism's life. That means that the immunological 'self' is not a given entity, but a process, during which it is constantly changing. Second, the immunological 'self' is non-reactive or silent in relation to the cells coming from other organisms, for example in the case of pregnancy. There is clear evidence that long after delivery, foetal cells are found in maternal bodies, creating a case of microchimerism. Why does the immune system not attack these cells? And third, why does the immune system *react* to the cells of the same organism in the case of autoimmune diseases? Why does the immune system treat the 'self' as if it were the 'other'? As Roberto Esposito points out, autoimmune diseases 'express, by their very name, its most acute contradiction: rather than a failure, a block, or a flaw in the immune apparatus, they represent its reversal against itself' (Esposito 2011: 162). Autoimmune diseases express an 'overactive defence' of the body, when the body is using a defence that is disproportionate to the actual size of the intruder.

Esposito argues that the antinomies of the immune system could be interpreted not as an alleged pathology, but, on the contrary, as its normal functioning. 'If the immune system works by opposing *everything* that it recognizes, this means that it has to attack even the "self" whose recognition is the precondition of all other recognition: how could the immune system recognize the other without first knowing the self?' (Esposito 2011: 164, emphasis in original). Here we see a certain antinomy: the immune system should recognise the 'self' in order to recognise the 'other'; however, this recognition is damaging because, after recognising this, it starts to attack itself. As Esposito points out,

> what needs explaining is not the fact that in some cases the immune system attacks its own parts, but the fact that this normally does not happen. This non-aggression is well known as being due to the phenomenon called 'autotolerance', or tolerance of self. What we want to draw attention to is how this leads to the reversal of a common perception: it is not autoimmunity, with all its lethal consequences, including death, that requires explanation, but rather its absence. (Esposito 2011: 164)

The question to be answered here is what is the primary and natural condition of the body: is it the absence of autoimmunity (so-called 'autotolerance'), or its necessary presence ('autoimmunitary attack')? As Esposito points out, 'Here we arrive at the key point of the argument: the destructive rebellion against the self is not a temporary dysfunction, but the natural impulse of every immune system. In countering all that it "sees", it is naturally led to *first* attack its own self' (Esposito 2011: 165, emphasis in original).

These philosophical reconsiderations force us to rethink the ways in which our bodies are defined, and, more importantly, make us question the assumption that our bodies are always already given and identical to ourselves. If the body is constantly changing during its life, at what point can the body be considered as 'proper', and, moreover, how can we determine our immunological 'self'? Commenting on recent biomedical research, Esposito comes to the conclusion that the immune system is not something definitive and identical to itself but is permanently changing and adapting to the environment. In this sense, the immune system can be thought of not as a defensive mechanism but as a network of relationships, or, as Deleuze and Guattari would say, as an assemblage, that creates temporal and non-hierarchical connections between heterogeneous elements. In this context the notion of immune tolerance could mean not only a lack of response but also a positive recognition of elements of the 'non-self'. The discovery that immune tolerance can be *induced* artificially demonstrates that the immune system can be taught to recognise the cells of the other body and respond to them positively.

> This means that tolerance is not a non-immunity, a kind of virtuous immuno-deficiency; if anything, it is a reverse immunity: that which reverses the effects within the same lexicon. But if so, if tolerance is a product of the immune system itself, it means that, far from having a single-response repertoire, that of rejecting other-than-self, it includes the other within itself, not only as its driving force but also as one of its effects. (Esposito 2011: 167)

In other words, the body should be thought of as a fusional multiplicity or as an assemblage where different molecular populations negotiate with each other.

All these questions signal that the notion of immunity is undergoing a conceptual shift. Rather than being understood as a defensive reaction towards an external, contagious element, immunity is now conceived as a network that keeps the balance in the organismal 'self'. In other words, it is not a negative reaction towards a foreign element but a normal functioning that needs to be explained. As Tauber points out,

> When immune reactions are conceived in terms of normal physiology and open exchange with the environment, where borders dividing host and foreign are elusive and changing, host defence is only part of the immune system's functions, which actually comprise two basic tasks: to

preserve host *integrity* (protection) and to establish organismic *identity*. (Tauber 2017: 117, emphasis in original)

In other words, immunity should be examined not in its negative and reactive state (as defence) but in its positive state (as 'tolerance' or immune silence). Examined from this perspective, immunity is explained not in terms of an opposition between 'self' and 'non-self' but as a self-organising system.

This conceptual shift can be related to immunologist Niels Jerne and his 'network theory', which explains immunity as a self-referential system. Haraway also points out the importance of Jerne's idea that the immune system has to be understood not as a protection of the individual 'self' but as a changing network based on self-regulation and self-organisation. 'Jerne's basic idea was that any antibody molecule must be able to act functionally as both antibody to some antigen *and* as antigen for the production of an antibody to itself, albeit at another region of "itself"' (Haraway 2013: 291, emphasis in original). In this sense, the immune system is understood as a network that is capable of recognising and mirroring the antigen in such a way that there is nothing external that the immune system has not already mirrored internally.

> 'Self' and 'other' lose their rationalistic oppositional quality and become subtle plays of partially mirrored readings and responses. The notion of the *internal image* is the key to the theory, and it entails the premise that every member of the immune system is capable of interacting with every other member. (Haraway 2013: 291, emphasis in original)

Thus, the immune system is understood as an internal network that reacts, not to an external 'invader', but to its internal structuring.

Tauber also examines Jerne's network theory as a major shift in immunity theorising. As Tauber explains, Jerne proposed the idea that the immune system is made of interlocking recognising units, so that each component reacts with the others within the system, and in this way they all together form a self-referential network. In this model the antibody has two roles, active and passive:

> So in addition to the active binding of antigen, Jerne suggested that antibody could also act as the target of another antibody by presenting itself as an antigen through its so-called *idiotypic* domains. On this view, immunoglobulin behaves as both antibody (as originally regarded) and antigen to a corresponding antibody that reacts with its unique *idiotope*. (Tauber 2017: 60, emphasis in original)

The immune system reacts to the external antigens only to the extent that these elements are recognised in the internal 'library' of antibodies. 'In other words, Jerne postulated that the amino acid sequences of immunoglobulins share structural homologies with all antigens to which the organism might respond – that is, "internal images" represent that external universe' (Tauber 2017: 60). Thus, the immune system performs a dialogue between antibodies that play two roles, the 'recogniser' and the 'recognised'. Neither the 'recogniser' nor the 'recognised' have any essential characteristics of 'self' or 'non-self'. Rather they are signifiers referring to other signifiers, and, in this sense, immunity can be understood as a self-referential structure of language. The 'other' is something that simply disturbs that structure and activates a response.

Seen from this perspective, the immune system cannot be explained by the 'self' and 'non-self' distinction because, strictly speaking, the immune network can recognise only itself. Every element is always already within the system, and what is external or 'other' is either invisible or appears as 'nonsense'. The distinction between 'self' and 'other' can be conceptualised only from the observer's point of view, whereas the immune network is always immanent to itself and cannot reflect its outside. As Tauber points out, 'Jerne's network conception [was] built on *self-recognition*, which then reconfigured "autoimmunity" (self-recognition) from aberrancy to the normative organizational rule of immune function' (Tauber 2017: 62, emphasis in original). Immune tolerance or silence does not need a special explanation because the immune system knows only itself. The originality of Jerne's model lies in the fact that it denies the subject–object structure, which implies the observer's perspective, and suggests that immunity is an immanent structure based on self-survey. As Tauber observes, 'Jerne's innovation offered a model of immune function independent of agency, and with that move, he highlighted the difference between the observer's perspective and the network's' (Tauber 2017: 65). This is a completely different epistemology, which might be compared to the notion of primary consciousness, as described by Ruyer. Similar to primary consciousness which knows itself in immediate self-survey, Jerne's immune network knows itself in self-referential loops.

The idea that the immune system is capable of recognising, responding and learning implies a close relationship between immune activity and cognition. At this point we can refer to Varela's theory of immunity, which he developed together with Nelson Vaz, Antonio Coutinho and others. Varela was trying to apply his theory of autopoiesis to Jerne's network hypothesis. His basic insight is that any autopoietic unit – from cells to complex living systems – is capable of cognition. In this sense, the immune system, similarly to the nervous system, possesses a certain kind of knowledge, which Varela and Anspach define as a 'immu-knowledge':

> We argue that the immune system is a cognitive network, not only because of properties which it shares with the brain, but also, more interestingly, because in both cases we have similar (or at least comparable) global

properties of biological networks giving rise to cognitive behavior as emergent properties. (Varela and Anspach 1991: 70)

The immune system has a cognitive faculty, which belongs not to some knowing agent but to the network as such. In this sense, the immune system is processing information, which is necessary to maintain the organism's integrity and identity. As Tauber points out,

> the immune system then is best regarded as an information-generating system, which continuously seeks its own *eidos* or steady state of immune identity. In this sense, immunity fashions *identity* as an ongoing self-seeking, information-organizing activity. To the extent immunology would fashion itself along these lines, the conception of the self partitioned from the world (and thus conceived defensively) would be replaced by a different 'ecological' character, one based on *in-formation*. (Tauber 2017: 144, emphasis in original)

In this respect, the immune system is understood as a cognitive system that processes information in a self-referential manner.

The application of an autopoietic model allows us to compare systems of different scales. In this sense, any living system – from cells and organisms to ecosystems – functions as a self-organising and self-referential cognitive network. Thus, Varela and Anspach draw a comparison between an immune system and a planetary system: 'the body is like Earth, a textured environment for diverse and highly interactive populations of individuals. The individuals in this case are the white blood cells or lymphocytes which constitute the immune system' (Varela and Anspach 1991: 69). The lymphocytes are generating different molecular populations within the body, similar to living species which generate diversity within an ecosystem. The immune system is like 'a microcosmic version of Gaia' (Varela and Anspach 1991: 69), which can maintain its balance through self-referential processes. Thus, the immune system, like the planetary system of Gaia, is shaped as an autopoietic entity, which is closed unto itself and can recognise only itself. However, what remains problematic in this autopoietic approach is how to define the other.[5] If the cognitive network knows only itself, how can it communicate with other organisms and other ecosystems? As Tauber explains, in this theory the 'non-self' appears as nonsense, or as informational noise:

---

[5] As Tauber points out, Antonio Coutinho, Francisco Varela and colleagues (the so-called Paris School) developed a two-tier schema in which a 'central' immune system (conceptualised as 'autonomous network theory', ANT) and a pathogen-driven 'peripheral' immune system (known as 'clonal selection theory', CST) operate in a coordinated manner. This approach fails to explain what holds these two systems together (Tauber 2017: 68).

the *other* (nonself) does not exist in this closed system as Jerne originally proposed. [. . .] ANT [Autonomous Network Theory], locked into seeing only itself and blind to the *other*, fails to define the other as other, which then can only be identified as 'foreign' from an exterior point of view . . . (Tauber 2017: 237, n. 7, emphasis in original)

Thus, if the immune system sees only itself, how can it coexist with other systems, and, in general, how is this autonomous network approach compatible with the notion of the holobiont?

The idea that the immune system works as a self-referential autopoietic network is an important theoretical elaboration in so far as it replaces the dualistic opposition between the 'self' and the 'non-self' and shifts the focus from a defence mechanism towards immune balance. However, the theory of symbiosis and that of the holobiont poses another challenge, because the immune system has to deal not only with purely exterior elements, or with an interior self, but also with difference within itself. Such biomedical phenomena as microchimerism, when genetically different molecules circulate in the same body, reveal a need for a new approach. Tauber asserts that in the future biology should create a model of ecological immunity which could examine immunity not as a defence, but as an interface. As Tauber points out,

Older understandings of immune identity based on autonomous, insular animals in competition with others omit the crucial mechanisms of tolerance that allow organisms to live as a holobiont. And to study such aggregates, eco-immunology shifts from the individual-based conceptions that have dominated the life sciences to considerations of the dialectical relationships that require tolerant mechanisms to mediate beneficial exchanges. (Tauber 2017: 221)

Immunology has to reconsider the mutualistic scenarios between competing or cooperating elements within an organism, and to take symbiosis into account. In this sense, the focus shifts from defence to immune balance, and, in general, from immunity towards autoimmunity.

## Hybrids and Chimeras

There are many examples of such symbiotic existence. First of all, eukaryotic cells themselves appeared as a result of endosymbiosis; it was demonstrated that mitochondria and chloroplasts possess their own genes; in other words, they used to be free-living bacteria which later merged into one cell. Second, multicellularity may have been initiated by interactions between bacteria and protists. Third, humans themselves are genomic chimeras: nearly 50% of the human genome consists of transposable DNA sequences acquired exogenously from microbes (Tauber 2017: 100–2). This biological evidence forces us to give up the idea of the biological individual and find appropriate terms to think of consortiums or assemblages within individuals. For example, Vinciane Despret encourages us to think in terms of 'combinations' and 'compositions': combinations create hybridisations that still reproduce certain features of 'parent' species, whereas compositions create chimeras open to surprise and chance. 'Co-optation, contagion, infections, incorporations, digestions, reciprocal inductions, becomings-with: the nature of being human, Haraway says, is at its most profound, at its most concrete, at its most biological, an interspecific relation – a process of co-opting strangers' (Despret 2016: 191). In a similar way, Margrit Shildrick differentiates between hybrids and chimeras: 'in a hybrid *each* cell consists in a combination of genes, while in a chimera each individual cell will contain genes from only one of the originating organisms. In short, the tissues of a chimera are populated by cells that are genetically distinct from each other' (Shildrick 2019: 11–12, emphasis in original). Thus, both hybrids and chimeras deconstruct the idea of the biological individual and provide new patterns to conceptualise biological existence.

In this respect, the phenomenon of microchimerism (Martin 2010; Shildrick 2016; 2019) found in humans can be a good starting point to discuss eco-immunity. Microchimerism appears in specific medical cases, such as organ or stem cell transplantation, or in natural situations, such as pregnancy. As Shildrick points out, 'Strictly speaking microchimerism indicates that no more than 1 in 1000 cells is *genetically* distinct from the majority, but in some cases such cells may come to predominate in a particular organ as well as circulating in low numbers throughout the body' (Shildrick 2019: 11, emphasis in original). The term chimerism is derived from the Greek word Chimera, a mythological creature which is composed of different animals such as a lion, a goat and a serpent. In a similar way, a donor's organ in a recipient's body or a foetus in a maternal body create a kind of microchimerism. Referring to Diana Bianchi's (1996) research, Shildrick argues that immunology 'has uncovered strong evidence, now widely accepted, that both maternal and fetal cells cross the placental barrier as a matter of course, effecting a kind of microchimerism within each body' (Shildrick 2016: 97). Thus, instead of rejecting the foetus, the maternal immune system remains silent and even contributes to a certain cellular mobility within the body. It seems surprising that the relationship between foetus and maternal body was never considered as an argument against the 'self' and 'non-self' distinction in immunology.

Thus, is microchimerism a short-term phenomenon, created in specific circumstances, such as organ transplantation or pregnancy, or is it a game-changing discovery? As Shildrick observes, one of Bianchi's most interesting findings is that pregnancy-generated microchimerism is not a temporal phenomenon, but persists in a maternal body many years after giving birth. Moreover, some of the women in Bianchi's research had never been pregnant, nor had had either organ transplants or blood transfusions. One acceptable explanation is that chimerism 'handed down' as it were from mother to child could entail the translocation of HLA deriving from a *previous* pregnancy, in which fetal markers (effectively traced as male ones) had entered the maternal body. In other words, every subsequent female offspring of the same mother could carry Y-coded HLA, not from any pregnancy of her own, but from the circulation of her own older male sibling's cells in the maternal body. (Shildrick 2016: 100)

From this it follows that microchimerism is not only an intercorporeal but also an intergenerational phenomenon, which can be passed to other generations. In other words, if microchimerism persists in the same body over several years, maybe it is not particular and random, but universal and continuous.

The discovery of microchimerism allows us to reconsider the notion of autoimmunity, since the immune response towards 'non-self' components might be not only defensive, but also protective. As Shildrick points out, 'there is emerging evidence that autoimmunity may not be the intrinsically self-destructive phenomenon that has long been assumed but that in addition to its pathological outcomes it may also serve a regular and necessary homeostatic function' (Shildrick 2019: 17). The discovery of microchimerism is also a challenge to modern philosophy, based on the image of the autonomous and self-reflective individual. If an individual body is always haunted by other bodies and also by other species (such as microbes), then immunity is more about creating a community, as Esposito claims, than about keeping the boundary between the 'self' and the 'non-self'. Every organism is an ecological system, where different cellular populations compete and collaborate with each other. In Derrida's words, every single body is haunted by the spectre of another body, thus creating a certain corporeal hauntology. In this sense, every organism is a spectre without clear boundaries, and, consequently, the science of immunology is more like a corporeal hauntology endlessly searching for components of 'non-self'.

At this point we can observe that the term sympoiesis refers to *poiesis*, meaning 'making' or 'art', which can be another possible way to examine our relationships with non-human others and to think along the lines of ecological immunology. Here I would like to discuss some artistic examples which examine the interaction between human and non-human animals not in a speculative, but in an actual physical way. The first is the project 'May the Horse Live in Me' (2011), created by Marion Laval-Jeantet and Benoît Mangin (Art Orienté Objet). The project constitutes an attempt to hybridise the human body through the injection of horse's blood. To achieve this, the artist had to exclude from the horse's blood some of the most cytotoxic red blood cells, as well as lymphocytes and macrophages; however, she saved for transfusion all other cells, including immunoglobulin, which transfers information within the body (Hirszfeld 2015). Over the course of several months Laval-Jeantet allowed herself to be injected with horse immunoglobulin, and thus progressively developed a tolerance to this foreign animal body. After having built up her immune tolerance, the artist was able to be injected with horse blood plasma during a ritualised performance on 22 February 2011 at Galerija Kapelica in Ljubljana. During the performance the artist put on a set of leg-extending stilts that 'were engineered to mimic the suspensory spring-and-lever structure of a horse's hind leg' and that allowed her to be high enough to achieve '"the horse's eye view" and line of vision, and to duplicate the swinging motion of a horse at walk' (Downey 2018). The artist and the horse walked around the gallery, thus conducting a symbolic ritual of bonding. After that, their newly hybridised 'centaur' blood sample was extracted and freeze-dried like a molecular sculpture.

Thus, the performance enacted a kind of chimerisation at the molecular level. The intention of this performance was that the horse immunoglobulin would bypass the defensive mechanisms of the human immune system, enter the artist's bloodstream and interact with it. In this respect, the horse blood plasma transfusion performance became a place of negotiation with otherness: on the one hand, the injected horse blood plasma was recognised by the artist's immune system and this recognition saved her from anaphylactic shock; on the other hand, some negative or defensive reactions emerged. As the artist herself points out, the first response to the transfusion was fever, which went up and down, then sleep disorder, a very strong appetite and panic attacks (Hirszfeld 2015). When the hybridised 'centaur' blood sample was extracted, it became completely clotted in ten minutes, thus showing symptoms of strong inflammation. The blood sample as such can be seen as a synecdoche of the performance, as a document of a new form of hybridisation of the performer.

This immunological experiment was followed by other performative attempts to overcome bodily boundaries. As Laval-Jeantet points out, 'After experiencing immune otherness through horse blood injection, we have become interested in eco-systemic otherness, including human and non-human animal microbiota as new milieu within which to perform' (Laval-Jeantet 2020: 158). This interest in eco-systemic exchange led to two new artistic projects which involved microscopic living matter as performance 'actors': 'May the Rain Forest Live in Me' (or 'May the Pygmy Live in Me'), and 'Holy Coli, the Mouse in Odour of Sanctity'. The first project, 'May the Rain Forest Live in Me' (starting from 2015), was inspired by the scientific discovery that Yanomami people in the Brazilian rainforest have the richest and most diverse microbiota in the world, and, consequently, the most exceptional immune system. The artist decided to approach another tribe, Pygmy, known from her previous journeys, and imagined that after grafting the same microbiota as a Pygmy, she would experience fascinating changes in her mental states: 'could I, in turn, also learn to feel the forest environment as my Pygmy friend does, thanks to the transplant of his internal ecosystem?' As it turned out, the experience was quite exceptional:

'It was followed by brutal colic, a violent eviction of this Indigenous world by my European internal ecosystem' (Laval-Jeantet 2020: 159). It seems that microbiotic multiplicity is not always a good thing and might lead to a lethal contagion; moreover, that it might be one of the reasons why people die young in this geographical location.

However, in the second project, 'Holy Coli, the Mouse in Odour of Sanctity', the transformation of the microbiota was more favourable for the host. The project aimed to transform the microbiota of a mouse with genetically modified E. coli, which made the mouse's faeces smell of violets. In this way the figure of the mouse is elevated to a certain holiness, because it is the animal that is most often used in laboratory research to save humans. Similarly, Haraway noticed this holy dimension of experimentation when describing the special case of the oncomouse, a genetically modified mouse that carries an activated oncogene and that was intentionally created to research breast cancer. In Haraway's interpretation, the oncomouse is both a scapegoat and a secular Christian figure that will be sacrificed to find a cure for breast cancer and possibly save many women – other mammal beings (Haraway 1997: 79). 'Holy Coli', then, suggests that the smell of violets potentially changes the status of the laboratory animal and restores it to its own existence. The project also suggests that in some medical or biological situations human bodies and animal bodies are interchangeable, transgressing the boundaries of the insular biological individual.

Maja Smrekar's project 'K-9_topology', in different forms and over different time periods, examines the potential hybridisation of humans and dogs. The first part of the project, the exhibition 'Ecce Canis' (2014), reproduced the smell of the hormone serotonin, which was biotechnologically extracted from the blood of the artist and her dog. This hormone defines reciprocal tolerance between humans and wolves, which were domesticated as dogs. In this respect, the smell of serotonin not only created the molecular environment for interspecies cohabitation, but also incites the spectator to become part of this process. Another attempt to create a symbiosis between the two species was the performance 'Hybrid Family' (2015–16), which took place in the Freies Museum in Berlin. During this performance the artist, using a special diet and mechanical stimulation of her breasts, produced a certain amount of colostrum, which was used to feed a puppy. In this respect, the performance questions the normative status of the heterosexual family and invites us to imagine 'unnatural' or 'aberrant' familial ties with other species. The project 'ARTE_mis' (2016–17) pushed these interspecies relationships even further by attempting to create a hybrid at a cellular level: after conducting research in the laboratory, the artist and her coworkers managed to perform in vitro 'fertilisation' of one of the artist's egg cells with her dog's somatic cell, taken from its saliva.[6] The merged cell was

---

[6] 'A reproductive cell has been in vitro enucleated in a laboratory with micromanipulators. Then it was left under a UVC light for 30 minutes, so as to achieve

maintained alive for two days; when the nutrition was stopped, it remained frozen as a molecular sculpture. Although the merged cell had no chance of developing because of large biological disparities between the two species, this frozen molecule can be seen as a virtual form of a wolf–human hybrid, which might potentially become real in the future, when (and if) the artist could legally use a dog's reproductive cells (instead of somatic cells). In this sense, the projects by Marion Laval-Jeantet and Benoît Mangin and by Maja Smrekar create chimeric or hybrid entities at a molecular level and question the dogma of bounded individual organisms.

These artistic experiments pose important biopolitical questions: to what extent can we manipulate our immune system, or microbiota, or reproductive system? To what extent can we manipulate other living beings? On the one hand, the 'actors' in these performances can be seen as being subjected to biopolitical manipulation and treated as 'bare life', in Agamben's terms. On the other hand, these experiments can be seen as a strategy to resist biopolitical power in so far as they help to overcome biological determinism, anthropocentrism and speciesism. How can we classify such entities as a blood sample containing molecules of horse and human blood, or a frozen fertilised cell containing human and dog cells? In Agamben's (2005) terms, it is a biopolitical *kairos*, a messianic promise of a different biological future. Biological *kairos* is this impossible, unthinkable moment, where life and death, animal life and human life, can be replaced interchangeably. Biological *kairos* is also a critical, decisive moment, which can involve danger for an artist, the danger of anaphylactic shock or of deadly contact. Thus, eco-immunity might look like a messianic promise of a different biological future, and might also involve the danger of lethal contagion.

---

decomposition of all DNA in the cell. The leftover membrane of enucleated reproductive cell was fused with a dog's somatic cell, isolated out of her saliva, through the process of electroporation. Since a reproductive cell "programmes" the nucleus to divide, after 7 divisions, the aggregate of 128 cells, on the 6th day, a blastocyst occures. ARTE_mis has been left to divide just up to the stage before the formation of a blastocyst. It was then frozen to −198 degrees Celzius, after a 3rd day of growth. It gets reanimated for the exhibition, with the nutrition and hormone feeding stopped, so that the cell stays frozen in time.' More about this project can be found at 'ARTE_mis', 2016–2017, https://www.majasmrekar.org/k-9-topology-artemis (accessed 1 November 2022). However, in an earlier interview the artist expressed her intention to use, not a dog's somatic cell, but dog's sperm: 'in my fourth project within the K-9_topology series, I am suggesting to inoculate in-vitro my eggs with dog sperm in order to eventually make a new species which would have better chances to survive in the very unpredictable nature of the future'. More about this can be found at Régine Debatty, 'Post-anthropocentric art. An interview with Maja Smrekar', 2016, http://we-make-money-not-art.com/post-anthropocentric-art-an-interview-with-maja-smrekar/ (accessed 1 November 2022).

## Conclusion

All of these performances imply a certain 'logic of contamination', to use Jacques Derrida's term, by establishing new experimental conditions. The performances 'May the Horse Live in Me' and 'May the Rain Forest Live in Me' by Laval-Jeantet created conditions under which the artist's body and her immune system became the place of negotiations with other species. The artistic and experiential practices created new conditions of immune (re)cognition. In a similar manner, the performance 'Holy Coli' by Laval-Jeantet, and Maja Smrekar's performance series 'K-9_topology', invented an experimental space where human and animal bodies became interchangeable. In both cases the immune system was expected to function not as a defensive mechanism protecting the 'self' from the contagious 'other', but as an ecological network expressing the relationships between the organism and the environment.

These examples shape the model of ecological immunity based on the (re)cognition of beneficial interspecies exchanges. In this respect, the functioning of the immune system is similar to the functioning of an autopoietic system: on the one hand, the immune system has to keep the organism's 'identity', its smooth functioning and internal organisation; on the other hand, to remain what it is, it has constantly to negotiate its boundaries and connect to its environment. In this sense, immunity necessarily involves a certain immune-knowledge, the investigation and cognition of other beings. However, to know these other beings, the immune system has to incorporate them, to introduce them in the form of an antigen that is recognised by a specific antibody. Hence, immunity is an open and changing network, incorporating and negotiating otherness.

The fact that immunity can be induced artificially makes it conceptually isomorphic to the practices of bioart: bioart creates unique conditions that help to establish 'structural couplings' with other species and in this way induce them into our environment. Thus, the artistic practices discussed above work in a similar way to the practices of vaccination: they introduce a certain part of a foreign element and force the performer to cope with it, to accept it as a part of its autopoietic system. Instead of explaining these interactions in terms of symbiosis, we can interpret them as the interaction between different autopoietic systems, which maintain their integrity but simultaneously are open to structural changes.

# Conclusion: Organism-Oriented Ontology

After examining different authors and approaches, what can we say about the ontological status of organisms? Even if the answer to this question might seem obvious to a biologist, it is not clear what place organisms occupy in contemporary philosophy. As we know, the discussion about organisms appeared in Kant's *Critique of the Power of Judgement* and has taken on different configurations during the recent history of philosophy. As Hui suggests, 'Kant's *Critique of Judgment* imposes the organic as the condition of philosophizing, which is to say that for any philosophy to be, it has to be organic' (Hui 2021: 16). But what does it mean that philosophy has to be organic? An organic form of thinking continued in the early twentieth century in the works of Whitehead and Bergson, and also became prominent in the later twentieth century, where it manifested itself in systems theory, process philosophy and cybernetics (Hui 2021: 54). As we have seen, the organic condition continues to be a preoccupation in the philosophies of Simondon, Ruyer, Deleuze and Guattari, and also takes new turns in the works of contemporary thinkers such as Stiegler, Malabou, Latour and Haraway. In one way or another, these thinkers reveal the organic as a condition of philosophy and thus can be seen as precursors to organism-oriented ontology. Rather than concentrating on individuals and identities, contemporary philosophy is more and more interested in processes, developments, entanglements and changes; in other words, it is defined by organic features and conditions. It was Kant, again, who found that a biological model of epigenesis could be useful for theoretical thinking because it opens the possibility of imagining 'pure reason' as an organic system that is self-organising, self-maintaining, creative and unpredictable.

Now, in retrospect, we can say that all the authors discussed in this book take some specific features characteristic of organic beings and make them the centre of their philosophy. The first feature, shared by all authors, is processuality: the idea that processes and individuations have ontological priority over formed individuals. In this respect, Simondon's insight that physical, biological, psychosocial and technical entities develop in an analogous way is very important. Simondon clearly demonstrates that the organic condition can be extrapolated towards other systems. Although the crystal, and physical individuation in general, cannot achieve an organism's flexibility, other systems, such as the psychosocial and technological, express a certain organic creativity. The inventor's imagination (discussed by Simondon) or the brain's organisation (examined by Deleuze and Malabou) express a certain biological plasticity and unpredictability, which is generated by its organic materiality. Similarly, technology changes and develops throughout the interaction with its inventor and the associated milieu. Both Stiegler's organology and Hui's cosmotechnics, and the theory of Gaia (examined by Lovelock, Margulis, Latour and Stengers), reveal the continuity between nature and technology. Smart technologies and the development of AI provide more and more evidence that technologies are becoming organic, and create huge organisms in which we live.

Processuality is closely related to another feature of organism-oriented ontology – that of potentiality. To develop means to actualise those virtual or 'embryonic' qualities that are perfectly real but still waiting in an abstract form. However, this does not imply that virtual or potential features are determined in advance; there is no place for preformationism. Rather, virtuality or potentiality, present in every living being, can be actualised through divergent and differentiating lines, through multiple encounters with the milieu. These encounters, as demonstrated in the last chapter, are not necessarily beneficial, but might be destructive and damaging. Therefore, the potentiality leading to growth and creation is, at the same time, an impotentiality leading to impoverishment and depletion. As Agamben argues, commenting on Aristotle's famous passage, 'all potentiality is impotentiality of the same and with respect to the same' (Agamben 1999: 182). Beings, which are capable of potentiality, are equally capable of their own impotentiality. In this sense, Deleuze and Malabou clearly demonstrate that ontogenetic development means not only the augmentation, expansion and prosperity of forms, but, at the same time, their explosion, impoverishment and degradation. In this respect, organism-oriented ontology can be distinguished from all orders of cybernetics, which promise the increasing efficiency of recursive operations. By contrast, organisms not only increase their potentiality, but also move towards impotentiality, finally reaching annihilation and death.

Processuality is also closely related to multiplicity. The notion of multiplicity has two meanings. First, multiplicity means that an organism develops in a multi-phased way, and, in this sense, it constantly differs *from itself*. In this context an organism as a multiplicity can be defined as virtual potential, which may increase or augment its potential, and, at the same time, may gravitate towards its destruction or annihilation. Second, multiplicity means that an organism contains multiple differences *in itself*. It is an actual multiplicity, which makes linkages and connections between different parts. However, what is important to stress is that multiplicities or assemblages are not identities, and their parts are not subsumed into totalities or wholes. As DeLanda explains, even biological organisms are assemblages: 'Conceiving an organism as an assemblage implies that despite the tight integration between its component organs, the relations between them are not logically necessary but only contingently obligatory' (DeLanda 2006: 11–12). In other words, conceiving of an organism as an assemblage means that, first, it is defined by relations of exteriority which imply a certain autonomy for the terms to which they relate; and, second, these relations are not necessary, but contingent, being the result of their coevolution. Such reconceptualisation of an organism allows us to include in its definition a holobiont, which relates several biological entities into one symbiotic assemblage. It also embraces organological entities, which connect biological organisms and tools, humans and machines, or machines and natural environments. It also includes the planetary Gaia, which interrelates biological and atmospheric multiplicities. In this respect, an organism-oriented ontology creates a continuous milieu for organisms, animal species, technologies and the planet.

And yet how does this organic condition of philosophising relate to the human subject? The problematic of the human individual does not disappear; however, attempts to reconceptualise the notion of cognition can change the position of humans in the continuum of living beings. Cognition can be attributed not only to humans but also to micro-organisms, animals, technological systems and the planet. It was Ruyer who argued that every organising activity, from atoms and molecules to more complex organisms, is a primary consciousness. All other forms of consciousness, characteristic of animals with motor schema, or of humans with reflective consciousness, derive from this primary form. Thus, primary consciousness is a forming activity that describes not only organisms, but also inorganic entities. This does not mean that Ruyer is advocating a kind of vitalism, or is trying simply to expand organic features to physical entities. Rather, he asserts the idea that a certain formative activity is schematically common to molecules, organisms and consciousness. In other words, this formative activity *is* consciousness. The human brain has no monopoly over consciousness, but rather it is participating in this common structuring activity.

Ruyer proposes the theory of forms which enable a certain continuity between inorganic entities, organic beings and reflective consciousness. Similarly, Damasio asserts a continuity between different forms of 'self', which form a continuous organismic unit. In this respect, Damasio's theory questions the mind–body divide. The most basic form of auto-affectivity is the 'proto-self', which is in the background of all organic processes. The 'proto-self' is 'the feeling of what happens' within the body, which provides both organismic and mental auto-affection. This means that the nervous system and the brain are not the only providers of mental phenomena because they are deeply rooted in non-nervous structures of organisms. 'Neural and non-neural structures and processes are not just contiguous but *continuous* partners, interactively [. . .] In plain talk, brains and bodies are in the same mind-enabling soup' (Damasio 2018: 240, emphasis in original). Malabou also examines this cerebral auto-affectivity, which she names the cerebral unconscious. In contrast to Damasio, who asserts that an organism, a nervous system and a brain are continuously interconnected by homeostatic recursivity, Malabou considers the rupture between cerebral auto-affection and subjective auto-affection, observed in such cases as neurodegenerative diseases or brain lesions. Cerebral auto-affection and subjective auto-affection might break apart, but that does not devalue the ontological status of these organisms, even if they cannot reconnect to themselves. This is a very important biopolitical implication – to ascribe a certain value or dignity to those bodies that are in a state of impotentiality, but that are still very much alive while they are moving towards their annihilation.

The notion of cognition, which can now be extended not only to human subjects but also to non-human animals, enables the invention of new configurations of subjectivity. Ruyer's concept of primary consciousness, Damasio's idea of the 'proto-self' and Malabou's idea of the cerebral unconscious – all these insights outline multiple processual subjectivities that run through human and non-human bodies, but which are not appropriated by any individual subject. As Brian Massumi points out,

> there should be no illusions that the mental power of processual subjectivity resides in a 'mind' (individual or collective). It is a subjectivity not only without an efficient cause behind it, but without a subject behind it either. The mental power of this processual *subjectivity-without-a-subject* may be considered spiritual, if by that is simply meant intensely, relationally enlivening. (Massumi 2014: 41, emphasis in original)

This subjectivity-without-a-subject is reflected in Massumi's concept of 'bare activity', which he invents following Ruyer's notion of forming activity. 'Bare activity' designates processual subjectivity that cannot be captured by any atomised individual, and that cannot reach any final cause or goal. On the one hand, this 'bare activity' is indeterminate and vague, lacking boundaries and determination; on the other hand, this indetermination allows it to resist biopolitical power and control. If biopolitical power functions by creating boundaries and hierarchies that lead to inclusions and exclusions, then processual subjectivity can be seen as an antidote to biopolitics because it is indeterminate, plastic and mutually inclusive.

Another aspect of this reconfigured notion of subjectivity is that cognition can be associated not only with human and non-human 'selves', but also with computational machines. Hui clearly demonstrated that the reflective 'self' conceptualised in German idealist philosophy might be compared with the recursivity of smart machines. In her recent works Malabou (2019; 2023) even argues that there are no clear criteria to distinguish between the 'subjective self' of the human mind and the 'technological self' of AI. She argues that AI does not simply 'imitate' the human brain, but, through this imitation, relates to its own 'technological self'. In this respect, there is a clear continuity between human intelligence and artificial intelligence. This idea also appears in N. Katherine Hayles's works, where she discusses the notion of non-human cognition, which embraces the cognitive capacities of biological, human and technological entities. According to Hayles, the great divide is not between humans and non-humans, but between cognisers and non-cognisers (Hayles 2017: 30). Cognition is a process of meaning-making which relates different kinds of cognisers – organs, organisms, animals, human brains and technologies – to their milieus. This makes cognition fundamentally different from the purely quantitative information described by Shannon and Wiener (Hayles and Sampson 2018: 66). The cognitive relationship with the milieu is not adaptive but rather creative and world-changing. Organisms are manipulating their milieu in such a way as to make the world more amenable for living.

This new organism-oriented approach allows us to tackle such persisting political problems as the question of the Anthropocene. On the one hand, the recent debates about the Anthropocene seem important because they draw our attention to the conditions that make our planet less and less suitable for living. On the other hand, we can ask to what extent the Anthropocene itself, as a discursive and visual apparatus, is trying to outsource responsibility for climate change to some fictitious Anthropos (Demos 2017: 17). The notion of the Anthropos is a dangerous fiction because it brings back the 'universal man'. It is as if the urgency of the approaching catastrophe allows us to wipe away all the theoretical efforts of postcolonial and feminist criticism to differentiate and define every condition. Another problem is that Anthropocene discourse is often associated with geo-engineering, which suggests solving the problem of climate change with the help of quantitative solutions. A good contrast to the quantitative discourse of the Anthropocene is Gaia theory. Gaia is a planetary cognition based on the complex knowledge of organisms that know how to endure and survive.

Organism-oriented ontology not only resituates the question of the Anthropocene but also allows resistance to biopolitical manipulation and control. As Malabou suggests, resistance to the biopolitical instrumentalisation of the living being might emerge from the potentiality of the living being itself. It is the capacity of living beings to self-organise, self-generate and change that might help them to evade the control of biopower. An organism, as was discussed earlier, is capable both of maintaining itself, and of transforming itself and the environment. Organisms are open for entanglements, interactions and symbiotic couplings. However, an organism-oriented ontology does not imply an organismic or vitalist philosophy; organisms are assemblages that include within themselves both inorganic materials and organological forms such as tools and machines. Organisms are plastic materialities that allow us to reconsider all these posthuman conditions in which we live. By conceptualising symbionts and holobionts, hybrids and chimeras as ontological conditions, we resist the biopolitical demand to differentiate, classify and decide which forms of life are worth living. In this respect, organism-oriented ontology is mutually inclusive, sharing ontological value with the cognisers of other species, those that are living and those that have become extinct. It also gives ontological weight to all conditions of human life, including trauma, disability, illness, decomposition and death. It also includes technologies, which are understood not as something external and hostile, but as extended projections of our internal organs and organisms. Let us hope that creativity, contingency and potential for change – the characteristics of organism-oriented ontology – enable us to evade the grip of biopolitical and anthropo-political power and create more liveable conditions for the future.

# Bibliography

Agamben, Giorgio. 1999. *Potentialities: Collected Essays in Philosophy*, trans. Daniel Heller-Roazen, Stanford, CA: Stanford University Press.
Agamben, Giorgio. 2005. *The Time That Remains: A Commentary on the Letter to the Romans*, trans. Patricia Dailey, Stanford, CA: Stanford University Press.
Allen, Barry. 2019. 'Unnatural Nuptials', in Michael James Bennett and Tano S. Posteraro (eds), *Deleuze and Evolutionary Theory*, Edinburgh: Edinburgh University Press, pp. 23–41.
Ameisen, Jean-Claude. 1999. *La sculpture du vivant: La suicide cellulair ou la mort créatrice*, Paris: Seuil.
Ansell Pearson, Keith. 1999. *Germinal Life: The Difference and Repetition of Deleuze*, London: Routledge.
Bains, Paul. 2002. 'Subjectless Subjectivities', in Brian Massumi (ed.), *A Shock to Thought: Expression After Deleuze and Guattari*, London: Routledge, pp. 101–16.
Barad, Karen. 2007. *Meeting the Universe Halfway: Quantum Physics and the Entanglement of Matter and Meaning*, Durham, NC: Duke University Press.
Bennett, Jane. 2010. *Vibrant Matter: A Political Ecology of Things*, Durham, NC: Duke University Press.
Bennett, Michael James, and Tano S. Posteraro (eds). 2019. *Deleuze and Evolutionary Theory*, Edinburgh: Edinburgh University Press.
Bertalanffy, Ludwig von. 1968. *General Systems Theory: Essays on its Foundation and Development*, New York: George Braziller.
Bhandar, Brenna, and Jonathan Goldberg-Hiller (eds). 2015. *Plastic Materialities: Politics, Legality, and Metamorphosis in the Work of Catherine Malabou*, Durham, NC: Duke University Press.
Bianchi, Diana W., Gretchen K. Zickwolf, Gary J. Weil, Shelley Sylvester and Mary Ann DeMaria. 1996. 'Male Fetal Progenitor Cells Persist in Maternal Blood for as Long as 27 Years Post-partum', *Proceedings of the National Academy of Sciences USA*, 93(2), pp. 705–8. https://doi.org/10.1073/pnas.93.2.705
Bogue, Ronald. 2009. 'Raymond Ruyer', in Graham Jones and Jon Roffe

(eds), *Deleuze's Philosophical Lineage*, Edinburgh: Edinburgh University Press, pp. 300–20.

Bogue, Ronald. 2017. 'The Force that Is but Does Not Act: Ruyer, Leibniz and Deleuze', *Deleuze Studies*, 11(4), pp. 518–37.

Bowden, Sean. 2012. 'Gilles Deleuze, a Reader of Gilbert Simondon', in Arne De Boever, Alex Murray, Jon Roffe and Ashley Woodward (eds), *Gilbert Simondon: Being and Technology*, Edinburgh: Edinburgh University Press, pp. 135–53.

Bryant, Levi R. 2011. *The Democracy of Objects*, Ann Arbor, MI: Open Humanities Press.

Canguilhem, Georges. 1947. 'Note sur la situation faite en France à la philosophie biologique', *Revue de métaphysique et de morale*, 52(3), pp. 322–32.

Canguilhem, Georges. 2008. 'Machine and Organism', in Georges Canguilhem, *Knowledge of Life*, ed. Paola Marrati and Todd Meyers, trans. Stefanos Geroulanos and Daniela Ginsburg, New York: Fordham University Press, pp. 75–97.

Capra, Fritjof. 1997. *The Web of Life: A New Synthesis of Life and Matter*, London: Flamingo.

Capra, Fritjof, and Pier Luigi Luisi. 2014. *The Systems View of Life: A Unifying Vision*, Cambridge: Cambridge University Press.

Changeux, Jean-Pierre. 1985. *Neuronal Man: The Biology of Mind*, trans. Laurence Garet, New York: Parthenon Books.

Changeux, Jean-Pierre, Philippe Courrége and Antoine Danchin. 1973. 'A Theory of the Epigenesis of Neuronal Networks by Selective Stabilization of Synapses', *Proceedings of the National Academy of Sciences USA*, 70(10), pp. 2974–8. https://doi.org/10.1073/pnas.70.10.2974

Changeux, Jean-Pierre, and Paul Ricoeur. 2002. *What Makes Us Think? A Neuroscientist and a Philosopher Argue about Ethics, Human Nature, and the Brain*, trans. M. B. DeBevoise, Princeton, NJ: Princeton University Press.

Clarke, Bruce. 2012. 'Autopoiesis and the Planet', in Henry Sussman (ed.), *Impasses of the Post-Global: Theory in the Era of Climate Change*, Ann Arbor, MI: Open Humanities Press, pp. 58–75.

Clarke, Bruce. 2017. 'Rethinking Gaia: Stengers, Latour, Margulis', *Theory, Culture & Society*, 34(4), pp. 3–26.

Clarke, Bruce. 2020. *Gaian Systems: Lynn Margulis, Neocybernetics, and the End of the Anthropocene*, Minneapolis, MN: University of Minnesota Press.

Colonna, Fabrice. 2007. *Ruyer*, Paris: Les belles lettres.

Combes, Muriel. 2013. *Gilbert Simondon and the Philosophy of the Transindividual*, trans. Thomas LaMarre, Cambridge, MA: MIT Press.

Crutzen, Paul J. 2002. 'Geology of Mankind', *Nature*, 415, p. 23. https://doi.org/10.1038/415023a

Crutzen, Paul J., and Eugene F. Stoermer. 2000. 'The "Anthropocene"', *Global Change Newsletter*, no. 41, pp. 17–18. http://www.igbp.net/download/18.316f18321323470177580001401/1376383088452/NL41.pdf (accessed 4 November 2022).

Damasio, Antonio. 1999. *The Feeling of What Happens: Body, Emotion and the Making of Consciousness*, London: Vintage.
Damasio, Antonio. 2018. *The Strange Order of Things: Life, Feeling, and the Making of Cultures*, New York: Pantheon.
De Boever, Arne, Alex Murray, Jon Roffe and Ashley Woodward (eds). 2012. *Gilbert Simondon: Being and Technology*, Edinburgh: Edinburgh University Press.
Debatty, Regine. 2016. 'Post-anthropocentric Art. An Interview with Maja Smrekar'. http://we-make-money-not-art.com/post-anthropocentric-art-an-interview-with-maja-smrekar/ (accessed 4 November 2022).
DeLanda, Manuel. 2002. *Intensive Science and Virtual Philosophy*, London: Continuum.
DeLanda, Manuel. 2006. *A New Philosophy of Society: Assemblage Theory and Social Complexity*, London: Bloomsbury.
DeLanda, Manuel. 2016. *Assemblage Theory*, Edinburgh: Edinburgh University Press.
Deleuze, Gilles. 1997. *Essays Critical and Clinical*, trans. Daniel W. Smith and Michael A. Greco, Minneapolis, MN: University of Minnesota Press.
Deleuze, Gilles. 2001. 'Review of Gilbert Simondon's *L'individu et sa genèse physico-biologique* (1966)', *Pli: The Warwick Journal of Philosophy*, 12, pp. 43–9.
Deleuze, Gilles. 2004a. *Difference and Repetition*, trans. Paul Patton, London: Continuum.
Deleuze, Gilles. 2004b. *The Logic of Sense*, ed. Constantin V. Boundas, trans. Mark Lester and Charles Stivale, London: Continuum.
Deleuze, Gilles. 2004c. 'The Method of Dramatization', in Gilles Deleuze, *Desert Islands and Other Texts 1953–1974*, ed. David Lapoujade, trans. Michael Taormina, Los Angeles: Semiotext(e), pp. 94–116.
Deleuze, Gilles. 2004d. 'On Gilbert Simondon', in Gilles Deleuze, *Desert Islands and Other Texts 1953–1974*, ed. David Lapoujade, trans. Michael Taormina, Los Angeles: Semiotext(e), pp. 86–9.
Deleuze, Gilles. 2005. 'Immanence: A Life', in Gilles Deleuze, *Pure Immanence: Essays on Life*, trans. Anna Boyman, New York: Zone Books, pp. 25–33.
Deleuze, Gilles. 2006a. *Foucault*, trans. Sean Hand, London: Continuum.
Deleuze, Gilles. 2006b. *The Fold: Leibniz and the Baroque*, trans. Tom Conley, London: Continuum.
Deleuze, Gilles, and Félix Guattari. 1994. *What is Philosophy?*, trans. Graham Burchell and Hugh Tomlinson, London: Verso.
Deleuze, Gilles, and Félix Guattari. 2004. *A Thousand Plateaus: Capitalism and Schizophrenia*, trans. Brian Massumi, London: Continuum.
Demos, T. J. 2017. *Against the Anthropocene: Visual Culture and Environment Today*, Berlin: Sternberg.
Dempster, M. Beth. 2000. 'Sympoietic and Autopoietic Systems: A New Distinction for Self-Organizing Systems'. https://www.semanticscholar.org/paper/SYMPOIETIC-AND-AUTOPOIETIC-SYSTEMS%3A

-A-NEW-FOR-Dempster/44299317a20afcd33b0a11d3b2bf4fc196088d45 (accessed 4 November 2022).
Derrida, Jacques. 1974. *Of Grammatology*, trans. Gayatri Chakravorty Spivak, Baltimore, MD: Johns Hopkins University Press.
Despret, Vinciane. 2016. *What Would Animals Say If We Asked the Right Questions?*, trans. Brett Buchanan, Minneapolis, MN: University of Minnesota Press.
Downey, Georgina. 2018. 'Becoming-horse: Jenny Watson, Art Orienté Objet and Berlinde De Bruyckere', *Artlink Magazine*, 38(1). https://www.artlink.com.au/articles/4657/becoming-horse-jenny-watson-art-orient C3A9-objet-and-/ (accessed 4 November 2022).
Driesch, Hans. 2020 [1908]. *The Science and Philosophy of the Organism*, Frankfurt am Main: Outlook.
Espinas, Alfred. 1897. *Les origines de la technologie*, Paris: Alcan.
Esposito, Roberto. 2011. *Immunitas: The Protection and Negation of Life*, trans. Zakiya Hanafi, Cambridge: Polity.
Favre, Alexandre, Henri Guitton, Jean Guitton, Andre Lichnerowic and Étienne Wolff. 1988. *De la causalité à la finalité. A propos de la turbulence*, Paris: Maloine.
Gane, Nicholas. 2006. 'When We Have Never Been Human, What Is to Be Done? Interview with Donna Haraway', *Theory, Culture & Society*, 23(7–8), pp. 135–58. https://doi.org/10.1177/0263276406069228
Gilbert, Scott. F. 2017. 'Holobiont by Birth: Multilineage Individuals as the Concretion of Cooperative Processes', in Anna Tsing, Heather Swanson, Elaine Gan and Nils Bubandt (eds), *Arts of Living on a Damaged Planet*, Minneapolis, MN: University of Minnesota Press, pp. 73–89.
Gilbert, Scott F., Jan Sapp and Alfred I. Tauber. 2012. 'A Symbiotic View of Life: We Have Never Been Individuals', *The Quarterly Review of Biology*, 87(4), pp. 325–41. https://doi.org/10.1086/668166
Gilbert, Scott F., and Sahotra Sarkar. 2000. 'Embracing Complexity: Organicism for the 21st Century', *Developmental Dynamics*, 219(1), pp. 1–9. https://doi.org/10.1002/1097-0177(2000)9999:9999<::AID-DVDY1036>3.0.CO;2-A
Grosz, Elizabeth. 2012a. 'Deleuze, Ruyer and Becoming-Brain: The Music of Life's Temporality', *Parrhesia*, 15, pp. 1–13.
Grosz, Elizabeth. 2012b. 'Identity and Individuation: Some Feminist Reflections', in Arne De Boever, Alex Murray, Jon Roffe and Ashley Woodward (eds), *Gilbert Simondon: Being and Technology*, Edinburgh: Edinburgh University Press, pp. 37–56.
Grosz, Elizabeth. 2017. *The Incorporeal: Ontology, Ethics, and the Limits of Materialism*, New York: Columbia University Press.
Grusin, Richard. 2015. 'Introduction', in Richard Grusin (ed.), *The Nonhuman Turn*, Minneapolis, MN: University of Minnesota Press, pp. vii–xxix.
Guattari, Félix. 1993. 'Machinic Heterogenesis', in Verena Andermatt

Conley (ed.), *Rethinking Technologies*, Minneapolis, MN: University of Minnesota Press, pp. 13–27.

Hansen, Mark B. N. 2009. 'System-Environment Hybrids', in Bruce Clarke and Mark B. N. Hansen (eds), *Emergence and Embodiment: New Essays on Second-Order Systems Theory*, Durham, NC: Duke University Press, pp. 113–42.

Hansen, Mark B. N. 2016. 'Introduction: Form and Phenomenon in Raymond Ruyer's Philosophy', in Raymond Ruyer, *Neofinalism*, trans. Alyosha Edlebi, Minneapolis, MN: University of Minnesota Press, pp. vii–xxi.

Haraway, Donna J. 1995. 'Cyborgs and Symbionts: Living Together in the New World Order', in Chris Hables Grey, Steven Mentor and Heidi J. Figueroa-Sarriera (eds), *The Cyborg Handbook*, New York: Routledge, pp. xi–xx.

Haraway, Donna J. 1997. *Modest_Witness@Second_Millenium.FemanleMan_Meets_OncoMouse: Feminism and Technoscience*, London: Routledge.

Haraway, Donna J. 2004 [1976]. *Crystals, Fabrics, and Fields: Metaphors That Shape Embryos*, Berkeley, CA: North Atlantic Books.

Haraway, Donna J. 2008. *When Species Meet*, Minneapolis, MN: University of Minnesota Press.

Haraway, Donna J. 2013 [1989]. 'The Biopolitics of Postmodern Bodies: Constitutions of Self in Immune System Discourse', in Timothy Campbell and Adam Sitze (eds), *Biopolitics: A Reader*, Durham, NC: Duke University Press, pp. 274–309.

Haraway, Donna J. 2015. 'Anthropocene, Capitalocene, Plantationocene, Chthulucene: Making Kin', *Environmental Humanities* 6(1), pp. 159–65. https://doi.org/10.1215/22011919-3615934

Haraway, Donna J. 2016. *Staying with the Trouble: Making Kin in the Chthulucene*, Durham, NC: Duke University Press.

Haraway, Donna J. 2017. 'Symbiogenesis, Sympoiesis, and Art Science Activism for Staying with the Trouble', in Anna Tsing, Heather Swanson, Elaine Gan and Nils Bubandt (eds), *Arts of Living on a Damaged Planet*, Minneapolis, MN: University of Minnesota Press, pp. 25–50.

Harding, Stephan. 2014. 'Daisyworld', in Fritjof Capra and Pier Luigi Luisi (eds), *The Systems View of Life: A Unifying Vision*, Cambridge: Cambridge University Press, pp. 166–8.

Hayles, N. Katherine. 2017. *Unthought: The Power of the Cognitive Nonconscious*, Chicago: University of Chicago Press.

Hayles, N. Katherine, and Tony D. Sampson. 2018. 'Unthought Meets the Assemblage Brain: A Dialogue between N. Katherine Hayles and Tony D. Sampson', *Capacious: Journal of Emerging Affect Inquiry*, 1(2), pp. 60–84. https://doi.org/10.22387/CAP2018.14

Heidegger, Martin. 1976. 'Das Ende der Philosophie und die Aufgabe des Denkens', in Martin Heidegger, *Zur Sache des Denkens*, Tübingen: Max Niemeyer, pp. 61–80.

Hirszfeld, Aleksandra. 2015. 'May the Horse Live in Me (interview with *Art Orienté Objet*)', in Piotr Zawojski (ed), *Klasyczne dzieła sztuki nowych mediów*, Katowice, pp. 174–80.
Hui, Yuk. 2016. *On the Existence of Digital Objects*, Minneapolis, MN: University of Minnesota Press.
Hui, Yuk. 2017. 'On Cosmotechnics: For a Renewed Relation between Technology and Nature in the Anthropocene', *Techné: Research in Philosophy and Technology*, 21(2–3), pp. 319–41. https://doi.org/10.5840/techne201711876
Hui, Yuk. 2019. *Recursivity and Contingency*, New York: Rowman and Littlefield.
Hui, Yuk. 2021. *Art and Cosmotechnics*, Minneapolis, MN: University of Minnesota Press (e-flux).
Husserl, Edmund. 1964. *The Phenomenology of Internal Time-Consciousness*, ed. Martin Heidegger, trans. James S. Churchill, Bloomington, IN: Indiana University Press.
Jeannerod, Marc. 2002. *Le cerveau intime*, Paris: Odile Jacob.
Kant, Immanuel. 1998. *Critique of Pure Reason (The Cambridge Edition of the Works of Immanuel Kant)*, ed. and trans. Paul Guyer and Allen W. Wood, Cambridge: Cambridge University Press.
Kant, Immanuel. 2000. *Critique of the Power of Judgement (The Cambridge Edition of the Works of Immanuel Kant)*, ed. Paul Guyer, trans. Paul Guyer and Eric Matthews, Cambridge: Cambridge University Press.
Kapp, Ernst. 1877. *Grundlinien einer Philosophie der Technik*, Braunschweig: Georg Westermann.
Latour, Bruno. 2005. *Reassembling the Social: An Introduction to Actor-Network-Theory*, Oxford: Oxford University Press.
Latour, Bruno. 2017a. *Facing Gaia: Eight Lectures on the New Climatic Regime*, trans. Catherine Porter, Cambridge: Polity.
Latour, Bruno. 2017b. 'Why Gaia is not a God of Totality', *Theory, Culture, & Society*, 34(2–3), pp. 61–81. https://doi.org/10.1177/0263276416652700
Latour, Bruno. 2018. *Down to Earth: Politics in the New Climatic Regime*, trans. Catherine Porter, Cambridge: Polity.
Laval-Jeantet, Marion. 2020. 'Art and the Microbiome: New Places for Microperformativity in the Work of Art Orienté Objet', *Performance Research*, 25(3), pp. 158–63. https://doi.org/10.1080/13528165.2020.1807778
Le Blanc, Guillaume. 2010. *Canguilhem et le vie humaine*, Paris: PUF.
Leroi-Gourhan, André. 1945. *Milieu et techniques*, Paris: Albin Michel.
Leroi-Gourhan, André. 1993. *Gesture and Speech*, trans. Anna Bostock Berger. Cambridge, MA: MIT Press.
Lovelock, James. 1972. 'Gaia as Seen Through the Atmosphere', *Atmospheric Environment*, 6, pp. 579–80.
Lovelock, James. 2000. *Gaia: The Practical Science of Planetary Medicine*, Oxford: Oxford University Press.

Lovelock, James. 2016 [1982]. *Gaia: A New Look at Life on Earth*, Oxford: Oxford University Press.
Lovink, Geert. 2019. 'Cybernetics for the Twenty-First Century: An Interview with Philosopher Yuk Hui', *e-flux*, 102. https://www.e-flux.com/journal/102/282271/cybernetics-for-the-twenty-first-century-an-interview-with-philosopher-yuk-hui/ (accessed 5 November 2022).
Luhmann, Niklas. 1990. 'Autopoiesis of Social Systems', in Niklas Luhmann, *Essays on Self-Reference*, New York: Columbia University Press, pp. 1–20.
Luhmann, Niklas. 1995. *Social Systems*, trans. John Bednarz, Jr and Dirk Baecker, Stanford, CA: Stanford University Press.
Magner, Lois N. n.d. 'Developments in Embryology'. https://www.encyclopedia.com/science/encyclopedias-almanacs-transcripts-and-maps/developments-embryology (accessed 5 November 2022).
Malabou, Catherine. 2005. *The Future of Hegel: Plasticity, Temporality, and Dialectic*, trans. Lisabeth During, London: Routledge.
Malabou, Catherine. 2008. *What Should We Do with Our Brain?*, trans. Sebastian Rand, New York: Fordham University Press.
Malabou, Catherine. 2012a. *The New Wounded: From Neurosis to Brain Damage*, trans. Steven Miller, New York: Fordham University Press.
Malabou, Catherine. 2012b. *Ontology of the Accident: An Essay on Destructive Plasticity*, trans. Carolyn Shread, Cambridge: Polity.
Malabou, Catherine. 2015. 'Will Sovereignty Ever Be Deconstructed?', in Brenna Bhandar and Jonathan Goldberg-Hiller (eds), *Plastic Materialities: Politics, Legality, and Metamorphosis in the Work of Catherine Malabou*, Durham, NC: Duke University Press, pp. 35–46.
Malabou, Catherine. 2016a. *Before Tomorrow: Epigenesis and Rationality*, trans. Carolyn Shread, Cambridge: Polity.
Malabou, Catherine. 2016b. 'One Life Only: Biological Resistance, Political Resistance', trans. Carolyn Shread, *Critical Inquiry*, 42(3), pp. 429–38. https://doi.org/10.1086/685601
Malabou, Catherine. 2019. *Morphing Intelligence: From IQ Measurement to Artificial Brains*, trans. Carolyn Shread, New York: Columbia University Press.
Malabou, Catherine. 2023. 'Epigenetic Mimesis: Natural Brains and Synaptic Chip', in S. E. Wilmer and Audronė Žukauskaitė (eds), *Life in the Posthuman Condition: Critical Responses to the Anthropocene*, Edinburgh: Edinburgh University Press, pp. 280–8.
Margulis, Lynn. 1997. 'Big Trouble in Biology: Physiological Autopoiesis Versus Mechanistic Neo-Darwinism', in Lynn Margulis and Dorian Sagan (eds), *Slanted Truths: Essays on Gaia, Symbiosis, and Evolution*, New York: Springer, pp. 265–82.
Margulis, Lynn. 1998. *Symbiotic Planet: A New Look at Evolution*, Amherst, MA: Basic Books.
Margulis, Lynn. 2001. 'The Conscious Cell', in P. C. Marijuan (ed.), *Cajal*

*and Consciousness: Scientific Approaches to Consciousness on the Centennial of Ramon y Cajal's Textura*, New York: New York Academy of Sciences, pp. 55–70.

Margulis, Lynn, and Dorian Sagan. 1986. *Microcosmos: Four Billion Years of Evolution from Our Microbial Ancestors*, New York: Summit Books.

Margulis, Lynn, and Dorian Sagan. 2001. 'The Beast with Five Genomes', *Natural History*, 110, pp. 38–41.

Martin, Aryn. 2010. 'Microchimerism in the Mother(land): Blurring the Borders of Body and Nation', *Body & Society*, 16(3), pp. 23–50. https://doi.org/10.1177/1357034X10373404

Massumi, Brian. 2012. '"Technical Mentality" Revisited: Brian Massumi on Gilbert Simondon', in Arne De Boever, Alex Murray, Jon Roffe and Ashley Woodward (eds), *Gilbert Simondon: Being and Technology*, Edinburgh: Edinburgh University Press, pp. 19–36.

Massumi, Brian. 2014. *What Animals Teach Us about Politics*, Durham, NC: Duke University Press.

Maturana, Humberto R., and Francisco J. Varela. 1980. *Autopoiesis and Cognition: The Realization of the Living*, Dordrecht: Reidel.

Maturana, Humberto R., and Francisco J. Varela. 1998. *The Tree of Knowledge: The Biological Roots of Human Understanding*, trans. Robert Paolucci, Boulder, CO: Shambhala.

McFall-Ngai, Margaret. 2017. 'Noticing Microbial Worlds: The Postmodern Synthesis in Biology', in Anna Tsing, Heather Swanson, Elaine Gan and Nils Bubandt (eds), *Arts of Living on a Damaged Planet*, Minneapolis, MN: University of Minnesota Press, pp. 51–69.

Meillassoux, Quentin. 2008. *After Finitude: An Essay on the Necessity of Contingency*, trans. Ray Brassier, London: Continuum.

Mensch, Jennifer. 2013. *Kant's Organicism: Epigenesis and the Development of Critical Philosophy*, Chicago: University of Chicago Press.

Mills, Simon. 2016. *Gilbert Simondon: Information, Technology and Media*, New York: Rowman and Littlefield.

Moore, Jason. W. (ed.). 2016. *Anthropocene or Capitalocene: Nature, History, and the Crisis of Capitalism*, Oakland, CA: PM Press.

Onori, Luciano, and Guido Visconti. 2012. 'The GAIA Theory: From Lovelock to Margulis. From a Homeostatic to a Cognitive Autopoietic Worldview', *Rendiconti Lincei*, 23, pp. 375–86. https://doi.org/10.1007/s12210-012-0187-z

Prigogine, Ilya, and Isabelle Stengers. 1984. *Order Out of Chaos: Man's New Dialogue with Nature*, New York: Bantam.

Roffe, Jon. 2017. 'Form IV: From Ruyer's Psychobiology to Deleuze and Guattari's Socius', *Deleuze Studies*, 11(4), pp. 580–99. https://doi.org/10.3366/dls.2017.0286

Roffe, Jon. 2019. 'The Egg: Deleuze Between Darwin and Ruyer', in Michael J. Bennett and Tano S. Posteraro (eds), *Deleuze and Evolutionary Theory*, Edinburgh: Edinburgh University Press, pp. 42–58.

Ruyer, Raymond. 1966. *Paradoxes de la conscience et limites de l'automatisme*, Paris: Albin Michel.
Ruyer, Raymond. 2007. 'Raymond Ruyer par lui-même', *Les etudes philosophiques*, 80, pp. 3–14.
Ruyer, Raymond. 2016. *Neofinalism*, trans. Alyosha Edlebi, Minneapolis, MN: University of Minnesota Press.
Ruyer, Raymond. 2018. 'The Philosophy of Morphogenesis', trans. Jon Roffe and Nicholas B. de Weydenthal, *Parrhesia*, 29, pp. 1–25.
Ruyer, Raymond. 2020. *The Genesis of Living Forms*, trans. Jon Roffe and Nicholas B. de Weydenthal, New York: Rowman and Littlefield.
Ruyer, Raymond, Tano S. Posteraro and Jon Roffe. 2019. 'Instinct, Consciousness, Life: Ruyer contra Bergson', *Angelaki: Journal of the Theoretical Humanities*, 24(5), pp. 124–47. https://doi.org/10.1080/0969725X.2019.1655283
Sabolius, Kristupas. 2019. 'Traversing Life and Thought: Gilbert Simondon's Theory of Cyclic Imagination', *Social Imaginaries*, 5(2), pp. 37–57. https://doi.org/10.5840/si20195213
Sartre, Jean-Paul. 2004 [1940]. *The Imaginary: A Phenomenological Psychology of the Imagination*, trans. Jonathan Webber, London: Routledge.
Sauvagnargues, Anne. 2012a. 'Simondon, Deleuze, and the Construction of Transcendental Empiricism', *Pli: The Warwick Journal of Philosophy* (special volume: Deleuze and Simondon), pp. 1–21, https://plijournal.com/volumes/special/ (accessed 13 February 2023).
Sauvagnargues, Anne. 2012b. 'Crystals and Membranes: Individuation and Temporality', in Arne De Boever, Alex Murray, Jon Roffe and Ashley Woodward (eds), *Gilbert Simondon: Being and Technology*, Edinburgh: Edinburgh University Press, pp. 57–70.
Shildrick, Margrit. 2016. 'Chimerism and *Immunitas*: The Emergence of a Posthumanist Biophilosophy', in S. E. Wilmer and Audronė Žukauskaitė (eds), *Resisting Biopolitics: Philosophical, Political, and Performative Strategies*, Abingdon: Routledge, pp. 95–108.
Shildrick, Margrit. 2019. '(Micro)chimerism, Immunity and Temporality: Rethinking the Ecology of Life and Death', *Australian Feminist Studies*, 34(99), pp. 10–24. https://doi.org/10.1080/08164649.2019.1611527
Simondon, Gilbert. 2008. *Imagination et invention (1965–1966)*, Paris: PUF.
Simondon, Gilbert. 2009a. 'The Position of the Problem of Ontogenesis', trans. Gregory Flanders, *Parrhesia*, 1(7), pp. 4–16.
Simondon, Gilbert. 2009b. 'Technical Mentality', trans. Arne De Boever, *Parrhesia*, 1(7), pp. 17–27.
Simondon, Gilbert. 2015a. *Communication et information: Cours et conférences*, Paris: PUF.
Simondon, Gilbert. 2015b. *Sur la psychologie (1956–1967)*, Paris: PUF.
Simondon, Gilbert. 2017. *On the Mode of Existence of Technical Objects*, trans. Cécile Malaspina and John Rogove, Minneapolis, MN: Univocal Publishing.

Simondon, Gilbert. 2020a. *Individuation in Light of Notions of Form and Information*, trans. Taylor Adkins, Minneapolis, MN: University of Minnesota Press.
Simondon, Gilbert. 2020b. *Individuation in Light of Notions of Form and Information*, vol. II: *Supplemental Texts*, trans. Taylor Adkins, Minneapolis, MN: University of Minnesota Press.
Smith, Daniel W. 2012. *Essays on Deleuze*, Edinburgh: Edinburgh University Press.
Smith, Daniel W. 2017. 'Raymond Ruyer and the Metaphysics of Absolute Forms', *Parrhesia*, 27, pp. 116–28.
Smith, Daniel W. 2019. 'André Leroi-Gourhan', in Graham Jones and Jon Roffe (eds), *Deleuze's Philosophical Lineage II*, Edinburgh: Edinburgh University Press, pp. 255–74.
Spemann, Hans. 1935. 'The Organizer-Effect in Embryonic Development' (Nobel Lecture, 12 December 1935). https://www.nobelprize.org/prizes/medicine/1935/spemann/lecture/ (accessed 5 November 2022).
Spemann, Hans. 1962 [1938]. *Embryonic Development and Induction*, New York: Hafner.
Stengers, Isabelle. 2015a. *In Catastrophic Times: Resisting the Coming Barbarism*, trans. Andrew Goffey, Ann Arbor, MI: Open Humanities Press.
Stengers, Isabelle. 2015b. 'Accepting the Reality of Gaia: A Fundamental Shift?', in Clive Hamilton, Christophe Bonneuil and Francois Gemenne (eds), *The Anthropocene and the Global Environmental Crisis: Rethinking Modernity in a New Epoch*, Abingdon: Routledge, pp. 134–44.
Stiegler, Bernard. 1998. *Technics and Time, 1: The Fault of Epimetheus*, trans. Richard Beardsworth and George Collins, Stanford, CA: Stanford University Press.
Stiegler, Bernard. 2010. *For a New Critique of Political Economy*, trans. Daniel Ross, Cambridge: Polity.
Stiegler, Bernard. 2011. *Technics and Time, 3: Cinematic Time and the Question of Malaise*, trans. Stephen Barker, Stanford, CA: Stanford University Press.
Stiegler, Bernard. 2017. 'General Ecology, Economy, and Organology', trans. Daniel Ross, in Eric Hörl and James Burton (eds), *General Ecology: The New Ecological Paradigm*, London: Bloomsbury Academic, pp. 129–50.
Stiegler, Bernard. 2018. *The Neganthropocene*, trans. Daniel Ross, London: Open Humanities Press.
Tauber, Alfred I. 2017. *Immunity: The Evolution of an Idea*, Oxford: Oxford University Press.
Thompson, Evan. 2009. 'Life and Mind: From Autopoiesis to Neurophenomenology', in Bruce Clarke and Mark B. N. Hansen (eds), *Emergence and Embodiment: New Essays on Second-Order Systems Theory*, Durham, NC: Duke University Press, pp. 77–93.
Thompson, William Irwin (ed.). 1991. *Gaia 2 – Emergence: The New Science of Becoming*. Hudson, NY: Lindisfarne Press.

Toscano, Alberto. 2006. *The Theatre of Production: Philosophy and Individuation between Kant and Deleuze*, Basingstoke: Palgrave Macmillan.
Uexküll, Jakob von. 2010. *A Foray into the Worlds of Animals and Humans*, trans. Joseph D. O'Neil, Minneapolis, MN: University of Minnesota Press.
Varela, Francisco J. 1991. 'Organism: A Meshwork of Selfless Selves', in Alfred I. Tauber (ed.), *Organism and the Origin of Self*, Dordrecht: Kluwer Academic, pp. 79–107.
Varela, Francisco J., and Mark Anspach. 1991. 'Immu-knowledge: The Process of Somatic Individuation', in William Irvin Thompson (ed.), *Gaia 2 – Emergence: The New Science of Becoming*, Hudson, NY: Lindisfarne Press, pp. 68–85.
Varela, Francisco J., Humberto R. Maturana and R. Uribe. 1974. 'Autopoiesis: The Organization of Living Systems, Its Characterization and a Model', *BioSystems*, 5(4), pp. 187–96. https://doi.org/10.1016/0303-2647(74)90031-8
Varela, Francisco J., Eleanor Rosch and Evan Thompson. 1991. *The Embodied Mind: Cognitive Science and Human Experience*, Cambridge, MA: MIT Press.
Voss, Daniela. 2019. 'Invention and Capture: A Critique of Simondon', *Culture, Theory & Critique*, 60(3–4), pp. 279–99. https://doi.org/10.1080/14735784.2019.1679652
Watkin, Christopher. 2017. *French Philosophy Today: New Figures of the Human in Badiou, Meillassoux, Malabou, Serres and Latour*, Edinburgh: Edinburgh University Press.
Weinstein, Jami, and Claire Colebrook (eds). 2017. *Posthumous Life: Theorizing Beyond the Posthuman*, New York: Columbia University Press.
West-Eberhard, Mary Jane. 2003. *Developmental Plasticity and Evolution*, New York: Oxford University Press.
Wiener, Norbert. 1985 [1948]. *Cybernetics: Or Control and Communication of the Animal and the Machine*, Cambridge, MA: MIT Press.
Wiener, Norbert. 1989. *The Human Use of Human Beings: Cybernetics and Society*, London: Free Association Books.
Wolfe, Cary. 1995. 'In Search of Post-Humanist Theory: The Second-Order Cybernetics of Maturana and Varela', *Cultural Critique*, 30, pp. 33–70.
Wolfe, Cary. 2010. *What Is Posthumanism?*, Minneapolis, MN: University of Minnesota Press.
Wolfe, Cary. 2020. 'What "The Animal" Can Teach "The Anthropocene?"', *Angelaki: Journal of the Theoretical Humanities*, 25(3), pp. 131–45. https://doi.org/10.1080/0969725X.2020.1754033
Wolfe, Cary. 2023. 'Jagged Ontologies in the Anthropocene, or, the Five Cs', in S. E. Wilmer and Audronė Žukauskaitė (eds), *Life in the Posthuman Condition: Critical Responses to the Anthropocene*, Edinburgh: Edinburgh University Press, pp. 195–221.

# Index

absolute form, 40–1, 43, 48, 52–5
absolute survey, 50, 52–4; *see also* self-survey
Actor-Network Theory, 123, 126–7
actual and virtual, 57, 59, 61, 63–6, 75
actualisation, 59–61, 63–4; *see also* counter-actualisation
adaptation, 7, 28, 113
affect, 7, 32, 34, 66, 69, 71, 74, 86–7
   auto-affection, 77, 86–8, 154–5
   auto-affectivity, 72, 85, 87–8, 154–5
Agamben, Giorgio, 76, 150, 153
allagmatic, 30
allopoietic, 7, 10, 129–30
analogical paradigmatism, 15, 19, 23, 55, 59, 106
Anthropocene, 11, 13–14, 110, 113–15, 128n, 132, 138, 156
anticipation, 35–6, 103–4, 108, 111
Art Orienté Objet, 147
assemblage, 1, 4, 10, 12–15, 17, 65–71, 125, 130, 134–6, 138–9, 141, 146, 153–4, 156
associated milieu, 99–100, 107, 112, 114, 153
autopoiesis, 2, 6–7, 9–11, 14, 17, 30–1, 55, 115, 118–23, 126–32, 135–6, 143

Bergson, Henri, 3, 16, 59, 63, 97–8, 106n, 152
Bertalanffy, Ludwig von, 4, 5, 108n
biopolitics, 1, 18, 95, 139, 155
biopower, 1–3, 95, 156

body without organs, 14, 65–8, 71, 74–5, 135
brain, 7–9, 15–17, 39–40, 45–6, 50, 53–5, 57, 71–5, 77–88, 90, 93, 106, 111–12, 119, 121, 143, 154–6

Canguilhem, Georges, 16, 38, 96–8, 106n
causality, 2, 7–8, 46, 92, 94, 99, 100–1, 109, 113, 127
   cause and effect, 2–3, 7–8, 39, 64, 95, 120, 125
   final cause, 7, 39, 44, 155
cerebral unconscious, 16, 77, 86, 88, 155
chronology, 30
closure, 6, 10, 45–6, 120–2, 127, 131
   operational closure, 6, 10–11, 30, 120
cognition, 7–9, 17–18, 30, 36–7, 50, 52, 53–6, 63, 73–5, 77, 81, 91, 112, 118–23, 132, 143, 151, 154–6
concretisation, 98–9
consciousness, 8–9, 15–16, 32, 34, 36, 39, 41, 43, 45, 47–55, 63, 71–2, 74, 77, 83, 87, 89, 100, 104, 105, 119, 121, 154
   organic consciousness, 15, 37, 45, 47, 50, 55, 63, 83, 87
   primary consciousness, 15, 18, 38–9, 47–8, 50, 52–5, 72, 83
contagion, 68–9, 134, 135, 139, 146, 149–50
contingency, 2, 7, 16, 61, 94–5, 97, 101, 108–110, 114–15, 126–7, 131–2, 157
cosmotechnics, 108, 112–14, 153

# INDEX

counter-actualisation, 64; *see also* actualisation
cybernetics, 2, 5, 26, 49, 96, 98, 101, 108–9, 114, 119, 122, 126, 131, 152–3

Damasio, Antonio, 9, 82–6, 88–9, 121, 154–5
dark precursor, 62–4
DeLanda, Manuel, 12n, 64, 154
Deleuze, Gilles, 1, 12–13, 15, 18, 20–1, 23–4, 31, 57–65, 74–6, 95, 153
Deleuze, Gilles, and Guattari, Félix, 12, 14–16, 18, 20, 51n, 56–7, 64–75, 77, 135, 141, 152
Dempster, Beth M., 17, 129
Derrida, Jacques, 78, 98, 104, 147, 151
Despret, Vinciane, 146
difference, 5, 7, 8–9, 12, 15–17, 19–20, 23–6, 34, 45, 56–66, 69, 75, 81, 101, 107, 110, 123–7, 136, 139, 143, 145, 153
differentiation, 12, 23, 29, 42, 45, 48, 57–8, 60, 63, 91–2
Driesch, Hans, 3, 4, 12, 46

embryogenesis, 38, 40, 46, 94
emotion, 9, 32–4, 55, 87, 112
environment, 1, 4, 6–9, 12–13, 15, 18, 23–4, 27, 30–2, 36, 42, 47–9, 78, 80, 83, 90, 92, 109, 113, 116–20, 122–4, 126–7, 129–132, 135, 139, 141, 144, 148–9, 151, 154, 156
epigenesis, 3, 12, 77, 90–5, 105–6, 112, 114, 152
epigenetics, 1, 13, 90, 92–3, 95
epiphylogenesis, 106–7, 114
equipotentiality, 13, 15, 39, 44–7, 53–4, 73–4
Esposito, Roberto, 140–1, 147
evolution, 13, 16, 68, 70, 75, 94, 97–8, 110, 114, 116–17, 127, 130; *see also* involution
exteriorisation, 49, 70, 103–5, 108
exteriority, 28–30, 32, 35, 103, 154

feeling, 9, 73, 82–7, 89, 121, 154
finalism, 39, 43–4, 74n; *see also* neofinalism

force, 1, 3, 6, 18–19, 24–5, 27, 29, 31, 39–41, 44, 46, 52–5, 60–2, 64, 67, 70, 73–4, 92, 96, 98, 100, 105, 108n, 110–14, 119, 125, 138, 141, 146, 151
form, 3–4, 9, 11–13, 15–17, 19–26, 28, 30, 32–5, 38–44, 46–56, 57n, 59–60, 62–3, 66–85, 89–92, 95, 99–102, 104–5, 108n, 109–12, 114n, 117, 121, 127, 129–30, 133–6, 138, 142, 148–9, 150–4, 156–7
Foucault, Michel, 1, 95

Gaia, 14, 16, 17, 115, 117–19, 121–33, 144, 153–4, 156
  Gaia theory, 10, 13, 17, 110, 115, 118–19, 121–3, 128, 132, 156
  Gaia hypothesis, 2, 16, 115–16, 118, 122, 132
Gilbert, Scott F., 13, 17, 129n, 136–9
Grosz, Elizabeth, 20, 24n, 27, 42, 47, 51n, 53–4, 73
ground and form, 99–100

Haraway, Donna J., 10, 17, 115, 128–32, 134–6, 138–9, 142, 146, 149, 152
Hayles, Katherine N., 56, 121, 156
Hegel, Georg Wilhelm Friedrich, 15, 24, 77, 78, 109
Heidegger, Martin, 103, 109
holobiont, 13–14, 17, 65, 130, 132, 134, 136–8, 145, 154, 157
homeostasis, 5, 82–3, 85, 90, 115–16, 120, 122, 126
Hui, Yuk, 2–4, 16, 20, 97–8, 101, 105, 106n, 108–110, 112–14, 126, 152–3, 155
Husserl, Edmund, 59, 103–4
hybrid, 10, 14, 17, 47, 123, 128, 145–6, 149–50, 157
hybridisation, 110, 134, 148–9
hylomorphism, 14, 21, 71

identity, 6, 9n, 10–12, 14–15, 19, 21–2, 35, 58–9, 63n, 64, 80, 87–9, 98, 102, 109, 122, 130, 140, 142, 144–5, 151
imagination, 35–7, 60, 80, 99–100, 104, 112, 153
immunity, 17, 70, 134, 139, 140–7, 150–1
immunology, 138, 140, 144–7

## INDEX

individual, 2, 11, 13–15, 17, 19–22, 24–7, 31, 34–7, 40–1, 43, 45, 52, 54, 59, 61, 64, 68, 75–6, 80–1, 88–90, 94, 99, 102, 104–8, 110–23, 126–7, 130, 136–9, 142, 144–7, 149–50, 152, 154–5
individuation, 11, 13–16, 19–35, 37, 44, 57–64, 71, 98–9, 106–7, 153
information, 4, 19–20, 22, 24–6, 29, 33, 35–6, 48, 86, 88, 96–7, 100–1, 114, 119, 129, 144, 147, 156
interindividual, 31, 34
interiorisation, 103–4
internal resonance, 22, 26–7, 32, 62, 99
invention, 11, 16, 19, 24, 33–6, 43, 45, 49–50, 53, 70, 81, 97–8, 99–100, 102, 104, 108, 110, 112, 155
involution, 68; *see also* evolution

Kant, Immanuel, 2–3, 39, 65, 74, 90–5, 97, 109, 152

Lamarck, Jean-Baptiste, 28, 98
Latour, Bruno, 12, 115, 123–8, 130, 132, 152, 153
Laval-Jeantet, Marion, 147–51
Leroi-Gourhan, André, 49, 70, 97, 102–3
Lovelock, James, 5, 10, 16–17, 110, 115–17, 119, 121, 124–5, 128, 132, 153
Luhmann, Niklas, 121, 127

machine, 3, 5, 7, 9–10, 16, 26, 49, 96–8, 101–2, 108–15, 123–4, 128, 154–6
machinic phylum, 57, 70–1, 75
Malabou, Catherine, 1, 3, 13, 15–16, 75, 77–82, 85–95, 111–12, 152–3, 155–6
Mangin, Benoît, 147, 150
Mangold, Hilde, 46
Margulis, Lynn, 5, 10, 16–17, 68, 115–19, 121–3, 125–6, 128–30, 132, 135–6, 153
Massumi, Brian, 18, 20, 26, 155
matter, 2–5, 8, 21–2, 24–5, 40–1, 70–1, 91–2, 94, 102–3, 114n, 121, 123, 129n, 146, 148
Maturana, Humberto R., 5–9, 17, 30–1, 55, 115, 119–21, 129, 136

McFall-Ngai, Margaret, 137
mechanism, 2–5, 7, 39, 42, 46, 96, 97n, 101, 108n, 109, 114, 139, 141, 145, 151
membrane, 26, 28–9, 32, 119, 132, 150n
memory, 35–6, 45, 53, 74n, 100, 103–8, 111
Mensch, Jennifer, 3, 95
Merleau-Ponty, Maurice, 33n, 34
metastable, 14, 21, 25, 27–9, 35–7, 58, 60–1, 100, 117
metastability, 21–2, 27, 29–32, 34, 37
microchimerism, 140, 145–7
mind, 8, 10, 16–17, 36, 52–3, 55, 63, 71–2, 74n, 77, 79–80, 83, 89, 91–2, 99–100, 102, 109, 121, 131, 154–5
molar structure, 40–1
morphogenesis, 11, 13, 15, 38–44, 47–8, 50, 57, 62–3, 65, 75, 80
multiplicity, 11–15, 17–18, 37, 52, 56, 59–60, 63–4, 69, 86, 114, 124–5, 134–5, 141, 149, 153–4

neofinalism, 38, 43–4, 50, 74; *see also* finalism

ontogenesis, 11, 13–16, 19–21, 23, 25, 28, 37–8, 97–8, 100, 107
ontology, 11–14, 17–19, 55, 58, 74, 88, 152–4, 156–7
open system, 4–6, 46, 82, 120
operational closure, 6, 10, 30, 120, 122
orders of magnitude, 22, 24–7, 31–2, 58, 60–1
organic consciousness, 15, 37, 45, 47, 50, 55, 63, 83, 87
 primary consciousness, 15, 18, 38–9, 47–8, 50, 52–5, 72, 83, 119, 121, 143, 154–5
organicism, 2, 4, 39–40, 42, 95–6, 108–10
organisation, 2, 4–7, 10, 14–16, 18, 29–30, 33–4, 39–41, 43–7, 54, 59–60, 65–7, 75, 82, 96–7, 100, 106, 110–11, 115, 119–21, 125, 129, 131, 151, 153
organology, 2, 16, 20, 96–7, 102, 106–10, 113–15, 132, 153

perception, 8–9, 32–6, 45–6, 50–2, 55, 73, 81, 84, 86, 104, 119, 140

# INDEX

plasticity, 12–13, 15–16, 18, 75, 77–82, 85, 88–90, 93, 95, 111–12, 153
potentiality, 1, 11, 13–14, 18, 22, 31, 36–7, 44–6, 55, 58, 61, 67–9, 74–8, 80–2, 90, 95, 99–102, 113–14, 153, 156
pre-individual, 13–14, 19, 21–3, 27–8, 31–2, 34–7, 57–61, 64, 99–100, 102, 107
preformationism, 11, 13, 15–16, 39, 43–4, 77, 90–2, 100, 153
Prigogine, Ilya, 4–5, 125
problematic, 23–4, 27–8, 31, 34, 36, 86, 154
processuality, 11–14, 18, 152–3
purposesiveness, 3, 39

recurrent causality, 7–8, 99, 113
recursivity, 7, 10, 16, 97, 101, 108–10, 112, 114, 122, 126–7, 131, 155
Roux, Wilhelm, 46
Ruyer, Raymond, 11–13, 15–16, 18, 20n, 37–55, 57, 62–3, 70, 72, 74, 77, 81, 83, 86, 88, 108, 118, 121, 143, 152, 154–5

Sauvagnargues, Anne, 20, 23, 29
self, 6, 9, 50, 83–4, 86–9, 112, 119, 126, 138–47, 151, 154–6
  autobiographical self, 9, 84
  core self, 9, 83–4
  non-self, 139, 141–7
  proto-self, 9, 83–7, 121, 154–5
self-enjoyment, 38, 51–2, 54, 74, 121
self-organisation, 5–6, 10–12, 15, 38, 44, 47, 54, 96, 118, 120, 142
self-survey, 15, 38–9, 41, 50–5, 57, 72–4, 86, 88, 121, 143; *see also* absolute survey
Shildrick, Margrit, 146–7
Simondon, Gilbert, 11–16, 19–38, 40, 44, 55, 57–61, 64, 71, 97–109, 112–14, 152–3
Smrekar, Maja, 149–51

Spemann, Hans, 46–7
Stengers, Isabelle, 115, 125–6, 128, 153
Stiegler, Bernard, 12–13, 16, 20, 97–8, 102–8, 110, 112–14, 152–3
structural coupling, 6–7, 10, 119–20, 123, 131, 151
substantialist atomism, 21, 24
symbiogenesis, 14, 115, 117, 129, 132, 135, 138
symbiosis, 12, 14–15, 17, 65, 68–9, 117, 129, 132, 135–9, 145, 149, 151
sympoiesis, 10, 17, 128–32, 134–6, 138–9, 147
systems theory, 2, 4–5, 11–12, 65, 115, 122, 125–7, 131–2, 152

technical object, 13, 16, 19–20, 34, 36–7, 97–104, 106–10, 112–14
technology, 16, 26, 49, 70–1, 97, 107–14, 123, 153
teleology, 7, 43, 118
tertiary protention, 111
tertiary retention, 104–6, 110–11
theme, 38, 41–4, 46–9, 62–3;
  developmental theme, 41–3, 74n
  formative theme, 41, 43–5
topology, 28–30
transduction, 20, 22–4, 26, 34, 44, 103
transindividual, 23, 31–5, 37, 102, 104–6, 114

Uexküll, Jacob von, 35, 48, 108

Varela, Francisco J., 5–10, 17, 30–1, 55, 63, 115, 119–22, 129, 132, 136, 143–4
virtuality, 24n, 59, 75, 90, 101, 153
vitalism, 1–5, 7, 11, 13, 39, 41–2, 46, 70–1, 74, 96, 108, 114, 154

Waddington, Conrad, 4, 90, 108n
Whitehead, Alfred North, 11, 152
Wiener, Norbert, 5, 33, 96, 98, 108, 156
Wolff, Étienne, 44

EU representative:
Easy Access System Europe
Mustamäe tee 50, 10621 Tallinn, Estonia
Gpsr.requests@easproject.com

www.ingramcontent.com/pod-product-compliance
Lightning Source LLC
Chambersburg PA
CBHW051128160426

43195CB00014B/2385